Cleo

CLEO LAINE

SIMON & SCHUSTER

SIMON & SCHUSTER
Rockefeller Center
1230 Avenue of the Americas
New York, NY 10020

Originally published in Great Britain by Simon & Schuster Ltd.

SIMON & SCHUSTER and colophon are registered
trademarks of Simon & Schuster Inc.

Manufactured in the United States of America

1   3   5   7   9   10   8   6   4   2

Library of Congress Cataloging-in-Publication Data is available.

ISBN 0-684-83762-5

Credits

Thanks to James Kirkup for permission to publish 'The Poet' on pp 175–76.

Picture Credits:

Jacket back: Phil Stearn. Jacket front flap: Kurt Gebauer. Page 5: Paul Smith (4); Brian Moody (7). Page 7: Skyviews & General Ltd (Sonoma). Page 8: Roy Campbell (8). Page 9: BBC (1). Page 10: David McCabe (1); Dee Knott (2). Page 11: ITC (4); Waring Abbott (5); Doug McKenzie (6). Page 12: Larry Bussacca (1). Page 13: Jim Henson Productions (3). Page 15: Kurt Gebauer (4); Gered Mankowitz (7). Page 16: Kurt Gebauer (1 and 2).

While every effort has been made to trace copyright holders we have been unsuccessful in some cases. We apologise for any omissions.

Acknowledgements

Faith Evans, for gently pushing me and editing along the way.

Kurt Gebauer, who guided me through my computer illiteracy, finding lost work after weeks of hard grind.

Sheila and Becky of our office, who helped Kurt discover the lost passages.

Alec Campbell, my brother, who jogged my memory on occasions and provided photos from the past.

And Carol O'Brien, who tidied me up with more editing at the end.

Love and many thanks to you all.

To John and the children

— and to all the musicians who have supported me through the years

Contents

1

A Southall Tomboy

'But what's going to happen to the children, Minnie?'

My mother was visiting her aunt, who lived in Penge in a large and (as I thought) grand house. Heavy well-polished furniture, heavy draped curtains and heavy mahogany doors gave it a feeling of portentious gloom. Or so it seemed to three exuberant children doing their utmost to clamp their energy into the chairs where they had been instructed to sit quietly.

I didn't like it or the atmosphere very much, and I don't think my brother or sister liked it either. However, my mother had told us that we had to be on our best behaviour, so I sat still, quietly eating my sandwiches and cake and trying not to drop any crumbs. Those that escaped I picked up carefully and surreptiously popped into my mouth, hoping I hadn't been spotted. But I guess I had, because the aunt suddenly suggested that we all go out into the garden to play.

The heavy door wasn't quite closed behind us. Alec and Sylvia ran ahead of me into the garden, happy to be free, but I lingered behind. I liked to listen to grown-up talk: it was whispery and it made my heart pound. I always imagined that they were saying suggestive secret bodily things when they whispered to each other. I really couldn't hear or understand what they were talking about – but I do remember that question to my mother: 'What's going to happen to the children, Minnie?', which came out loud and clear, followed by 'What can you have been thinking of?' All I knew was that my aunt was berating my mother for something naughty she had done.

It was all very exciting, but after a while the door was pushed shut, so I never heard what it was she had done. Relieved not to have been discovered, I joined my brother and sister in the garden. In keeping with the house, it was a large and pristine garden, and the domain of my aunt's husband, who seemed nice and kindly, allowing us to help him tend his precious plants without too many anxious looks. We were just beginning to enjoy using up some of our pent-up energy when we were called to leave for home.

We never visited Penge again, but the incident remained to fuel my imagination for years. Until, that is, my mother told me what it was she had done that so upset her aunt who lived in a grand house that we all went to visit one day in Penge.

My mother was the daughter of Charles Hitchen and Elizabeth H. Hillier. A small farming family. He was from Cleverton in Wiltshire, and she was from London. My mother, Minnie Blanche, was born and brought up in Swindon along with two brothers, Frank and Arthur, and a sister, Emily. It seemed to be a happy family until the deaths of their parents. Mother's father died when she was twelve years old of a heart attack. He was harnessing a pony in the stable when he called out, 'I'm going now, mother,' but there was something in the sound of his voice that made my grandmother run out to him, followed by mother. They found him lying on the ground and he soon passed away in the arms of his wife. This is how my mother told it to me. Five years later, my grandmother died from cancer of the womb, when my mother was seventeen.

After that things changed drastically for my mother. Without her parents protection, life became a nightmare for her. The property was inherited by her eldest brother Frank, who according to mother did not look after his young brother and sisters.

I'm not aware of the full story – I always regret not sitting down with my mother later in life to ask more detail about her family – but I do know that from then on my mother had not only to find her own way in the world, but to fend for her brother and sister too.

Over the years little bits of information were dropped from time to time when my mother was in a chatty mood. I know that her brothers were tall and sandy-haired and that Mother and Aunt Emily had brown hair. Mother had an eighteen-inch-waist as a girl, brought about by corsetting. At dances, young girls would often faint because of the tight encasing in their iron girdle – Mother never fainted because her waist was naturally so small. Though not a beauty she was handsome and strong-faced with a square chin, good eyes and a fair complexion. She would have been considered good-looking today, but in those days not 'pretty' enough. Her attractive qualities would have been her strong friendly personality and a care for the underdog that sometimes got her into trouble.

My mother was a bigamist. Her first marriage was to Fredrick Bullock in Swindon. She told me he was a quiet, well-mannered gentleman with a club foot, who had been educated at Oxford University. He did not have a liking for work, and they had two businesses that failed – two restaurants. Fredrick suffered from migraines, which he used as an excuse for not helping her in the cafés (thought the excuse appeared more often than the actual migraine, she thought). The other skeletons in the closet, which she found out later in the marriage, were his love of the horses and a monkey he kept as a pet. The horses got rid of any profits they acquired, the monkey of customers and crockery.

The monkey was kept on a perch or in a cage in the café. She never explained . . . why a monkey? One day it escaped and went too far with its trickery – this was the straw that broke her marriage. Mother had opened for the day and was laying the tables when she heard several loud crashes, one after the other. Rushing to investigate what it might be, she found the

3

monkey trying to do the trick of pulling the tablecloth off the table without disturbing the newly laid plates and cutlery – not very successfully. She caught the monkey, closed up shop and went home to find Fredrick fast asleep in bed. She woke him, handed him his monkey, called him a milksop and left.

Swindon was a railway and farming town: not the place to hold an angry, ambitious, wilful girl unless you happened to be dotty about engines or besotted with cows and sheep. It turned out that neither attracted my mother. So she moved on, using the train to get her to the big city of London in the hope of exciting adventures ahead. Though Mother didn't have a good education – only the normal one for a country girl from a farming community before the Great War – she was bright and intelligent and she knew her three Rs well. She also played the organ a little – a small, foot-pumping, squeeze-boxy kind – mostly Methodist hymns. However, apart from her domestic and café experience she had no qualifications, so she had to take many different kinds of jobs when she arrived in London. She was continually tinkering with her age – up when they wanted a manageress for a shop, down when youth was what was required. Even we children never knew how old she was. When we asked her about her age she always replied, 'as young as my little finger, but older than my teeth'.

The stories she told made us laugh a good deal when we were small. After having children she put on quite a lot of weight, and one story that particularly amused us was about her having to run up the back of a ladder as part of some kind of training to strengthen her legs and arms for her work in the fire brigade during the First World War. It seemed unbelievable to us. We couldn't imagine our tubby mum being able to run at all, let alone whiz up a ladder backwards. We would all hoot with laughter and try it out for ourselves in the back yard, finding it almost impossible to do. The thought never entered our cruel young heads that she had been young, childless and considerably thinner when she had achieved that feat.

It was after the war that my father and mother met, though just how they met and how they earned a living before then remains a mystery that I shall now probably never solve. Alexander Sylvan Campbell came from Jamaica. His reasons for leaving home and family at the tender age of fifteen are also a puzzle to me. I do know he didn't get on with his father, and the story that has been told by relatives is that he had a terrible row with him, packed his bags, kissed his tearful loving mother goodbye and just left. Another version, told by my father, who was quite a romancer, was that he left Jamaica with a doctor travelling to Holland – what as, he never made clear to us, or maybe we were so used to hearing tall stories from him that we didn't pay attention to the details. He could have been the doctor's servant, I suppose, but my father was such a snob he would never have admitted to that. He just skimmed over any inconvenient factual information or else he made up stories that had a smattering of truth in them. Nobody really knows how he got to Europe or under what circumstances: he was just there.

As a soldier during the 1914–18 war mustard gas affected my father's lungs – or so he said. He also said that he had bladder trouble stemming from the war. He never went into detail, but I can remember the mad dashes he made to reach the toilet in time.

Pa wasn't very tall, just a bit taller than mother. His colour was an attractive dark brown, and his hair, which he kept cut close to his head, was black and tightly curly. His eyes always seemed black to me and they darted in all directions, taking in everything that was going on. His mouth was not large, with lips quite nicely shaped but with a slant that gave him a cynical look. It was an interesting face – a grand mixture of many races – a Mongolian face.

After the war Pa came to Britain, meeting Mother sometime, somewhere, in the early twenties. My father and mother knew each other for at least four years before my eldest sister, Sylvia Beryl, was born, out of wedlock, twenty-one months before I was born, also out of wedlock, in October 1927 in Clarence Street in Southall, Middlesex – near the gas works, the poor end of Southall, in a tiny terrace house with a small back and front garden. I was given the name Clementina Dinah.

Mother and Pa went out to work together selling things from door to door – 'on the knocker', it was called. (Mother hired a young girl to look after us while they were away during the day.) It must have been a God-forsaken job, having to go out in all kinds of weather. They rode bicycles all over the areas they covered. I don't know how it came about or whose idea it was, but they were doing it long before any of us children were born. To replenish their stock they paid regular visits to to Petticoat Lane, in London's East End, a colourful, vibrant street full of lively characters selling their wares to gullible Sunday tourists and bargain-hunters. Mother and Pa were not part of that fleeced flock, though: they had cards that admitted them to the wholesale warehouses that were in abundance in the area.

Buying goods cheaply this way enabled them to keep their heads above (just about) the poverty line. So my parents became loud and lively characters of Southall on bicycles. Until Mother had to come off the knocker when she was literally knocked off her bicycle by a passing car and fell heavily to her knees, which gave her terrible trouble from that time on, always swollen and painful. She developed water on the knees, and she swore it was caused by that fall.

I don't think Mother had much respect for doctors in those days, blaming them for not attending to her injury in time. She was also against the new practice of vaccination, because she had heard of a local woman who had supposedly lost a child as a direct result of having been inoculated. I doubt if she made any serious enquiries about this – more likely she just listened to the rumours and general gossip that would have been rife in such a close-knit community about one of its own. Anyway, she would have none of her children inoculated, and 'I don't believe in it' was her usual reply when challenged on the subject.

I contracted pneumonia when I was very young at a time when the illness meant almost certain death for a young child. Mother swore that if it hadn't been for her keeping vigil by my hospital bed nobody would have been there to see my eyes roll up into my head, seemingly going into a coma or death, whereupon she grabbed me from the bed and walked me all night, talking and cajoling to keep me awake. By the morning, the story went, little Clemmie was through the worst of the fever, saved by determination, anger and love. My mother also nursed me through diphtheria, bronchitis and most of the children's ailments that I seemed to get more quickly than Alec or Sylvia.

Mother said she had a hard time birthing me, at home in Clarence Street. I arrived in the early morning after many hours on her part struggling in labour. When I did arrive I was not terribly attractive, so her hard work might have been a bit of a disappointment to her. She always said I looked like a skinned rabbit – long and thin and hairless. Oh, how I wish I had remained long and thin! but it was not to be. Though I continued to be completely hairless for the first two years of my life – no eyebrows, no lashes, no hair on my head – when it did come through, it did so in abundance. It was sandy; Mother called it corn-coloured. My eyes were green/hazel and I grew to be a chubby-chops, with a head that was large, square-jawed and set with a bulldog determination. Not a very appealing infant when compared with my sister, who had dark brown hair, dark brown eyes and a small heart-shaped face.

Eighteen months later Alexander Sylvan the Second was born, in wedlock – well, wedlock of a kind, as my mother was still married to Mr Bullock. She hadn't seen him for seven years, which meant that by law he could be presumed dead. It is questionable whether she had any contact with him during those seven years. I am sure she knew he was alive, indeed I think she continued to help him financially for quite a few years. He may have blackmailed her when he found out that she had married. Whatever the truth, my mother was dogged by the fact of her bigamy, and also by her two husbands.

Like us two girls, Alec was born in the house in Clarence Street. When mother and the new baby were ready to receive visitors, Sylvia and I were allowed in to see our new brother. I was but a baby still myself, and had been deprived of my mother's attention long enough to be pretty angry with the reason for the deprivation. So when I saw the little bundle in my favoured position, in the arms of my mummy, I greeted him with: 'We don't want him, put him under the bed!'

This was the beginning of a hateful jealousy of Alec that lasted well into my teens, with a strong feeling of resentment on my part towards my mother for making him her favourite. At least, that's how it always seemed to me. Sylvia didn't seem to mind me or Alec. She was a caring, loving child. Alec was beautiful, with dark eyes and black hair – the complete opposite of mine, which was a bush. His was sleek and wavy and manageable, everything a girl should have had. So – he became the favourite and I became a green-eyed monster. Soon after his birth, Mother declared that she would have no more children.

Most of the Clarence Street stories are from the memories of my parents, told to us as we grew up, about our amusing baby antics. But certain things come back to me because they were uncomfortable, or because they ran counter to what I wanted as a small child. My mother had a large twin-carriage pram that was called 'the boat', and we were pushed around in it, either by her or by the girl who looked after us, when they went shopping or visiting. It was a big-wheeled, highly sprung monster, but I loved it. When they stopped the consoling movement to chit-chat with strange grown-ups who meant nothing to me, or to go into a shop, it was more than I could bear. So I would let them know I didn't like being left unpropelled, by moving it myself rocking back and forth in such a manner that the boat looked dangerously near to toppling its contents on to the pavement. Sylvia, who behaved more like little ladies should in large carriage prams, did not greatly appreciate this fairground boat ride with her impatient bloody-minded sister.

The boat was eventually retired to the garden of Clarence Street as a swing. Where (so the story goes) I was put one day, by the young girl who was looking after us, without any knickers, though the seat in the boat was soaking wet from the rainstorm the night before. Clemmie caught a severe cold and had another battle with death – all because she had wanted to be on the move again in a wet swing.

My eyes were in the wars at about this time, too. How they survived blindness, only Clemmie's guardian angel can say. Twice I almost lost my sight. Once when I was a terrible two-year-old, sitting in a high chair close to the table that was laid with knives and forks. Not being content with my spoon, I leaned over to grab a fork. The chair didn't stay on its feet for long. Unbalanced by my forward lunge, chair and child hit the floor with the desired fork stuck just under the right eye. According to Mother my bellowing sounded as though all hell had been let loose, and panic reigned until they discovered that the eye was still in its socket, undamaged.

The second attempt on my eye was made by my brother. On hearing the doorbell ring one day I ran to the door with my mother. She sent me back and when I turned I ran into my brother, who for some unknown reason was carrying a poker which collided with my left eye. Once again I roared. Eye once again survived, and lungs got some good preparation for the future. (I also thought my brother was out to get me.)

Not long after these eye accidents my parents made the first of their many moves into different houses in Southall – to a flat in the High Street over a butcher's shop. It was there that I first became aware of my parents' failure to see each other's point of view. It happened late one night, after my father had come home very late, missing the family supper. We had been made ready for bed and had stayed up so that we could say our goodnights to him and share cuddles and goodnight stories. But Pa didn't turn up, so eventually we were packed off to bed. I knew Mother was displeased because she wasn't as gentle as she usually was at bedtime. When he did come home it was very dark. I got up to listen to the grown-up talk, not really understanding what it was all about, though Mother's voice was loud, even weepy. I

9

walked into the room at the very moment when she threw the teapot at him, with boiling hot tea in it. She aimed to miss him and caught me instead – luckily her aim was low and hit my foot. This stopped the row immediately and I was the centre of attention, with a lot more lung exercise. Not an easy way to become a singer.

I can't say it was the happiest period for the family. The number of rows was growing and I was always in scrapes. I was also becoming a terrible tomboy, preferring the rough and tumble of boys to girls, who seemed unadventurous and concerned with things which didn't appeal to me. But I paid for my preference from time to time. Once I was in the garden with a young boy whom my brother and I played with from time to time. I can't remember much about him now except that he was Welsh, and older than me: I suppose I've wanted to erase him, to wipe away the unpleasing moments of childhood. There was a big wooden clothes wringer in the garden, and the boy thought he'd have a bit of fun by telling dumb Clemmie to put her finger 'just there'. 'There' was between its rollers. Quite a safe place if the handle wasn't being turned, but he felt the need to turn it, to see what would happen to my left index finger. Well, I could have told him; indeed, when I started to howl he darn well knew, but didn't hang about to learn the details. I was left attached to this giant clothes wringer lamenting the loss of the top of my finger. I was eventually discovered, unwrung and sped to the doctor, who stitched me up and put some strong-smelling disinfectant on that made me yell yet again. That I will never forget, ever: as I write I can still smell the powerful odour. For many years I hated all Welsh people, till I reached an age when I could reason things out a bit.

Meanwhile our parents were keeping us entertained with rows and music. My father had an excellent singing voice, and he loved to air it at any opportune moment, often embarrassing his children, his wife or anyone close at hand with his sudden vocal outbursts in the street, on the tops of buses, in the cinema queue or along with the performer up on the screen – when I at least would cringe and slip further down in my seat, pretending I was not with him. As we all had to leave together at the end of these humiliations, I wasn't very successful with my pretence. Everyone knew it was my dad who sang at the drop of a hat – anytime, anywhere. So I eventually came to terms with it, knowing he would never change. And I loved his singing, anyway, at home! He would sit us (two at a time – sometimes he managed three) on his lap and sing all the current songs of the day, from Al Jolson to Bing Crosby and tell silly, funny folk stories that we insisted on hearing whenever we could grab him. He loved telling us stories so it wasn't hard to persuade him. I also liked watching him shave, for he still sang as he did it – with a cut-throat razor. Seeing him pull funny faces along with the songs fascinated me, but there was a macabre touch to it too, as I wondered how many cuts he would inflict today upon his face and neck, then count the bits of paper stuck all over him, totting them up against the count of the day before. It was his singing that gave him all his cuts. How can you shave, sing, talk, laugh, be watched and come out unscathed? He often came out of the washroom besplattered with bloody bits of newspaper from cheek to jowl, with the most thrilling ones on his neck. Later on in life I wondered – was it the songs that fascinated me or the possibility of a cut throat? Oh, children are so cruelly inquisitive.

Another fascination for me was my father's smell. He used to put Pond's face cream on his face which gave him a warm wonderful aroma. As I think of him now I recall it quite clearly, though it wasn't overpowering, but subtle and reassuring. It was good to be cuddled by Pa and I got close to him whenever I could, to lap up more of him. In fact, Pa may be responsible for the one luxury item I indulge in – perfume. Smell is really important to me, and I have a strong sense of it – both good and bad.

My Pa was a slight man, no more than five foot five or six, and he was wiry and athletic: I can't remember him ever with an ounce of fat on his body. He loved the ladies, flattering and joking with both beautiful and plain: he managed to make those who weren't obviously attractive feel pretty and sexy. Extremely aware of his good looks, he was a dandy who never lost this Don Juan side of his personality, and he flirted well into his eighties.

Pa was always very fair to us children: if one had something, the others were given it too, or else no one had anything. Mother wasn't the same, certainly not after Alec was born. As I said, he became her little angel, and the girls took a back seat for a while. I think he reminded her of her adopted son Bertie, who had died of meningitis at the age of thirteen. Bertie was always a complete mystery to me – I have no idea who he was or where he came from. He was simply an angel as far as I was concerned. But it must have been a traumatic time in my mother's life when she lost that little boy, and maybe Alec took his place. She dressed him just as she had Bertie. We children always thought the large portrait of Bertie that hung prominently in every house we lived in was up in Heaven. He looked so angelic, posed in a little Lord Fauntleroy suit, sitting on a table, ankles crossed, in white ankle socks and patent leather shoes. Framing the picture was a design in mother-of-pearl of flowers, birds and curlicues, that to me at least looked like Heaven. Bertie in Heaven who died of meningitis: I didn't know what it meant, but it added to the mystery, as did the regular visits to his grave with Mother to cut the grass, place fresh flowers in the vase and take home (to clean) the globe filled with plaster flowers and birds on the wing. It was all so very reverent. I loved it, quite often crying for young Bertie in Heaven – who was not the threat to me that Alec was. I'm not sure how my father felt about this obsession with both the living and dead boy children. It's possible he felt like me – jealous, but unlike me he could do something about his jealousy, and he did.

It was becoming apparent to Mother that her children were musical like their father. I was the singer and Sylvia the dancer; Alec was also a singer. We were all sent to a lady called Madame De Courcey to learn to dance: ballet, tap, and acrobatics. We also took singing and piano lessons.

A Southall Tomboy

How they were able to pay for these I have no idea, as
the Depression was affecting every working-class family in
Southall. Pa was still on the knocker and Mother by that time
had opened a café in Regina Road, the third move of many
that we enjoyed or hated as kids. The café didn't work out,
for many reasons: Mother always said it was because Pa argued
with the customers or even rowed with them, sometimes coming
to blows. They eventually came to an arrangement whereby Pa
worked behind the scenes in the kitchen while Mother worked
up front, serving the men labourers who frequented it. But Pa
didn't like being the back-room boy – washing up, cooking and
being a dog's-body. So instead of being a partnership it became
a rocky ship, with arguments between them that involved the
customers who wanted to eat rather than debate Pa's position in
the workforce.

For me this was the time that music started to become an
important part of my life. I loved the lessons, though I was
too young to take them seriously: it was like playtime really.
Madame had a sprung shed in her back garden, where all the
little tots would assemble. Most of them, of course, only wanted
to be fairies, flitting about with wands and things. But Madame
was a good teacher, and she disciplined us little monsters into a
semblance of a chorus line. It amazes me, looking back, how she
put up with it all those years, when she was such a professional
and theatrical traditionalist. For instance, if you whistled while
in the shed you got sent outside, where you had to turn around
three times before knocking on the door and waiting until you
heard Madame say 'Come in'. If you mentioned Macbeth you
were really in trouble, but there was very little danger of any of
her charges revealing a knowledge of Shakespeare.

It was the whistlers who suffered, and me in particular.
I was an inveterate whistler, spending a lot of my dancing
classes whirling around outside the shed. I perfected the whirl
movement. Mother wasn't very keen on whistling either: she
would say, 'a whistling woman and a crowing hen is neither
good to God nor men'. My sister just said, 'It isn't ladylike,'

13

and told on me if she caught me at it. So I did it to annoy her. I still like to whistle and often pucker up for my own enjoyment, so they weren't able to cure me. Funny thing though, if I'm asked to whistle to order I can't do it. My lips start quivering and my muscles won't perform. So the world lost a singing whistling dervish.

Madame prepared us for concerts that were given for the working men's clubs of Southall, old people's clubs and anyone who wanted cheap entertainment. My first concert performance was at a very early age for a working men's club along with all the other fairies. Sylvia, Alec and I were an act – not a very good act, but we were cute. Mother dressed us up to the nines, with large bows in the girls' hair. Oh, my poor hair, it was so fuzzy and tangly. When I had to be properly dressed my hair and I went through a torture that the Marquis de Sade would have delighted in. My lungs had more exercise because of my hair than because of any of the accidents or near-deaths I had previously encountered. Along with the painful bows, there were white socks and patent leather ankle-strap shoes and a frilly dress for me. Sylvia, who had to acrobat, wore a tarted-up swimsuit. Alec, who for some reason had a tin drum slung around his neck with string, was dressed (like Bertie in Heaven) as Little Lord Fauntleroy, with long curls that the poor child had to live with long after he passed the baby stage.

Our moment in the concert finished the first half. Our routine had been worked out so that sister Sylvia was to go on first to grab the audience with her dynamic acrobatics. I would come on halfway through to knock them out with my song, while Sylvia still cavorted behind me. Then Alec, the baby, would steal their hearts with his drumming. As we were all babies really, nothing could happen for certain. That first time, Sylvia, being the most responsible and intelligent of the three, did her thing professionally then gave me a nod to come on, but I didn't move. Either I had stage fright or I didn't feel like it – but whatever the reason I wasn't going on, and all the cajoling backstage couldn't make me budge. As Sylvia came to the end of her routine she got exasperated with me, and walking to the side of the stage grabbed me and dragged me on. It did the trick. I stood on my given mark and sang my little heart out.

Once there, they could not remove me from centre stage. I loved it! I even loved the ridiculous song that had been assigned to me, 'Let's All Sing The Barmaid Song'. Strange words coming from a frumpy three-year-old with fuzzy hair and a big red bow on top of it all! But I was not to be removed. I absolutely enjoyed being the centre of attraction, so much so that the silly song was sung over and over again. Eventually Sylvia came to the rescue, breaking off a high kick to push me to one side, away from my limelight, to allow Alec to start his awful drumming. The audience by this time must have been in hysterics at our goings on. Eventually Sylvia managed to shuffle us into line, persuaded us to bow – almost at the same time – and then shoving, pushing and pinching us in the direction of the exit cleared the stage for the interval.

Our act went from strength to strength, and Southall dancing teachers began to vie with each other to train us and to put us in local concerts. We were unfaithful to Madame De Courcy only once, when friends and lower fees enticed us to other terpsy trainers. But she taught us well, and probably put her fees down when she saw that she might lose her little darlings to the competition. After all, she was the first on the scene and had won our hearts.

A favourite routine of Madame's was to make us waltz from one end of the shed to the other, with books on our heads. If the book didn't make it to the end you had to start over again until it did. Boring for those who could do it easily, embarrassing for the droppers. I was at a disadvantage because of the bush on my head – until I discovered how to make a ditch that the books could lie in, protected by the surrounding hair. It worked most of the time, so I became a straight-backed, long-necked waltzer. Ballet was another thing altogether. I adored it, and wanted so badly to do it well. But the skinned rabbit of birth was no longer: I was becoming a Jumbo (eventually that became my nickname in the family). The shed and Madame couldn't stand the pounding of Jumbo pirouetting around in such an ungainly fashion, and she suggested I give up ballet and stick to singing and tap. I guess she was right, but I have since regretted not ignoring her advice. Dancing has always been a great love of mine as well as singing, but dancing came first because I couldn't do it. I desperately wanted to dance like Fred Astaire, and at home I tried to all the time.

Singing I could simply do. I had various singing teachers over the years when I was small, much too early to do anything more than encourage an interest, and I already had that. But they might have done a lot of damage. One almost did – a Mrs Williams, who was fat! not just fat, but immensely, excessively fat, with fingers like sausages which grasped my ribs in an attempt to see if I was breathing correctly. Of course I wasn't – I was holding my breath so that I didn't have to breathe in her body odour. It wasn't her fatness that was the problem – I wasn't thin and mother was no sylph – she just didn't smell good, poor woman. So there was no hope of her teaching me anything except breath control. I was not kind to Mrs Williams and she eventually resigned, telling Mother that I was not practising and she was wasting her money. I was over the moon. No longer would I have to suffer being pulled into the arms of the offensively smelly teacher. She also taught the piano, so my pianoforte lessons ceased too. But there was always music in our house, so I didn't mind a bit.

2

Unwillingly to School

One after the other the cafés crumbled as the Depression deepened. For most of the time my father was out of work, but we children went on singing, dancing and performing for Ma, Pa and the clubs. Once again there was a move – to a large four-storey house almost next door to an abandoned mental asylum in Featherstone Road. (All these homes were rented, nothing ever belonged to my parents.) The time in Featherstone Road was one of the happiest I can remember, although Ma and Pa were fighting hammer and tongs now. Lack of work didn't help my father's moods, and too much work didn't help make my mother amiable.

At Featherstone Road they started a boarding house which roomed and fed mainly Irish labourers, single men and women and families. It must have been successful because they soon rented the house next door as well, which was even nearer the asylum. The gardens were wonderful, with large long playgrounds for all the children in the two houses and stables at the end of each one, which must have been built before the houses fell on hard times. Alec, our friends and I spent most of our free time being cowboys, Indians, doctors and nurses. Sylvia, the little lady of the family, had her own friends and didn't participate. She really wasn't keen on our rough and ready kind of play, objecting strongly when I chased after her with a worm in my hand. You could not belong to our gang without first touching a worm or you were a cowardy custard: Sylvia preferred to remain a coward.

We all had bicycles that we rode everywhere – we couldn't have survived without them. They became passports to exciting adventures. Pa insisted that we looked after our escape-machines properly so every Sunday it became a ritual – newspaper on the floor, tools out for changing or mending tyres. We had to clean the bikes and repair any damage we had done during the week. Pa inspected them as strictly as an army sergeant, himself a fanatical cyclist who rode the streets of Southall with pipe in mouth, trilby on head, and cycle clips around the ankles to keep his pin-striped trousers away from the wheels.

Pa was known as 'darkie' in Southall. As a nickname it didn't seem to bother him, any more than it bothered the paddys, taffs, or – his favourite – jocks to be called such. To him and them it was like being called 'mate', and unlike today it wasn't considered an odious term. Had it been, Pa would have been the first to let the offender know he wouldn't get away with it, even if it meant fisticuffs. Pa was an eccentric character and was considered to be so by the community. He would stand on a soapbox at Hyde Park Corner and in Southall, spouting out his grievances to all who would stop and listen, along with Prince Monolulu of 'I've-got-a-horse' fame, and all the political spouters of the day. Meanwhile Mother, Sylvia and I would be peeling bushels of potatoes to be cooked and eaten by the returning ravenous labourers who had to be fed a substantially filling meal, mostly stews with lots of bread and 'tatoes to mop up the gravy. Mother fed them well, getting a good reputation as a landlady in Southall. The men and women were happy-go-lucky, doing back-breaking work with not much to show for it in their pockets at the end of the week – though more than they could have earned in Ireland, if they were lucky enough to have a job at all.

I had many Irish friends, both young and old; and with them Sunday became a wonderful day in my life. It wasn't a school day, and so within reason I was free to do whatever and go anywhere I liked. Most of my friends were practising Catholics who went to the church across the road opposite the two boarding houses, next door to the pub that the night before they had got stinking rotten drunk in, ending with a good punch-up or getting a girl into trouble or committing some other sin that they'd confess to on Sunday, which confused me because they'd repeat the sins again the next Friday or Saturday. I didn't understand it and maybe few of them did. But Mary and Grace, who I'm sure would have had to rack their brains to find any sins to confess to, would take me to Sunday mass.

But first I had to submit to our once-a-week bath ritual. (The copper was lit first thing in the morning on both Sunday and Monday, for bath day and wash day.) The tin bath which hung outside the scullery door was brought in as soon as the water was hot enough to be ladled into it, and then we stepped in, Sylvia first, Alec and me together – all in the same water, of course. Inevitably a fight would break out between Alec and me because he wanted the soap when I had it, or the flannel, and both floor and Mother usually ended up getting a better wash than we did.

After the water fight we had to settle down so we could be prettied up for whatever Sunday arrangements had been made. Mine was church with the girls. It meant clean everything: underwear, socks, and shoes highly polished by Pa, who was the official shoe-cleaner for the family, and got the best shine for a Sunday. Clothes were Sunday best – garments that were not touched any other day of the week unless we were going somewhere special. So, with my head pulsating after a tug-of-war with the tangles in my hair, a large bow atop it all and sparkling body and face, I was considered ready and in the right condition to enter the church across the road with Mary and Grace.

It was my first dramatic role. As I entered I became solemn, quiet and still, whereas a few moments before I'd been laughing and yelling and carrying on like a whirlwind. Once again a smell, the heavy pungent clinging smell of incense, became exotically

19

important to me. What it was that filled my lungs and made being there special I didn't know at the time, not until much later. I followed the girls' moves religiously (pardon the pun): a dip of the knee at the entrance, before dipping my finger in the holy water to cross my body just like them. Feeling suddenly grown up and knowing, we took our places in the pews.

It was then that the drama really began for me. The incense came from young boys and men swinging long gold chains. The cassocks they and the priests wore were much more glamorous than anything I had ever had to dress up in for a Madame De Courcey show. The service I couldn't understand, as that was in Latin, but I wasn't alone – Mary and Grace didn't either. They seemed to know when to respond and interject, so I just did it their way. The music was a love affair that swept me up, off and away into another world I did not understand, intellectually or emotionally. It touched parts of me in a way that even when it happens today I still can't explain. When a church organ soars it's difficult for me to contain tears and an imagined swelling of the heart, either in joy or in sadness, as certain orchestral music also affected me as a child. I often sat listening to music unable to control my tears, and had to be consoled by Pa or Mother.

The indignity of getting ready for this wonderful spectacle was well worth it. I was always sorry and slow to come out into the real world, and it puzzled me to see the men going into the pub after going through (I assumed) the same experience as I had. Once I even saw one of the priests go into that other place, after being the light-filled creature who only a few moments ago had stood before me in splendour, in that exotic-smelling place so close to heaven.

Of course I went through a period of wanting to be a nun, quite convinced it was the life for me. Mother, Grace and Mary didn't think it was such a good idea so the visits seemed to tail off for one reason or another. Like outings to Penge or to other friends of Mother's? Pa was an atheist and never did approve. This was one of the things he spouted about quite regularly in the house, as well as in Hyde Park. He thought all believers were hypocrites. He'd had some unpleasant experiences when he was younger with church attenders, which he never forgot. He felt that he'd been ostracized by the whole of Christian society because of his dark skin. He didn't distinguish between them: as far as he was concerned they were all guilty of shutting him out of work, making him unable to support his family or succeed in life. All except the Scots, whom I suspect he liked because he was a Campbell and of Scots descent. Later on in life he regularly visited Edinburgh searching for evidence of a fortune lying in a bank left by an aristocratic great-grandfather. It was true that his mother was a Stuart, so there were strong Scottish ties however they came about. It's possible, I suppose, that the aristocratic ancestor might really have existed, a disgraced son sent to the colonies to mind the sugar estate, but Pa was never able to prove it.

Mother had been brought up as a Methodist, but she was certainly not a practising one, so none of us was baptized or had any strict religious training. School, of course, taught the Bible and after falling for the wonders of the Catholic church I became besotted with the Salvation Army, because of the band and the uniforms. I followed them all over the place. They were the pied pipers of Southall, opening doors to glorious crashing and quite often swinging music.

I joined the Young Sunday School classes where we played with lead figures in sand. The figures were dressed in strange long gowns; their heads were covered and the men had beards. They lived with palm trees, donkeys and camels, and we were told the magic story of a baby boy who was born in a stable. But it was the music that held me, as it did in the Young Sowers League – well, the music and the outings.

The three of us joined various scripture classes, Brownies, girl guides, cubs and scouts to acquire badges for knots and good deeds. But most of all for the outings and tea parties that went along with belonging and paying your halfpenny every week so you could eventually have a beano with your friends. Sometimes these took place in a field in the country, but best of all was when we all got into a charabanc and went to the seaside for a wonderful wild day, free from being told of the advantages of being good Christian girls and boys.

Meanwhile we also had to go to school. We all went to Featherstone Road school, Infant and Junior. I liked the infant school as it was playtime rather than learning to me; I guess it was meant to prime one for the shock of going on to the higher school. They were next door to each other, possibly the same building. In the infants we did what starters do today. Nothing much has changed – painting, cutting coloured paper, banging things, lying down in the afternoon for a nap even when you were not in the least bit sleepy. I don't have any memories of unkindness or misery to do with that school, but the junior school was a different matter.

Why I disliked it so much or what accounted for my unreasonable behaviour there has faded with time. It could have been the shock of moving from looseness to discipline, and on to mix with unknown children or teachers. In retrospect I can't think why I was such a lackadaisical schoolgirl. Could it have been because too many wonderful things were happening at home and I was missing them? I recall the time when my pa was building a radio set with all the paraphernalia scattered over the kitchen table – valves, wires, accumulators and the rest – with the occasional successful sound that emanated from the clutter, which eventually gave us so much joy and pleasure. While he worked on his radio he sang, as he always did, and I stood by his side, watching and listening. Many of the songs I learnt during those radio days became part of my musical vocabulary and I have since recorded them.

We also joined the Ovaltinies Club, a weekly radio show on Radio Luxembourg, singing the theme song with passionate, loyal gusto and fervour. 'We are the Ovaltinies, happy girls and boys, at your request we're here to please you.' Commercials influenced what our mother bought us then, as it does today's mothers. Another favourite was Sonny Jim, a logo for Force, a breakfast cereal, which you could acquire if you stuffed enough of it for breakfast, so that you could eventually send off the requisite number of packet tops. They insisted you had to get the little fellow. Sonny Jim was a stuffed cloth doll of a man dressed in eighteenth-century clothes with a white wig which had a curled-up pig-tail, because he was in the act of jumping over a fence after eating his Force. His jingle went: 'High over the fence jumps Sonny Jim – Force is the food that raises him.' With a cupboard groaning full of Force, we all possessed him.

Whatever Force did for Sonny, Sylvia or Alec it certainly didn't do it for me. More like it weighed me down in the mornings when school was imminent. Poor Mother had to pull me out of bed, wash and dress me, still half asleep until the hair had to be tackled; then life arrived in the form of protest. Mother then had to walk behind me to make sure I reached school. It wasn't very far from our home and in those days a child could walk to school safely: I can't remember ever being taken to school by Pa or Mother for safety reasons – they escorted me only to make sure that I went. Meanwhile my brother and sister were already in the playground. I might have been the original model for Shakespeare's 'whining school-boy, with his satchel/ And shining morning face, creeping like a snail / Unwillingly to school'. Who would have thought with my record I would ever be quoting Shakespeare?

Things went from bad to worse. I began to play truant, spending whole days in the park, on the swings and roundabouts until home time. But I was eventually discovered when the dreaded school board man came to the house enquiring why Clemmie hadn't been to school – there had been no note of explanation. Then all hell was let loose, not only from my parents but also from the headmaster, who really didn't mince his words or his cane when he got hold of me. Mother also had a cane that was hung over the mantelpiece in case we should get out of hand, more of a threat than anything. It was taken down deliberately by Mother or Pa, flicked ominously a couple of times and that was usually enough. But on this occasion I felt its wrath, and Mr Brown's.

23

Cleo

The headmaster invited me into his study, on that and future occasions, and my hand got many a stroke from his cane for being persistently late or talking when silence was requested. Miss Owen was possibly my saving grace. She was the music teacher who, having at sometime heard me sing in her class, kept an eye on me. One day, from out of the blue, a message came to my classroom: 'Could Clemmie be spared for a few moments to show the music class how a certain song should be sung?' The song was 'Shenandoah'. This did my ego good – here I was centre stage, all by myself, with no brother or sister to take the spotlight away from me. I sang it beautifully as far as I can remember, with much expression and feeling. God, I must have been quite sickening, but Miss Owen liked it, and took me under her wing.

Her music lessons were inventive and adventurous for those days. She had a wind-up gramophone and played music that the class was unlikely to hear in their homes or tune into on the radio. She also had a leaning towards American music, and along with 'Shenandoah' she played us Longfellow's 'Song of Hiawatha', which we also had to learn. I was in my element, singing along like my Pa might have done without any embarrassment, just great joy in letting rip. The other pupils must have thought me a terrible show-off as well as being teacher's pet. I didn't much care. I enjoyed singing, and I was not going to stop for anyone now I had been given the opportunity.

However, my enthusiasm was starting to get out of hand by the time Miss Owen organized the school concert. She of course gave me a couple of show-off songs to sing: 'The Last Rose of Summer' and 'Rock a Bye Your Baby', two songs that did not need belting out or yelling. But I came on strong, giving that poor audience everything I had. It makes me go hot inside with shame now as I remember it. I violently dislike the precocious child performer who goes way over the top. Now I know why – I was one myself.

Miss Owen didn't like the performance at all, and proceeded to let me know it. The audience, however, thought this bushy-haired brat divine. Not because she had sung the song well, for she hadn't – it was a tasteless performance – but because I had nerve or chutzpah (a good Jewish word for neck or a lot of bottle). I'm afraid this phase lasted a long time, although a lot of friends along with Miss Owen tried to curb it. I said to myself, if people clapped and liked it, I was good.

My poor mother had to suffer me performing at the foot of her large iron bed. Oh how she loved that bed, so looking forward to getting into it after a gruelling day of cooking, mending and cleaning. A big feather bed that enveloped her as she sank into it, waiting for sleep to eliminate the aches and pains of the day. But Clemmie was going to perform her latest song, just for her alone, 'So don't you go to sleep!' Egged on by me, the others joined in and she had a full variety show, whether she liked it or not. I think she did like it. We were company for her and she loved to hear us. We would give her our full repertoire of singing and dancing. Alec, who was learning to play the violin, scraped away to Mother's delight – but not to Sylvia's or mine.

3

Ice-cream and Daydreams

The mid-1930s was a period of political chaos shadowed by the threat of world war – but I was too young to understand much about it. I had the vague sense, though, that Mother was unhappy, partly because Pa was finding it hard to find work. I must have been seven or eight when he started to busk as a street singer, which didn't do much to improve the family finances.

Then I remember two young girls suddenly coming into our lives: tall, thin, fashionably dressed and glamorous. One was black-haired and exotic and called Dinah; the other, fair, called Rose. We called them both Auntie, and we adored them because they were great fun and took us on outings. However, they were a disruption in the household because Pa also liked them and showed it. I don't know if he was having an affair with one of them, but Mother thought he was, and the rows grew worse as she was left alone to do most of the work and attend to us.

Saturday night had always been our family night out – a visit to the pictures. We generally went to the Gem Cinema, the local flea-pit where we had to queue up because it was so popular. Pa always bought Mother her favourite sweets, which were almonds covered with toffee. These were not cheap so she only got a few, but we always pleaded with her to give us just one. 'Only one, Mum, please!' After a little toing and froing she would finally give in so that she could enjoy the rest of them herself, alone in the darkness of the cinema, sucking the toffee away first until the nut was released. That's how I did it too. They last a long time that way, and when you finally reach the nut, you can really crunch. What a sensuous delight it was, enjoying that sweet in the dark, while watching and hearing the images up on the big screen! Stars like Jeanette MacDonald, Nelson Eddy, John Boles, Jean Harlow and Wallace Beery.

My mother and father were not drinkers, and they seldom went to pubs, but the big treat after the pictures was a glass of brown ale. Pa would buy a bottle at the off-licence, then come home to enjoy it with mother, who'd be listening to the radio or pottering about, while we ate our fish-and-chip supper before going off to bed. This kind of treat started to vanish at this time. Work was getting harder to find for everyone now, and Pa found it even harder than most, though he never gave up trying to earn a penny somehow. If a labouring job became vacant hundreds applied. I can remember my father practising in the garden (to the delight of the three of us) carrying a hod of bricks up a ladder. Faster and faster he would go, up, down, up, down – timing himself at each ascent and descent. After filling the hod with bricks at the bottom he would tear up the ladder, unload them on the garden wall, then speed down again. We thought it was a party trick, not understanding that there was a serious purpose to it.

One summer Pa decided to be an ice-cream man. The excitement began with the arrival of the wooden tub with the canister in the centre that was going to be filled with that delicious cream. We were all at home for the event and the working out of how it was to be done: Pa taking command, Mother making the mixture. They had to buy ice and salt, of course, so they got in touch with the ice man, who arrived at our house with his horse and cart, lifted the heavy blocks of ice on to his leather-covered shoulders and carried them into the scullery where the ice-cream was to be manufactured. All our friends in the street gathered round to watch. This was something really special – and even better, it was happening at our house, and people were asking about it. I felt real cocky, because these others were not going to be included in the mystery of ice-cream making.

Tub, mixture, ice and salt all assembled, we got to work. The boiling hot concoction was poured in and ice was broken off by chipping at the large block and put between the wooden tub and the metal canister. The lid was clamped down, a handle was inserted and we were ready to go. We argued and fought over who was to turn the handle, but it had to be done by either Mother, Pa or Sylvia, who had to keep at it until the cream became frozen hard. It was not an easy job as the lumps of ice often got jammed, so a strong arm and patience were necessary. Rough salt was thrown on at these tough moments to melt the ice a little, so that work could continue unimpeded. We were a family production team.

When the commanders pronounced the product finished the next step (before Alec and I ate it all) was to sell it. The plan was to go to Runnymede, by the River Thames near Maidenhead, which we often visited for family outings. We always jostled for a place on the back seat of Pa's bike, but in the end we had to take it in turns, as he wouldn't favour one over the other. When it wasn't your turn you went on the bus with Mother, riding on the top. She loved the top front seats so that she could see all around. But once Pa became the ice-cream man we had to forgo our turns for the sake of filthy lucre. What a sacrifice it was for me not to be sitting close to Pa with my arms around him, getting a good close warm whiff of that perfume of his! It was sissy to ride on the bus with Mother. When we arrived though, all that nonsense was soon forgotten: we had a great time picnicking, bathing in the river, exploring the fields and hills, worm-digging to fish with Alec.

Pa would arrive a bit later than us, even though he'd left a lot earlier, with the ice-cream strapped on the back of his bike. Then he'd set to work, singing out the name of his product at the top of his lungs. Ice-ah-cream, ice-ah-cream! He was a scream. I think he made a few shillings or he wouldn't have

29

persevered. But I shouldn't think it was enough to say we were rising above our near-poverty level. That the bills could not be paid was never of great concern to us children. Both parents seemed to want to protect us from it, but Sylvia always knew, keeping us in our place when we asked for things that were too expensive.

Mother was a great habituée of rummage and auction sales: treats for us, but essential money-savers for her. I don't think we ever had a new piece of furniture or clothing. Once I had a long and steamy argument, that I lost, about a pair of boots that had to be buttoned up with a hook. They really were lovely – today they would be in the height of fashion – but not for me then. I hated them, their only redeeming feature being the time it took to button them up in the morning. Delay tactics with tantrums about the awful boots I had to wear to school. I realize now that my behaviour was truly awful.

Mother picked up some magnificent items of furniture, as the houses in Featherstone Road were so big, with high impressive ceilings and huge rooms that were able to take pieces that the little houses had no room for. Big Victorian wardrobes, chests, tables and chairs galore, that would cost the earth today. She had an extremely good eye for a bargain, choosing wisely. One piece that particularly interested me was a pianola with a box full of piano rolls that went into our front room. This room was very large, taking up the whole of the ground floor, facing the street one end and the back garden the other. Hung in the centre of it was a pair of mahogany folding doors that you could pull out to make two rooms if required. We seldom did this as the room was the family entertainment centre where dogs, cats and birds as well as humans sang and danced, and general chaos reigned. Along with the pianola there was a wind-up gramophone, and between them they fitted into my dream world perfectly, especially the pianola. I would try to pick the times when the room was empty, so I could enjoy my fantasy world undisturbed. I would put a roll in, then prepare to pedal away, controlling the tempos of any choice of music I felt like. There was enough in the box to keep me entertained for hours at a time – from classics to popular songs.

It was not only a dream world, it was a learning experience for me. Many of the classical pieces that I know today I learnt from those rolls. I never closed the screen where the roll was located because it was such fun to see the patterns of the music go by, sometimes at great speed if my legs were not too tired. If they were, then the mood would be more romantic. That was what I liked best. It was then that I became the concert pianist, closing my eyes, swaying my body, dipping my shoulders. It must have looked pretty awful to my brother when he caught me at it – he didn't like all that sloppy stuff – and my sister would have thought I was just showing off. Friends who had to suffer it from time to time really knew it was a sham, but I didn't care. I was making music with no hard work attached to it, unlike all the other lessons.

Apart from the arguments, fights, lack of money and hard work, it was a loving family and, as far as we children were concerned, all very much together. But unknown to us, boiling and brewing underneath, all was not well. Dinah and Rose were certainly catalysts for future events whether they intended to be or not. My nosy-parkering never found that out, but things were changing, and not for the better. At the outset we were not aware of this because we were having such a great time. The girls took us to places we had never gone to before: to London to visit their friends, to Hyde Park, to museums. Sometimes Pa came with us, but I can't remember Mother ever being along.

I think the girls were in show business – dancers or showgirls. Pa might have thought that they could get him into the profession. He did audition for Jack Payne, the famous bandleader of the day, but he didn't pass. Desperately wanting to be a professional, he did the rounds of all the available auditions. The stories he told us when he returned home about how he conducted himself make it unsurprising that he never suceeded. Pa was no diplomat; he was opinionated and dogmatic to a fault about the way people should or should not behave, and if anyone offended him or if he thought he had been slighted, he would immediately let fly with a tirade of words.

Having been through the experience of a few auditions myself, I know now that they do nothing for your ego if you are in the least bit sensitive – you just hurt. My father was sensitive to a painful degree. Walking into a room of laughing people, he would instantly assume they were laughing at him. From a very early age he lectured us that it was wrong to stare at people who were different from us in any way, as it would hurt their feelings. Not an easy thing for a small child not to do, but if he caught us we were in trouble.

So Pa didn't become a professional singer and the girls disappeared from our lives as mysteriously as they had appeared. That meant that Alec and I had to fall back on old delights for our enjoyment. One of them was a creepy, thrilling game: the asylum almost next door to us was a deserted mysterious haunted house with shadowy ghosts and goolies behind a twelve-foot wall. Alec and his friends challenged me and my friends to climb over this wall with them to see if we could spot any of these frightening creatures. A challenge from my brother was like a red cloth to a bull, so I scaled the wall like a trained commando along with the boys.

Once over the other side the excitement began to mount in earnest. All was quite desolate. Overgrown gardens with broken statuary, rooms bare but for boxes of medical books, magazines and bottles strewn all over them. We couldn't believe that anyone would leave such valuable stuff behind unguarded. Surely, we thought, there must be a guard at least, and possibly some loonies who might jump out at any time. But we overcame our fear enough to flick through the books and see that some contained nude pictures – of men, women and children who in some cases were deformed. We thought these were rude, and that we'd be punished if we were caught with them. But each of us risked taking a couple back over the wall to pursue in secrecy later.

The garden of delights kept us entertained for quite a while – until it was turned into another mysterious delight: the Dominion

Cinema. This was a wonder palace for us. Until then we only had the Gem flea-pit, which was small, not too comfortable and certainly not a modern dream palace. As well as going for the Saturday night treats with our parents, we belonged to the Gem's Saturday Morning Club, which cost sixpence to join, and was run by a gentleman (who was not so gentle, at least not with the boys) with a long bamboo pole which he used to bang the offending party or parties on the head with. This pole could reach along a full row easily. It almost always came into use during the love scenes in cowboy or adventure films when the boys would boo, hiss, whistle, throw orange peel at the screen and create general mayhem until the kissing stopped or their heads were sore from the bamboo banging they got.

The Gem couldn't stand up to the competition the Dominion brought into the district, with its modern façade, its large opulent foyer, but most of all its movies. They were the latest to come out of Hollywood, whereas the poor old Gem only showed older ones. The Dominion had another trump card in its stage, which was large enough to put on band, variety and amateur shows, bringing famous radio stars to appear in the flesh.

It was expensive, though, and since we didn't have to pay to climb the asylum wall, we saw no reason why we should not climb into the pictures. This was the heart-pumping experience the new building was to provide. We called it 'bunking in'. Sometimes we had to wait an age for someone to come out of the side exit of the cinema before we could put our foot in the door to stop it closing. But once in we always managed to find a seat empty, sinking down into it in the dark. We tried to become invisible or to give off the air of having paid – whatever air that might be. In this dark illegal luxury Fred, Ginger, Garbo, Garland and many more fuelled my deepest desires. The music in the musicals was amazing, and the singing and dancing matched up to it. I dreamed that given the chance I could be up there too. This was a time when the cinema was making breakthrough after breakthrough. Both technically and artistically it came of age, and I managed to see a great deal of it – with or without paying. I

33

devoured the Shirley Temple films – *The Littlest Rebel*, *Curly Top*, *Bright Eyes*; I adored Mickey Rooney; and oh, I wanted Dorothy Lamour's hair so badly.

It was about now, when I was ten or eleven, that Mother started to become a half-hearted stage mum. She took to dressing and primping us up to look like Shirley Temple – though I, of course, much preferred the tomboy Jane Withers. Although her singing and dancing didn't match up to Shirley's, I could identify with her more, because she was a natural rebel. Mother began to take us to auditions for films and shows. How she got wind of them I don't know, and we didn't fare any better than Pa. There was a rumour that Sylvia could have gone to Hollywood, but mother was not allowed to go with her as a chaperone, so her screen chance was missed.

At one point Mother also had hopes that we might all join the 'Corona-Babes', a group of child performers named after the popular fizzy drink of the day; they toured all over the country extolling its virtues. When the Corona-Babes appeared at the Dominion Mother was asked to house them for the week. Most of them were fed separately by the couples assigned to look after them on tour, though two or three lucky ones ate with us. Mother fed them more heartily than those who had chaperones, and the others would plead with Mother, telling her of the meagre rations doled out to them by their chaperones and claiming that they were pocketing the food allowance money. There was so much discontent that eventually she gave up on getting us into the troupe. Our launch into the world of show business was not to be. Yet we made several visits to the show as guests of the Corona-Babes, and seeds were being sown in my mind as to what I was going to be later on in life.

I daydreamed constantly about how it would happen, and fell asleep making up stories of my rise to fame on the stage, looking unbelievably glamorous, with long black hair like Dorothy Lamour that I was able to swing over my shoulders. In my dreams I could comb through it with ease and as many times as I wished without a single tweak of pain. They were such wonderful dreams that they kept me happy when all about us seemed to be falling apart.

There was no need for dreaming at No. 8 Featherstone Road during the Christmas period, though, because it became a real-life dream world, an exciting time for all three of us. First, the writing of letters to Santa, and making coloured paper chains all together in the kitchen. I liked doing family things, writing present lists, and making Christmas puddings with silver threepenny bits hidden inside them. All of us got to stir the mixture then lick the spoon and bowl when the puddings were safely wrapped in their white cloths and tucked in the basins ready for the big steam-up day. Of course, we all had to make a wish as we stirred, hoping that on Christmas Day when we got our slice we would bite down on the threepenny bit, which was a lucky thing to do. Very little in our household was bought, so the kitchen became a cottage industry. Months before, Mother had prepared onions bottled in large jars of vinegar (her favourite), and hundreds of mince pies and tarts. We did help her a little by getting rid of a few surplus tarts, acting out the old nursery rhyme, but mostly we just got in the way, especially when she started to ice and decorate the Christmas cake.

Mother was a genius of a pastry cook. She had a large slab of marble, rescued from a Victorian washstand on one of her auction visits, as her pastry board. Her hands were always cold and she swore that this was one of the reasons her pastry was such a success: the trick was marble, cold hands and as little handling as possible.

Christmas shopping was left as late as possible because purchases like birds, fruit, vegetables and toys were so much cheaper if bought at the last minute. On Christmas Eve we'd go along to the auction at the butcher's, so that we could choose the bird we wanted: chicken being a luxury in those days for any poor family, it was an important buy. I remember us all standing outside the shop, which was decorated with mistletoe and holly, lights ablaze to show off the still feathered birds hanging from hooks in and outside the shop. The butcher – aproned, jolly-faced, with a piece of mistletoe suggestively stuck in his straw hat (a boater tipped at a saucy angle) – flirted with all the ladies, cajoling them to hurry, hurry, hurry before his little beauties disappeared before their very eyes. As the time ticked away the bargaining became brisker. This was the best fun for the children, with lots of repartee between the butcher and our mothers and fathers. If he didn't think he'd been offered enough he'd announce: 'Lady, 'owder ya think I kin feed me brood with an offer like that?' 'Ow about our lot, ya stingy bugger?' would come the reply. 'Tell ya what, give us a tanner more, an it's yourn.' Someone would agree in the crowd and he'd slap his hands together and at the top of his lungs yell 'Sold – to the lady in the green 'at!' Mother and Pa were good at holding out for what they thought they could afford.

The excitement stirred up by the butcher and the shoppers kept us enthralled, even though it was sometimes freezing. But we wouldn't be sent back home, so we stomped our feet, played games with the mysterious breath coming from our mouths and licked at snowflakes. Ignoring the cold we held out until the last orange, pomegranate, banana and nut (all exotic once-a-year buys) was hauled back to No. 8 along with the bargain of the evening, the prized chicken. If the snow was lying really thick in the garden when we got home we still wouldn't give up – out we would go again for a snow fight before being called in for bed. Even Sylvia, who seldom participated in such tomfoolery, couldn't resist the lure of romping in the snow late at night.

The day often ended in tears as frozen hands and feet started to come to life in the warmth of the kitchen. Pa would rub the hands and feet of one child, Mother another. Pa was always Father Christmas – we suspected it, but never caught him out: he was cleverer than we were at that game. In the morning we never knew how we had fallen asleep, when we'd been so determined to stay awake and watch the door like hawks. By then the pillow cases we had placed at the bottom of our beds had been filled with all sorts of precious goodies. Each of us had an orange, nuts and sweeties and at least one of the requests on the notes we had written to Santa. We became believers again for another year.

Ice-cream and Daydreams

Christmas Day was show-off day. We dressed in our Sunday best and paraded the street with all the other children, flaunting our new acquisitions. A bicycle if lucky, a doll, a pram to push it in, maybe skates. There was always one big gift that was our heart's desire, our wish come true. My parents paid for these expensive items by joining Christmas clubs at the beginning of the year, which paid a dividend if you kept up your payments regularly. Mother also belonged to the Co-op, with a dividend number we all had to remember – 482117. This gave a percentage on each purchase in the shape of tin coins marked up to a pound in value. They were saved in a tin box for a whole year, if possible, so that the Christmas luxuries could be afforded.

Cares and anxieties seemed to disappear during the hectic days leading up to Christmas and into the New Year. We were on holiday from school with new toys to occupy our interest. Books, jigsaw puzzles, a new record or a piece of music to struggle through, but best of all for me – not having to go to school. If only it could have lasted for ever, life would have been exactly how I wanted it to be – with just a few adjustments here and there.

Mother had many idiosyncrasies. Some that amused, some that irritated us like hell, and some that caused rows between her and Pa. She loved vinegar, pouring it on everything she ate, which angered Pa intensely. He'd hold forth on the many reasons for giving it up, the main ones being that it would dry up her blood and it was a bad influence on us. He was right there – I love it too, but my blood seems to be surviving the influence. Tea was another argument-provoker. Mother drank gallons of it: it was her cure for all distressful moments in life. Pa never touched it – coffee was his drink, the liquid kind called Camp Coffee, with an Indian soldier standing to attention beside a tent on the label. Nobody could make it properly for him, and he always complained if he hadn't made it himself.

There were so many things that my parents couldn't agree upon that they made a queer couple. Mother was a feather-bedder – mattress, pillows, eiderdowns. She loved to sink down into the luxurious softness of feathers. Pa did not approve – a real matrimonial problem to be solved. He certainly solved it as far as we were concerned: he simply would not allow us to sleep in such unhealthy beds, so we slept on hard and pillowless beds for as long as I can remember.

Ma had green fingers. On our walks with her she would break bits from bushes or flowers as she passed by, popping them into her handbag. We walked hurriedly ahead of her, utterly embarrassed. When she got home she would plant her snippets, and nine times out of ten the little devils would not only survive, but grow and develop into fine specimens. Another idiosyncrasy of hers was that she found it impossible to pass a bit of coal that lay in the street. She would pick it up, spit on it, wish – and put that into her bag as well. I don't think anyone attempted to pinch a penny from that handbag. I certainly never tried it.

My friend Pat, who lived next door, would sometimes come around to dream with me about all the good things that could happen for us one day. Pat had more reason to dream than I did. She had a pretty miserable life: her father was a bully and her mother was deaf and dumb, so Pat was the little skivvy of the household. Her father beat her mother regularly, without caring if he broke anything or blackened an eye. Pat was scared to death of him but still tried to protect her mother and often got badly beaten in her place. Sometimes he would allow Pat to stay overnight with us, but she was always worried about her mother being left alone with him, and would fly back in the morning early to make sure she was all right.

Mother, who was not at all afraid of this man, offered Mrs Smith a safe refuge whenever she couldn't bear it any longer. However, such support was sometimes of questionable value. She could not leave her husband, since he was her only means of support; and then there was Pat to think of. When Mother insisted she come to us after a particularly life-threatening beating, Mrs Smith had to face up to returning to the brute's anger at her having gone next door for sanctuary and, as he put it, 'letting the world know our business'.

We had three more house moves while living in Southall. Often we had no time to say goodbye because we didn't know what was going on. I think Mother did moonlight flits, avoiding payment of rent or bills that had piled up. Although leaving friends behind is never pleasant, for me, at least, these upheavals were sometimes filled with excitement. One move, which I think was less of a flit than an attempt to attract summer holiday-makers' money, was to the seaside, to Cliftonville, Margate, where once again a house was rented. A lorry was hired, and goods and chattels loaded, together with Mother's adored cats and dogs and children. Pa had decided not to travel with this gypsy caravan but to wait until we had settled in and got the house in some kind of order, with guests installed, cheerfully enjoying Mother's hospitality.

We arrived late at night, and all the furniture that Mother had seen fit to bring was dumped in one room to be sorted out in the morning. She had found a young girl to act as maid and generally help her out. Jessie smelt fishily of winkles, but she was very jolly, laughed and joked a lot, and adored Mother and us kids. I didn't like winkles, so with my strong sense of smell I avoided Jessie as far as possible.

That night the grown-ups slept in deck-chairs in the kitchen, which had a giant built-in dresser with the largest drawers I had ever seen. The drawers became Alec's and my beds for the night, while Sylvia slept in the space where the drawers had been. This was adventure time again for Alec and me. We had no electricity – Mother had to wait for deposits to come in from guests before she could get it turned on – so all was done by candlelight.

It was a hand-to-mouth existence my parents lived but they were determined that this wasn't going to affect us children if they could help it. We were at the seaside, and we could scarcely contain our excitement at the prospect of tomorrow, and exploring the beach, which was only a stone's throw from the house.

As at Christmas we were surprised to wake up and find it was morning. I had been absolutely sure I would never fall asleep again – life was too wonderful to waste time sleeping.

Alec and I started exploring at once. We investigated the house first, tearing up and down the stairs, picking out the room the three of us would share and make home for the season. After that the really important stuff had to be taken care of, like sorting out buckets, spades, fishing nets, jam-jars and cossies. We were then gone for the day. A bit of bread and an apple seemed like a grand picnic, with a drink from the water fountain that was sure to be found somewhere near the beach. If we could squeeze a few pence out of Mother we'd go for pony and donkey rides – and then there was the pier . . . the town held very little interest for either of us.

Music was not forgotten during the summer holidays – where Mother found our Cliftonville singing and piano teacher, Michael, I never knew, but he was quite mad. The front room, which was the guests' sitting-room, had a piano cluttered with an embroidered runner, vase, pictures and music. Music lessons were timed to be when the guests were out at the beach, and at the appointed hour, he would sprint into the room – having been for his daily swim. He would sit at the piano in plimsolls and swimming trunks, with a long mackintosh to cover his nudity, though every time he used the pedals his knobbly knees popped out. The songs he had prepared had to be gone over phrase by phrase, till I knew them. He was a stickler about the ends of words being properly enunciated and singing in tune. He was obsessed with 'September In the Rain'.

I had already learnt the song as my daily exercise. The introduction was played; knees displayed – and giggling I began 'The leaves of brown came tumbling down rememb'. The lid of the piano would be slammed down suddenly and quite violently – 'No! No! No! No! It's *rememberrr – ber – let's have the ends of the words please.*' Again, introduction, knees, and this time not only was there no beerr, but sloppy intonation, which sent him into a paroxysm of fury. I knew exactly what he would do the next time if I didn't sing the 'bers' clearly and precisely. Once again he would play the introduction, and I would start the song, singing every 'ber' perfectly for him until the last one, which

I would deliberately swallow. Driven to the point of despair, with a great sweep of his hand he would clear the top of the piano of everything, and stomp out of the room. I thought he was a good teacher. Apart from the amusement he gave, he also taught me the importance of diction. I'm also acutely aware of out-of-tune singing, which practically sends me into paroxysms of fury myself. Michael didn't last long, however; either Mother thought I was having too much fun, or she felt I was in danger. I never felt I was, but maybe if I had gone too far it might have been me and not the piano top that was swiped. Anyway, he disappeared one day with no explanation and my music lessons and fun ceased.

4

The Thief of Baghdad

The season was drawing to a close, but for some holiday-makers it was hard to let go of summer, so Mother was still hard at work. That meant we would be staying, and that we children would be going to school. Strangely this didn't disturb me much. It was a Church of England school, so besides the lessons, I had to go to church again, but this time every morning, whether I liked it or not.

I had to wear a smart uniform – pleated navy-blue skirt, white blouse, striped tie, topped off with a straw hat which sported the school badge. This was dress-up time for me, preparing for my performance in church, though not quite so dramatic as my Catholic experience. I enjoyed being religious: it let me off all my wickedness to my family. The one bit of serious bother that I had to live with was that hat. It would not stay on my head – it was continually springing up to sit on top of my mop, unlike the other girls, whose hats behaved themselves. It was a tug-of-war between the hat and me. Sitting in church listening to the lesson or singing 'Onward Christian Soldiers', me and my hat went through the daily routine of pull down–bounce up, until the inevitable happened: the brim became a necklace and the crown a basket in the next pew. This made all the girls and me break into

43

uncontrollable giggling – a scene that disturbed the oh-so-serious proceedings.

I was given black marks for lack of control, and for not wearing a school hat in church, which I felt extremely unfair – and my planned melodramatic performances slid into unplanned comedy that landed me into a lot of trouble, at home and school.

But this was a happy, almost carefree summer and autumn. We had three more moves ahead before arriving at Hayes End, Middlesex. One was to another café close to Southall Station, which gave Alec and me train-spotting to add to our amusements as well as bike-riding down the steep hill from the station to the café, pretty fearful, dangerous stuff on the main road. Alec and I escaped unscathed from these brakeless journeys, but not Sylvia. On one trip down, she lost control and crashed into the lamp-post at the bottom, giving her black eyes and a badly bruised body. She was in quite a state and was brought home in a faint. We were forbidden to ever ride our bikes down the hill again.

I think this café venture was successful, being close to the station; the most popular meal was pease pudding and faggots, which customers could either eat in the café or take away. The windows were always covered with white writing, telling of the special prices, the freshness of the faggots and the pudding, or of any other working man's delicacy Mother had cooked that day.

Our next move was to a farmhouse, close to Heston airport, now swallowed up into Heathrow. It was a mysterious move, a moonlight flit and an attempt by my parents to patch up their ailing partnership. For us it was a wonderful experience. The house was large, rambling and well-appointed: it had been owned by a well-to-do farmer who had sold the land and house shortly to be transformed into an airport. In the meantime it was rented out.

This time it was farm teas, with tables set out on the lawn. Where Mother expected customers to show up from I have no idea. I don't think she had thought about doing it at all until she got there and decided to capitalize on the lovely surroundings; catering was what she knew how to do, so why waste the opportunity, if someone passed by? Few customers materialized, except for a very large African who was cutting down the trees in the fields and who came every day. His name was Mr Samples, and he reminded me of a favourite film star of mine, Paul Robeson, so I liked going to visit him, hoping he would burst into one of the songs I knew so well. He never did oblige, so I just sat and looked at him.

Alec and I loved to watch the men working on the airport, interrupting them to ask questions galore. Mr Samples had a son who came from time to time to help him, but he did more playing about with us than work for his dad. We called him Samples: if we were ever told or knew his Christian name, it is lost in the fields that were our playground, now under concrete. Mr Samples, his work team and Samples Jnr, who became our best friend, were just about Mother's only customers.

Samples Jnr was older and a great deal more sophisticated than we were. He taught us how to smoke behind the barn – not a good experience for me – but we spent most of the time playing in the fields. It was with him that I found out that bulls were not friendly animals: trespassing into a field to challenge the animal, and test our courage, it was me who got stuck on the barbed-wire fence when the bull took exception to our presence and charged. We bolted, taking flight over the fence; my knickers got well and truly ripped and I landed in a bed of stinging nettles. The cure for the pain and white bumps was supplied by Pa, who wrapped me in dock leaves while Mother rubbed vinegar all over me. Pa also admonished Samples Jnr (he felt that being older he should have known better) and us for going on to other people's land, threatening to tell Samples Snr, who was a strict disiplinarian. Samples was not so cocky in Pa's presence as he was with us – he feared his father.

It was during our farm stay that we also met and made friends with some Spanish children, refugees from the Civil War. We met them in the bluebell woods nearby, where we were all picking flowers; I remember that one had an arm missing, another a hand. We didn't know why at the time: to us they were lonely and different, so we wanted to play with them. The friendship didn't last long, however, as we were soon on the move again, this time to a flat, back in the centre of Southall, on the main road called Broadway.

After all the large, people-filled houses, the attempts at business and the debt, this relatively small flat-living was almost like normal family life. I had been complaining that I wanted to live in a doll's house, like my friends – I don't know why, as I certainly had more fun than they did, with bigger gardens for dogs, cats, rabbits and the other fun things of childhood which they couldn't have because their mothers said there wasn't room. I was just a discontented child who thought her friends were better off than she was. I had no reason to complain, except that I wanted my parents all to myself.

In 1936 the Spanish Civil War, Hitler and the death of King George V were using up the airwaves: what with the radio and my father between them there was a lot of talking going on, although we tended to resist Pa's lectures on the unfairness ladled out to the working man all over the world (and especially to him). We were told about King George's death at school, and we all became extremely solemn as we listened to the radio. I cried as I heard the lowered voice of the commentator explaining events; and then the dirge of the funeral march set me off to such an extent that my Pa did not know how to pacify me: it took a lot of cuddling and cajoling to get me to stop, I was enjoying it all so much. When we went to the pictures, they had to go through all the blubbering again, when Pathe and Movietone News showed the film of the funeral cortège.

We did of course have Edward VIII as a new king to revere, but not for long. When he abdicated to marry Mrs Simpson, with no real understanding of events we children all sang silly rhymes like, 'Hark the Herald Angels sing, Mrs Simpson's stole our King'. We accepted the next king quite happily, as we were all given a holiday for the coronation, with lots of flag-waving, and two princesses for Mother to try and dress us up like.

While the world was churning out disaster after disaster, my own world wasn't going the way I wanted it to. I knew it all too well because of my love of tuning in to grown-up conversations – as Mother put it, 'You want to know the ins and outs of a cat's behind.' My brother was very ill in hospital, so he was getting all my Mother's attention which, selfishly, didn't suit me at all. I was seething with jealousy; and at the same time Mother and Pa were not being kind to each other, so the arguments were often hard and vicious.

Alec was eventually sent to a hospital in Seabourne, where he had a long convalescence before coming home. This meant Mother was away a great deal of time visiting him, which made me feel more and more unwanted. From being a fairly outgoing, social child, I became more of an inward-looking unsociable dreamer, and when Alec came home, our relationship was not so close as before, with the minutest incident triggering off a fight between us.

I was really going through a difficult period. I was a sullen, suspicious brat who thought she did not belong and that she must have been adopted. This fantasy kept my overbearing, aloof manner going strong for quite some time. Looking back at myself during these years I must have been a demanding handful for Mother to have to cope with, along with all the other problems that were making life pretty disastrous for her. But I was only concerned with mine, real or imagined – mainly the latter.

Moving to Hayes End was our last move as a family. It was there that my parents finally separated, after eighteen years or so of calms and tidal waves between two strong, independent, free spirits. It finished with an explosion I shall never forget, it was so frightening; but before that there were a few years more of family happiness together. At least for us children it felt secure.

We had to go to another new school, Mellow Lane Senior School, and amazingly I loved it. I liked being early, I was a decent pupil who wanted to learn, and started enjoying lessons that seemed as interesting as the music ones. Music still held my attention, but drama was for a while to take its place. I appeared in *A Midsummer Night's Dream* as one of the mechanicals, and in other Shakespeare plays as sword-bearer or rabble-rouser. To me it was extremely important stuff that had to be worked on and got right so that the drama teacher would give me a bigger part next term. I think the school was advanced in its teaching methods for its time. It was a modern building, bearing no resemblance at all to the old Victorian Featherstone Road school in Southall. You could look out of a window and see sky, trees and flowerbeds; I even had my own flowerbed, assigned to me to keep in good health. I loved it and looked with pride at the work I'd put into it.

Lessons were varied and made interesting by discussion; we were encouraged to ask questions. We were having a lesson about India and its people when the teacher said something like, 'When they are capable of ruling themselves, they will be allowed to, but they are still like children.' This really got my goat; influenced by my belligerent Pa, I'm sure, I had to stand up, even though I had a bit of the collywobbles, to say, 'I think, Miss, that if they had been given an education to prepare them for self-rule, they would not be like children, and anyway I do not believe that grown-ups should be treated like children', or words to that effect. It stunned her, but I was not shouted down or told I didn't know what I was talking about.

I was starting to be an argumentative child, following in the footsteps of Ma and Pa. I would not take anything as read just because a teacher said it was so. Though I was only nine I seemed to be more aware of the world and its problems than a lot of the other working-class children in the class: my Pa saw to that. We could not escape being influenced by him, by the multi-racial households all around us and, most important of all, by our own parents' mixed marriage. We certainly got both sides of every picture that cropped up, and my brother and I became great arguers – Sylvia less so, although at this stage she was considered the bright, responsible one, always serious about her school work, the one in the family who, when asked to do anything, did not have to be reminded umpteen times, and did whatever it was well.

Visiting the fair that annually came to the park was a big event in our lives, and we couldn't be kept in for love or money. Bill Betts was one of our favourite attractions. Bill guessed your weight – sixpence for grown-ups, threepence for children – before putting you on the scales. If he guessed right, which seemed to be always, you lost your money; if he misjudged (or more likely, to please the crowd and lull them into a false sense of security, deliberately got it wrong) you won – you were given your money back and a small stuffed animal or an African knick-knack. Bill was very popular: he felt the muscles of your arms and shoulders, looking keenly at you all the time. He made remarks about your physique that would flatter you and make the crowd hoot with laughter, but he was never hurtful. He would always dress in African robes and affected an African accent, but though his colour was blue-black, he was a Londoner. Pa knew him, I guess from his Hyde Park orating, so he was invited back to our flat when he'd finished his day's work. This became a regular visit that we all looked forward to.

Bill had an old motor car in which he took us out for Sunday spins. We children would sit in the rumble seat at the back of the car whilst the grown-ups sat inside. I grew extremely fond of Bill and his wife Olive who, like Mum, was white and a deeply commited socialist – but it was always Bill who was the centre of attention.

After one Sunday jaunt we got back home hot, tired and in need of a long cold drink. Mother was making dandelion wine, her summer fun, so the conversation turned to how she made it, the fermenting time, how strong it might turn out and whether they would like to try a glass of last year's brew. A bottle was brought out and they all partook of Mother's ruin. It certainly laid Bill out cold. This immense six-footer collapsed on to the couch, silenced for the rest of the day. Mother's wine was treated with great respect after that, mostly avoidance.

It was when Bill finally came to that he suggested something that turned out to be the start of my professional career in show business. As a member of the 'Actors Extra Union', Bill had heard that they needed children for crowd scenes in the film *The Thief of Baghdad*. Would Mother agree to us going along to try for it? And did we want to do it? If we didn't he wouldn't bother to put in a good word for us. Did we want to! Do cats refuse milk? The room became a circus of joy in which we jumped, cart-wheeled and hollered.

Just in case Mother refused we started to butter her up, but she was used to us soft-soaping her when we wanted something, and although she had winked at Bill beforehand she kept us on tenterhooks for a while. She hung out a little too long for comfort and had us quite scared. When she declared a win on our part, could you stop us going into all our party pieces that just might get us the job? It was a battle of the acts that our parents and visiting friends had to suffer for hours before they finally calmed us down.

It was the summer holidays so school wasn't a problem. All we had to do was try to live and sleep until we had our interview. It is one of the most unsettling, insecure, distraught-making periods for experienced artists to live through, the waiting to hear if you have the part of your life. And this for the three of us was the part of our lives, especially for me.

'We got the job! We got the job! We got the job!' we sang, skipping hand in hand around Mother; we had been told right away, after nothing more than a look at us to see if we could look reasonably Arabic and urchinlike. We were literally jumping for joy. Luckily we had no neighbours underneath: it was a shop that Mother rented in which she was selling off the furniture from the larger houses, yet another non-profit-making business. But soon we were to be earning vast sums of money playing dress-up: two pounds ten shillings a day. This was more money than we as a family had ever had to play with: fifty-two pounds and ten shillings a week!

Of course, we never knew from day to day if we would be asked to return the next day. When we were told to come again tomorrow big grins would appear on our faces – which might have kept us working a little longer; we were not so blasé as some of the other children on the set. Our smiles kept us in work for three of the happiest weeks of my life, getting up wildly early in the morning to catch the Greenline bus that would take us all to the dream world of Denham Studios. We would arrive in time to have makeup applied, wardrobe to dress us as Arab urchins and lunch boxes handed out before our day began. I was in heaven, a fantasy world in the alleys of old Baghdad.

Sabu, the young fourteen-year-old Indian actor, who was discovered when he was a stable boy in Mysore to play the lead in *Elephant Boy*, was the star of this film. We saw very little of him, except for one scene, when he had to tip a basket of oranges over to escape from Conrad Veidt's evil threats. The urchins (the extras – me) had to dive after the fruit with glee, helping him to get away in the confusion. I did my whooping and hollering wholeheartedly, flinging myself on the oranges and keeping a couple to eat later. Rex Ingram, the impressive black actor who played the Genie in the film, was very visible though throughout my period of filming, calling out 'Hi!' to us all every morning as he passed on his way to makeup or wardrobe. He had a very friendly manner towards us lowlier participants in the film. Most of the other stars, if they passed by, passed with nothing to say – Rex Ingram was really most unusual. But for me it was enough to be on the same studio lot as all of them, picking up the vibes.

One morning an assistant director came to pick out a group for a special scene; he wanted four or five of us to leap on to a six-foot-four, heftily built palace guard, diverting his attention from Sabu, who was flying by on his magic carpet. We had to imagine we had seen the carpet, realize the danger our friend the thief was in and spring from all directions over the guard's giant frame, to try and fell him to the ground. I was one of the hand-picked jumpers; my stardom had started at last.

The scene was set up, we were put into place for action, the clapper board was clapped, 'Scene one take one' shouted, then, action! The director wanted the six-footer to stand unmoved, like a statue, under the sudden impact of the leaping urchins, who would be left dripping from his arms and legs; he wanted nothing to move except his eyes, which at the moment of impact spotted Sabu flying past. Unfortunately the impact was so strong that the giant of a man crumbled to the floor. The director was of course sympathetic. We had caught the towering hulk offguard. It was the first take; next time he would know the strength of the impact from the little dears and be able to place his feet, to withstand our force.

Several falls later, everyone started to get hot and bothered, with the exception of us urchins, who were enjoying every wild leap and collapse to such an extent that we became hysterical with laughter. Told to control ourselves as this was a serious scene, we tried once again, but the fun was too much for me still – I ruined the next take because I giggled. This set the rest of the children off, and the great mountain couldn't contain himself either, laughing helplessly at the ludicrous situation he was in. So I was out, along with a couple of other gigglers, after which all went well. I had lost my moment of stardom.

The journeys home were extremely embarrassing for sister Sylvia, who saw no reason to bring her work home when it was done for the day. Not me though: I was now a movie actress, who had to polish up her act continually. We would both get on the Greenline bus to Hayes End and home, sixpenny fare in hand, and wait for the conductor to confront us with 'Fares please'. Sylvia, in her best English, would ask for her sixpenny fare. When it was my turn, ignoring the fact that we were together and obviously related, I would plunge into a most idiotic accent that had nothing to do with Sylvia's. Manic sounds that bore no resemblance to any known language poured from my mouth, only one word emerging that made any sense at all: my version of how a foreigner from who knows where might say 'sixpence'.

'Seexerpineez' didn't fox the conductor who probably came into contact with a lot of nutters on his daily route. I'd get my ticket, but it was too much for Sylvia. Indignant and hurt, 'Why are you talking like that? You're daft!' she said, so my cover would be blown.

Soon after the joy of a fantasy land, three weeks of being paid to play in paradise, the world was plunged into a real horror story – six years of war. The first twelve months were quite uneventful in Britain, but I managed to turn the issuing of gas masks into one of my melodramas. They were first handed out before war was declared, and we were told that we had to walk around with them at the ready.

Now I could wear the mask for real, thumbs on the alert, ready to pop under the straps, whiz it out and voilà, on to the head – that is, if my hair allowed it to happen that way; I was always the last to get the mask on at the daily school drills. I knew I would be gassed: there was nothing I could do except practise daily and get my speed up, or die a horrible death.

I made the most of it. The sirens went almost daily: they were always false alarms at the beginning and a nuisance, but they had to be obeyed. If they sounded while we were at school, we would all leave what we were doing and march to the shelter until the all-clear. We would read or draw or paint, or the teacher would lead us in a sing-song. Lessons came to a virtual standstill, until the teachers worked out a plan of action to continue some form of education during all the interruptions.

Despite all that I was happy. Combined with the film experience, the new school and new friends, Hayes End was an idyllic time for me. There were four of us – Sheila Patterson, a new friend as devil-may-care as we were, Samples Jr, who had reappeared in our lives from nowhere, Alec and I – and together we enjoyed being free spirits. We explored the countryside, we ran, we fought, enjoyed each other's company. We fell out of tree houses and smashed fingers in slammed car doors, we acquired countless scars that would remain for ever to remind us of the fearless days in the playground (we called the reck), where disaster could and often did strike leading us screaming towards home, blood seeping into sock from wounds to shins

or knees, to seek comfort from Mother, only to be scolded for
not being more careful. Like all mothers, her anger was only
a cover for the pain of her own worry for our safety. So the
wound was tenderly attended to, soggy socks removed, face
washed of dirt and tears, another admonishment to be careful,
a kiss and away we'd go again: to inflict ourselves and Mother
with another scar.

5

War

Children often sense that something is wrong, or they worry whether they have been just too naughty this time, and overstepped the mark. I couldn't remember doing anything so wicked as to cause what I saw happening to my Mother. The memory of her sitting spread-legged on the floor in the middle of the living room, screaming, just screaming, screaming hysterically and purposefully, her eyes screwed up tight, her fists clenched, pressed down on her chubby knees, helping those wild screams to come out at last, will always be quite vivid in my memory. I cannot remember anything or anyone else, except the screaming – my strong, self-possessed, tenacious, take-charge Mother, falling to pieces.

Looking back at that incident with more knowledge now, I realize that it was the start of a nervous breakdown. Mother must have been well into the menopause by this time, and fights and arguments with Pa were more than she could cope with. Not long after this incident she left him. They never divorced, but they didn't ever live under the same roof together again: although Pa tried several times later to patch up their differences, she would have none of it – she had had enough. She moved back to Southall with my sister Sylvia, to a small terraced house in Orchard Avenue.

Cleo

Pa, Alec and I remained behind in Hayes End. Alec and I were not put out by Mother's leaving – to us it was just another move, and we thought we would be joining her as soon as the new house was settled and put in order. Pa of course knew otherwise, but didn't tell us. I dare say he expected to be able to talk her out of the decision she had made eventually, as he had before, but it was not to be. So life carried on as it had been before the ghastly screaming fit and Mother's disappearance. Pa cooked for us and did it well – mainly stews, nothing fancy – he would leave them on a low heat for us to help ourselves when we got home from school. But Mother wasn't there to see that we came straight home from school and keep us in order, and we started to run wild for a while.

The 'rafts', as we called them, were nothing more than disused gravel pits, dangerous places that were off bounds in most parents' books. Our Pa forbade us to go anywhere near them and so did Samples' father. We disobeyed: one afternoon, at a loss for something to amuse us, we found ourselves near one, and the temptation was too much for us.

On this day Samples decided was to be a game of pirates. Each of the three of us, Samples Alec and I had found a plank raft on which to punt across the water. Samples' aim was to topple, by hook or by crook, one of us into the water, by getting the tip of his raft under one of ours and then, running quickly to the end of his plank, lift ours out of the water and the punter too. He tried this tactic unsuccessfully several times, all of us enjoying the tricky balancing acts we had to perform to keep upright and dry. Trying just one more time, he dashed to the end of his plank, with a big grin of success this time on his face as he saw me steadying myself, ready for the upsurge of his raft under mine. This was going to be it for me. He thought that I, being a girl, was the easiest prey. But I was determined not to be toppled. Then I saw the grin on Samples' face change to fear. He grappled desperately to keep on his raft, before finally losing his balance. He had misjudged the run back to the centre of his raft. In he went. It was then we discovered that he couldn't swim, because he was yelling 'Help me, I can't swim!'

Luckily he was near the edge, so he managed to scramble out. But he was well and truly soaked. We were delighted until we saw that our cocky friend was crying and terrified at what had happened, because if he went home in that soaked condition, his father would whip him. We took him home with us, with no thought of how we were going to solve his problem. Alec had the first and only brilliant idea: sit him in front of the fire to dry off, then he could go home, and his father would never know.

We all sat in a huddle watching as the steam started to rise from his sodden clothes. Suddenly – panic – the sound of the front door opening. We shoved Samples behind the settee, just as Pa entered the room, bicycle wrapped round his shoulders in a collapsed condition (the bicycle not Pa). He was not in the jolliest of moods. When we said, 'Hi Pa! Oh! What's happened to your bicycle?' he let us know, as only Pa in a temper could, which made us tremble in case he had noticed that all was not well at the home fire. We tried standing in front of the evidence, but the steam rising from behind the couch was making the atmosphere deadly damp and with the added marshy tang it could be but one person in hiding.

'Is that you there, Samples?' Pa's insight was working faster than ours. Samples rose slowly, with his steam, from behind the sofa, and Pa let rip. We were never to play with Samples again, with all the reasons why. By the time Pa had finished Samples was almost dry.

Our visits to the rafts were ended, but we continued to play with Samples – we couldn't drop a good playmate just because Pa objected to him. So we still went out everywhere together. But Pa knew. We always dropped our h's and talked sloppy when we'd been out together, he said.

Meanwhile the war was stepping up its pace, blackout curtains had to be put up, and windows criss-crossed with strips of glue-backed paper to avoid the glass splintering into the rooms. The air-raid siren meant that the enemy was near and could drop in, on your doorstep. As we were close not only to Heston aerodrome but also to the Fairy Aviation works, we used to get a lot of warnings.

Material things started being difficult to obtain, though this affected my parents more than it did me. My Pa proudly brought home some cups he had bought in Petticoat Lane, swearing that they were unbreakable. They were very thick canteen-type cups. I looked at them in disbelief, not only at their ugliness, but also at the lifelong guarantee. I thought I would put one of them to the test by dashing it to the kitchen floor. As it hit the lino, it shattered into a earthenware jigsaw puzzle. Pa and I stood looking at each other for what seemed for ever, in amazement, before he exploded: 'It wasn't to be dropped like that!' I countered, in my weak defence, that he'd said it was unbreakable. More splutter from Pa, but he couldn't defend the cup, or the Petticoat Lane wide boy who'd sold him the questionable crockery, so I just about got away within an inch of my bottom.

The accidents and misdemeanours piled up against Alec, me and our friends; we could tell that Pa wasn't coping with us too well. Everything seemed to come to a head after a series of incidents, starting with my friend Sheila who decided to run away from home and to take refuge in my room, mainly under the bed, until she was discovered by Pa and taken home. Then over Christmas, when Alec and I had overdecorated the family room with paper chains, I stood with a candle (imitating the Nativity) just a little too close to the chains and they went up in flames. We got bowls of water and threw it over the walls and decorations, making the mess of all messes.

In the New Year we found ourselves back with Mother and going to a new school. I was thirteen by now. No. 48 Orchard Avenue had gas lighting, an outside lavatory for downstairs use, one upstairs, no bathroom, and a copper and an earthenware sink in the scullery, next to the kitchen. Two rooms led off a passage that went to the front door and a flight of stairs led to one small and two large bedrooms. They were always occupied as bedsitting rooms, occasionally even the kitchen, by a stream of human flotsam flung together by the war in the shape of billeted soldiers, evacuees from London's bombing, factory workers, and young girls whom my Mother looked after when they were in trouble and had no one else to go to. There was a lady who owned a greengrocer's shop in the High Street who also did abortions, and a lot of the girls were attended to by this backstreet opportunist before being mothered by Mother. This lady did one abortion that went wrong, and it happened to be on a policeman's wife, who turned her in, so she went to prison.

As well as taking in lodgers Mother was working in a food canning factory called Poulton & Noels (which always came out as 'Poltnernols'). The employees were mostly young girls, many from the North of England, along with Irish and other nationalities. They all seemed to end up at our house.

Mother was on night-shift, so we saw a lot of her during the day: she would wake us when she got home, see that we had washed and had breakfast and that we had remembered our gas masks and then pack us off to our new school, in Montgomery Road. We all walked there and back for lunch, then back again for the afternoon until school finished, with another long walk home.

My new friend at Montgomery Road School was called Ann Gill. She was pretty, and very interested in clothes and makeup, which hadn't entered my mind until meeting her, because we never had the money or coupons to indulge in luxuries like that. We had just enough to buy school clothes and bare necessities. As for makeup, it was a scarce commodity and I had no idea how to apply it, but Ann knew all the tricks and tried hard to impart her vast knowledge to me, without much success.

I had more interesting things to do. Music was still uppermost in my mind, and it didn't mean as much to Ann, at least not the music that appealed to me. Lots of wonderful songs were now being sung, and played in films, on radio and record. I listened to Anne Shelton and Vera Lynn with envy, singing songs I knew by heart. Any money I had was saved to spend on records or films. Bunking in wasn't being done any more, Samples was no longer in our lives and Mother kept a keen eye on us all, as she didn't want Pa to accuse her of not being able to cope, so enabling him to return to the fold. He came regularly to plead with Mother to change her mind, but she was adamant. I never heard her say she would like to try again, in fact she often turned her back, refusing to talk, eyes filled with scorn. Whatever had happened between them in Hayes End had, for her, wiped out the eighteen or more years they'd had of ups and downs together, but Pa never gave up trying to make it up.

Mother became known as the compassionate lady in Orchard Avenue: anyone who needed help was sent to her. At the age of thirteen I helped deliver a baby boy for an Irish girl called Kathy. Mother wasn't home at the time, and Kathy went into unexpected labour. She'd had a baby before, so she knew what to do. Grasping on to the frame of the iron bedstead for grim death, she lay in agony, sadder, maybe not wiser, confessing for all the world to hear, especially me, 'Mary Mother of Jesus never again never again' over and over. I can remember thinking at the time, as I stood looking in frightened sympathy: why had she done it again? I knew she had another child, also that she was unmarried, she wasn't all that young, and it seemed pretty stupid to go through all that agony. Eventually things started to happen, the baby was born very easily and it was a boy. Mother was still not home so I was told by Kathy what to do next. She was an expert with her instructions: I tied the cord exactly where she told me to and cut. When I think of it now I shudder at what could have gone wrong. Luckily for me and Kathy, Mother eventually arrived, was amazed at what I had achieved and took over. I became the teagirl, a bit of a demotion from head midwife.

I was surprised that I hadn't been nauseated by this experience, but it all seemed to be so natural, and apart from the 'Mary Mother of Jesus' beginning, fairly painless. Kathy was deliriously happy with her baby boy, even though she had no idea who the father was or where. She was a Catholic and abortion was out of the question for her, no matter how many mistakes she made, and knowing Kathy, I guess that wasn't the first time she'd yelled her Mary Mothers, so expert was she in giving birth.

The baby was named Alec, and I became a godmother, although because I wasn't a Catholic the church didn't give its blessing, but I was at the christening, and Kathy recognized it.

War

So girls came and went, some of them so beautiful that I couldn't understand why anyone would abandon them or the babies. Often the man was married, with a wife at home in the North of England, and sometimes it was for purely religious reasons, a Catholic who would not marry a Protestant. This seemed to me daft, and started to put me off all religions: Pa was right.

The war was worsening and despite our proximity to Heston airport, and factories such as Fairy Aviation, we had evacuees billeted with us after the blitzes on London. An elderly gentleman came to us after having his home blasted and burnt to the ground. He was in a terrible state of nervous shock on his first night with us: there was a heavy raid aimed at the airport and ammunition factories. He became hysterical; nothing any of us could say or do would calm him down, he was so upset. We had three air-raid shelters at our disposal: an Anderson shelter in the garden, a reinforced concrete shelter available to the tenants of houses in the street, and a Morrison shelter in the kitchen. This was an iron cage-like construction that could also be used as a table during the day, under which we dived in an emergency. Most nights the family slept in the Anderson shelter. Southall wasn't too heavily bombed, but there were quite a few fire bombs, and we eventually had our share of buzz bombs, V1s and V2s. The V2 was the most dangerous; when the sound cut off, it became the silent dropper of death. You never knew where it was going to land, so it was fingers-crossed time.

For us children it was exciting rather than dangerous. Danger didn't start sinking into our understanding until much later. Alec and I went about our daily life much as before, we fought each other as we had always done, yet at the same time enjoyed each other's company; he became extremely interested in aeroplanes, spotting them and making them, so I got to know a lot too, but I think I hindered rather than helped with the making of planes, and also canoes, another interest of his. Most of Alec's hobbies became mine too: when he and his pals went fishing, I tagged along as the worm digger-upper.

But as we grew older we started to go our separate ways. More

61

and more girls were staying with us, wives of servicemen, with their children, and soldiers: we had two Polish airmen billeted with us. One remained in Britain after the war and became a close family friend, the other went to the States.

A group of girl lodgers from the food factory, in the shape of Joan, Maggie, Olwen, Majorie and Ida, a wife of one of the men working there, and I haven't forgotten the already resident clown, Kathy, kept the house at Orchard Avenue a lively, happy, funny, and sometimes sad dwelling – rather like the plots in some of the musicals I loved on screen.

Maggie was tall, extremely skinny, standing like a question-mark, with a tomboyish air about her. She had a great sense of humour, always keeping the others' spirits up if they were going through a bad time, and she did wonderful imitations of the American comedians Zazu Pitts and Ned Sparks; those two were her party pieces whenever we all got together in the kitchen late at night. Cigarettes were in short supply during the war, so she rolled her own, keeping a tobacco tin full of fag ends and cigarette papers. She would cut open the butts, extract the tobacco, and carefully roll a new and skimpy cigarette. She was in love with an Irish soldier she called Paddy, who also loved her. She worshipped the ground he walked on, but because she wasn't a Catholic, he kept delaying marriage until he learnt he was being sent overseas.

Joan was small and exotically beautiful, with jet black hair that she styled with Spanish kiss curls on cheek and forehead; she put vaseline on her eyelids and brows that seemed to make her eyes darker, and sparkle. She could have had her pick of lots of men, but she loved a man who treated her mean. Why she should chose such a relationship when she could have said eeny-meeny-miny-mo, I'll have you, foxed us all. We gave good advice, from best friend Maggie to unsophisticated me, when she came home sobbing after being let down on a date with him. Everyone tried to cheer her up – Ned Sparks imitations, a song and dance from me, Sylvia and even Alec, jokes galore, strip poker into the night, with long stories of love and rejection from all-knowing Kathy. Poor Mother would be on night work and didn't participate in all this girl talk.

6

The Pawnshop

The time soon came around when we all had to think of our
uneducated future lives. We hadn't excelled academically in
school, though none of us had ever been bottom-of-the class
students. We didn't go on to further education for obvious
financial reasons: Pa wasn't contributing to the new household,
because Mother wanted to be independent of him.

Mother didn't abandon us to high-wages factory jobs with no
future. When the time came for us to leave, she sat down with us
to talk about what we would like to do; we'd discuss whether or not
it was a realistic wish and how to go about achieving it. Sylvia was
apprenticed to a local furrier and tailor, successfully finishing her
apprenticeship and becoming a much-loved and respected worker
in the shop until she married and started a family. Alec went to
Fairy Aviation as an apprentice draughtsman, until he was called
up and joined the Air Force. When my turn came, and I told
Mother what I had told everyone so far what I was going to do,
she felt I was being unrealistic: my father had had a similar wish,
and she too had tried to get him started, with no success; here was
another dreamer. I was apprenticed to a hairdresser.

So it was that at the tender age of fourteen I started my first
job in Perivale, for Mr and Mrs Hanson in their shop called
Maison Hansons, next to the Hoover factory. I was paid seven

shillings and sixpence a week, for which I washed the towels in the ladies' and men's saloons, swept the floors and handed pins to the accomplished, who were doing sets and perms. I stood watching them, and when they were not too busy, I got a lesson in Marcel waving or wet setting, on a piece of hair fixed to a wig block. I was also required to serve behind the counter, selling handbags, belts, and knick-knacks of all kinds. In other words, I was a dog's-body. It was a cheap way of getting a cleaner. But luckily I did want to learn, and one of the hairdressers made time for me, teaching me quite a lot in the end. I remained in that job for about two years, leaving on medical grounds, because the hair was irritating my lungs and breathing became difficult. I was singing in talent competitions, going to local auditions and rehearsing at this time, so I couldn't allow anything to ruin my voice. Mother got a doctor's note, and I was freed.

What I missed after I'd left were some of the girls I'd become fond of, who'd been kind to me, and who'd gone through the same skivvying experience; also the occasional trips I had made to London, to get supplies for the shop from the wholesalers. I used to take advantage of these trips to window-shop and people-watch. Like the studios at Denham, London became a wondrous dream place, where I imagined being discovered one day, on one of these expeditions.

Now at a loose end, looking for another job to fill in the time before I was discovered, I met Peter, my first teenage love, a young soldier living a couple of streets away from ours with his mother, who was a widow. His father had died when he was very young and he had become a bit of a mummy's boy; his upbringing had made him more naïve than I was. However, it was a first love experience for both of us and although we were overpowered one evening by the strength of our emotion, we remained virgins. He didn't know what to do, and neither did I, so between the pair of us it was an embarrassing failure – we couldn't help each other out (luckily).

After this Peter felt much more strongly about me and wanted to see me more often, but the feeling I'd had for him wasn't sustained; it cooled considerably. He was so serious about our relationship that he insisted I come to meet his mother, but I was uncomfortable in her company. He wanted to become engaged as he was soon to go abroad, but I avoided him and the answer. His mother got in touch with me, telling me he was unhappy, but I couldn't continue, so I made a date to meet him and broke it off completely. His mother continued to write to me about him, hoping to change my mind, eventually saying he had been sent abroad to the war zone and would I write to him – so I relented and we wrote to each other for a few months, until she informed me one day that he had been killed in action.

I was shaken by this news and extremely saddened for a long time. Even though I did not want to be married to him, I had loved him and now I would never see him again. For a while I thought it was my fault that he had died, feeling that if he had gone away to war engaged to me he would have looked after himself better and not got killed: a romantic sixteen-year-old's imagination running wild. But the war had become a reality for me for the first time: I was never the same again. Suddenly I had grown up. I had been in love, made love (albeit unsuccessfully), fallen out of love and lost my first love permanently. I vowed never to fall in love again, it was too painful.

My next job was nearer home with a hairdresser/milliner learning how to trim hats, selling them and keeping them clean in the shop window. My boss was a Mrs Brooker, a tall, heavy-busted woman from the north of England, who superficially seemed a strict disiplinarian. But she was a warm, understanding, considerate boss, who taught me more than I had learnt in my first job about working in a shop, and how to dress smartly cheaply – 'Black, luv, always black, from head to toe, you'll not go far wrong if you stick to that, and a clothes brush, specially for you.' She had noticed I wasn't the tidiest young lady she had had under her wing, and would need pulling into shape. Her daughter Sybil worked upstairs in the saloon; she had finished her apprenticeship and was now a fully fledged hairdresser, and we became close friends.

I helped out when they were busy, shampooing, handing out

pins and so on, but my job was hats! the things that would not stay on my head in any shape or form. Believe me, while I was there I tried them all, but the hair still had to be tamed and I hadn't yet found a solution to the problem. Once again I was really nothing but a glorified sweeper, a duster and brusher of hats.

Weekends were always busy with weddings and do's, and then, at Easter and Christmas, we were rushed off our feet. The best part of the job was when I was sent off to London to pick up ribbons, feathers, flowers, cherries and birds, enabling me to indulge my dramatic hobby. I was never Clemmie Campbell picking up the stuff, I was the owner of the shop or a great actress, or better still, the singer I wanted to be on her way to an important audition. In my head I would develop a situation where everything came out right, just as it did in the musical films I adored.

It was all day-dreaming, but I was getting there slowly, doing local auditions and talent contests that I never seemed to win (it was always the comedian or a wobbly soprano singing 'Oh My Beloved Father' – some things never seem to change); also I would sing off the cuff at the dances that Mrs Brooker's daughter Sybil and I had started going to. The buying trips started taking longer and longer, as I wandered around the West End of London, instead of getting straight back to unexciting Southall. I was reprimanded by Mrs Brooker about it a couple of times, but twice was too often: after the third time she said the owner had given her orders to give me notice. So I left before they sacked me. But Sybil and Mrs Brooker always remained close friends of mine: I listened to their problems, and they listened to mine.

My next occupation was on the same street, but it was an almighty change from the others. It was in a chain library. A job I fell in love with, because I could legitimately sit and read all day long, so that I was able to advise the customers, when they asked, about the latest books that had come in; I was expected to tell them what they were all about, and whether, in my opinion, they were any good (poor authors). Most of the books were romantic novels, mysteries and thrillers. But tucked away in a corner was a section with a few classic novels just 'in case'. With the help of the manageress, I became an 'in case'. Maybe this was the start of my proper education, and my love of books. I sopped up more classic literature than had ever come my way at school and re-read some that had, in a totally enjoyable, unpressurized way.

The man who interviewed me couldn't have known how wide a door he'd opened for me: it was my first good audition, perfect casting for my personality and needs at that time. I read everything and anything, from the limited good to the vast amount of rubbish they had on the premises. It wasn't a highbrow library, but for the first time it made me want to read.

Mother asked me to bring home all the 'Charlie Chan' mysteries that came out. Dutifully I brought them home to her every week, such an avid fan was she of these Chinese mysteries. One evening we were discussing the current thriller when Mother surprised and made me laugh at the same time, as she confided to me in a sheepish and guilty fashion: 'Do you know, Clemmie, that if a Chinese gentleman came to the door, I just couldn't put him up; I'd be afraid.' I could not believe what I was hearing; it was so laughable. Here was a woman who all my life had never turned anyone away from her door if she had a bed to offer – the list of different nationalities reads like the United Nations Assembly – Africans, Indians, Irish, French, Polish, Czechs, Jamaicans and Germans as well as all the British.

It was Dr Fu Manchu not Charlie who had done the damage: along with the films that were also popular at that time, these books had influenced her thinking. Had she been put to the test, I am sure she would not have thought twice about her decision. I can't remember her ever being put to the test, except for a Jamaican airman whom I met at a local dance and who had obvious Chinese ancestry. We became good friends and I occasionally went out with him. He'd call for me at the house and Mother would always invite him in to chat while he waited. He was extremely charming and she fell for his appealing manner. Mother's confession might have been the dawning of my realization of the powerful influence books can have, if you choose to read them without thinking, so with a little help along the way, I began to think things out for myself. Some thoughts went wrong, others wonderfully right.

Sadly, the library didn't last for ever: it closed, leaving me to look for further work, but the time I spent among the hotch-potch of books there was a privilege and an influence that I didn't fully comprehend until later. Then, it just seemed like the end of another job that was a fill-in until my real work came about, but it had changed my views on learning for ever.

My next job was not so illustrious: it was on Ealing Broadway in a pawnshop and clothes store combined. The clothes were very cheap, aimed at a family market that paid weekly for purchases or joined a club that enabled mothers to clothe children for school, Christmas and holidays. It was exactly how Mother had managed her few pence when we were at school.

I didn't get paid very much and the manager wasn't very attractive: a tall skinny man who opened the store at nine a.m. sharp, never late, and the assistants – that's what he called us – had to be there and waiting as he unlocked the doors at ten minutes to nine. Shutters covered the shop front, which was glassless, and once they were unlocked, we were exposed to the elements. He pushed the shutters, with the help of the assistants, as high as his long arms could manage, then two of us would finish off the exercise with long hooked poles. The poles were then used again to hang clothes outside. No artistic arrangement here, as there had been in the milliner's window: this shop move closely resembled an Arabian bazaar, with tressle tables outside displaying the bargains of the day to catch the eyes of passers-by.

The manager would don his working overall, a long brown cotton coat to protect his suit, and the day would begin. He would never allow me to stand around doing nothing: if I had swept and dusted already, I had to do it again if a customer wasn't taking up my time. When I had finished the transaction with the customer I went to the shelves and tidied them and tidied them and tidied them again. It was quite a relief when the weekend came and there was a rush of customers, or I was told to help in the pawnshop.

The Pawnshop

I didn't do much assessing – once again I was an apprentice, a dog's-body. And I hated the indescribable sadness when customers parted from priceless wedding rings, brooches and family silver, even though it might be for just one week.

I still remember one woman who brought in a cameo brooch to pawn: she was young, but grey and depressing to look at. Apparently she was a regular weekend visitor whose precious brooch was her escape from the beating her husband would give her if she hadn't saved something from her meagre houskeeping money. It brought relief for a few days when she was able to pass on the few pounds the brooch recognized (after the minimum of haggling for more than it was worth). They always gave her a little more, and this perked her up enough to put a smile on her face, so that as I handed her her ticket, tagged the brooch and placed it in the case that held pieces for short stays, the smile revealed a pretty girl beneath the gloom. I never saw this woman again while I worked there, and eventually a 'For Sale' ticket was written out for the brooch, this time placed in the window. She often crosses my mind, especially when I pass the three large golden balls in my travels, and glance in the windows where they put the pieces that have not been redeemed.

One day I was called into the pawnshop to give a hand, writing out tickets and non-stop tidying. It was the start of the day, and I hung my coat up in an old wardrobe set aside for the pawnshop staff. Business wasn't too brisk at the start, but the tempo perked up later on in the day once people realized that their weekend drinking would be curtailed after all the weekly bills had been paid, like coal, food and new booties for the baby. (This was another saying of Mother's when she had a financial windfall: 'Well, it will buy new booties for the baby.')

At the end of the working day, all the clobber outside was brought in, shutters pulled down, coats taken out of old wardrobes and hurriedly scrambled into, as we called out our goodnights to workmates: 'See you tomorrow! Don't be late!' There were cheerful exits all round; I was always happy to be on my way out,

69

to run across the road to the bus stop, and wait for my number 607 trolleybus.

That evening as I stood at the bus stop my back suddenly began to itch like mad. It was most irritating: no matter how much I squirmed and wriggled to ease the discomfort, it wouldn't go away. I thought I'd attack it from the inside. Putting my hand down behind my neck, and thrusting it as far down my back as my single joint would allow to give it a good scratch, my hand grasped a warm, soft, round object that was either settling down for the night or trying to escape. I had disturbed a mouse. As I realized this, in utter disgust I scooped it out from the warm hideaway it had found on my back, and dashed it to the cold pavement. I was appalled, and my body went rigid for a moment before going into an epileptic-type fit as I relived the experience. An army of mice started walking over my grave and continued to do so during the bus ride home, and again when I told the tale to all at home.

'How did it get there?' they asked.

'It was that bloody wardrobe,' I said, 'and that's the last it's going to see of my coat and me!' And I gave in my notice.

Teenage Marriage

My love life was faring no better than my working life; for most of the time, I was going through adolescent hell. Either I was dismissing young men who liked me, or drowning in passionate, emotional, anguish for ones who (in some cases) were not even aware of my existence, but preferred my sister or friends. Those feelings were so crushingly debilitating, I wonder how anyone can survive them. And yet looking back at some of my desired love objects I wonder what I saw in them.

A couple of the loves of my life – needless to say they didn't feel the same way – lived with us as lodgers. Frank was a budding writer, who had articles and essays accepted from time to time. He came into our lives in the company of an older man, who encouraged him in his endeavours, a sort of guardian. Frank was very very handsome, beautifully blond, with the most dazzling blue eyes. He became fond of me as a sort of sister, and we talked a lot, often into the early hours of the morning. I would do my darndest to get him to make love to me, but his kisses always remained brotherly and quite devoid of passion. I was naïve enough to think that if he wanted to sit up so late talking, liking my company, that he must be in love with me.

I don't think Frank would ever have fallen in love with me or any other girl. I knew nothing about homosexuality then, and it's possible that Frank didn't either, but I'm now convinced that that was the reason our close relationship never got to be more than a friendship. Eventually he was called up and went into the army. When he came home on leave, he looked so wonderful in his uniform – I drooled over him and waited eagerly for every leave. He was sent abroad and killed. I was consumed with my imagined lover's loss; I would never fall for anyone again. Until Mick came to live with us.

Mick was a Czechoslovakian vagabond. A refugee who had come to England when very young, his mother and father having been killed during a Jewish massacre, he spoke perfect English, and was extremely intelligent, funny and full of life. Everyone loved Mick – his charm just oozed into 48 Orchard Avenue, enabling him to have almost anything he wanted. But he had an addiction that got him into an amazing amount of trouble. His great love was gambling – dogs, horses, cards – and he abhorred work, so he was never able to earn enough money to feed his addiction. The solution for him was petty crime.

Mick had a tall, elegant body that looked good in clothes, and when he had a win he would don new gear and play the peacock. Nobody enquired where the clothing coupons had come from. At first we assumed he'd saved up his quota, but as events progressed we learned otherwise. Mother and the local police officers were on friendly terms: they kept in touch with her because of the different characters who had streamed through her boarding houses, past and present, in Southall. So when the plain-clothes policeman came to the door for a chat, she wasn't surprised, nor were we. But it soon became apparent that Mick had been up to no good: he had been involved in a robbery with some well-known naughty boys of Southall. It was a first offence for Mick, so the officer was asking Mother to vouch for him, to see that he didn't stay out late at night and to make sure he attended his appointments with his probation officer. She agreed to keep an eye on him, because he had charmed his way into her heart as he had into every woman's in the house – but not as deeply as into her youngest daughter Clemmie's.

Teenage Marriage

Because Mick was grounded he spent more time in the house and my days were happiness once again. He took me out dancing, to the Hammersmith Palais, a dream palace to me. Once again I could indulge my play-acting; my partner was as much of a Walter Mitty as I was. I felt so grown-up and sophisticated, but I was merely the cover for him to be in London to meet his gambling wide-boy cronies, who were up to something that turned out to be a disaster for him and sadness for me. The police came around again, this time to search his room, and they found what they were looking for: jewellery, not very successfully hidden. So he was taken away to spend time in prison, where I kept in touch by letter. It had been nothing more than friendship for him, but my heart had taken yet another beating.

George, my first husband, was also around during this period. I had met him when my friend Joan was going out with his brother John, and I with his brother's friend – they were both in the same regiment. Paul (the friend) and I were not serious about each other, we just tagged along because Joan and John were our best friends. Their relationship was just a wartime infatuation: she was married to a soldier posted abroad, and her family naturally didn't approve. John was a deserter, who was eventually caught and court-martialled. Joan tried to hang on by visiting his family, whom she'd got close to, and that was how George and I started our relationship. I accompanied Joan several times on her visits, and George was often there, on leave from the Navy.

George was quieter than his brother and had qualities that were attractive to someone eight years his junior – I was seventeen when we met. He was kind, considerate, attentive, with a good sense of humour, and he was a man of the world. He also looked good in his sailor's uniform. On one of these visits I became aware that the reason he was on leave was me.

I grew very fond of George and George fell in love with me. He was steady and solid as a rock, but he wasn't romantic like Mick, and I knew I could never be more than fond of him. When Mick departed from the scene, George saw his chance, working hard at becoming the courting Romeo. He asked me to marry him but I was undecided, so he spoke to mother. He had already asked her and she'd told him I was too young; she also told me I was too young, and that he drank too much. That, I guess, was enough to make up my mind to do the complete opposite of what she wanted. It also proved that she was right – I was too young.

I said I was going to marry George whether she approved or not (I needed her legal approval because I was under age). George and I began to plan our wedding. Everything was in short supply – food, clothes, drink – but somehow we got it all together. George wore his demob suit, and I had saved enough coupons to buy a blue outfit that I would be able to wear on other occasions. Friends rallied round and helped as much as they were able. Mother made the cake, and by the time the day arrived she had come to terms with her wilful daughter's decision to get married. Though she never came to terms with some of his habits and the age difference, she did recognize that he was a kind man who adored her daughter and would look after her.

After the register office service, which took place in Uxbridge, we had pictures taken and all the usual congratulations. I can't remember a great deal about the ceremony or how I felt, but I do remember, very vividly, the drive back in the hired limousine, with George holding my hand. The thoughts that I had were not the thoughts a young bride should have: I suddenly realized that I had started something I wasn't sure I wanted. For a moment I panicked, then I said to myself, 'Oh well, if it doesn't work out, I can always get divorced.' What a way to start married life.

Yet for eight years, apart from the frustration of never having a home of our own, we jogged along without incident. I was always the disrupter of harmony, never satisfied with my lot. I felt George could do better for himself than tiling roofs. He was intelligent, and the only reason he didn't go on to higher education was the death of his father, which left his mother to raise five children by herself. He had been very good at maths and English at school, so I talked him into doing a correspondence course on those subjects, and I took in work from a local factory to do in the evening as well as my daytime job in a shoe repair shop. George continued his job as a tiler, which wasn't highly paid: if the weather was bad he was laid off, which meant the pay packet was light at the weekend.

Things were tight and I was always trying to find ways of easing the tightness. The housing situation was never resolved: we had our name down for council housing in both Southall and Croydon and had to move from one mother's home to the other in order to qualify. We were so low down on the list that it was a hopeless visit each week to see if anything had turned up. We always turned up, but the house never did.

I always felt more comfortable in the front room of 48 Orchard Avenue, and was miserable when we had to do our stint in Croydon: it was a close-knit community, which revolved around the local pub, the only social outlet for all age groups; even the little ones would sit outside eating crisps and drinking lemonade until they were of an age to enter the inner sanctum and to join all the clubs: summer outing club, Christmas club, clothes and darts clubs.

George was a darts expert, and he was an excellent all-round sportsman: his great love was football, and he played for the junior team of Croydon Football Club, though the war curtailed his rise to the senior league.

There was a ladies' summer outing and also a men's, which allowed married people to flirt and carry on as if they were single, and single people to maybe find romance. Whatever happened on those outings no one discussed – if they did and were found out, they were ostracized. The meeting-place for the start of the outing was always outside the local pub, where the whole community would turn up to see the charabanc leave. I remember only sunny days, so the mood was always gay and ribald, and suggestive jokes and comments flew back and forth between the trippers and those left behind.

The ritual was always the same: as the bus was about to leave for Margate, Brighton, or any place with a smashing pier, we would throw pennies out of the windows of the chara as compensation for the wide-eyed children. For the women it was freedom from them and the chore of cooking the Sunday lunch, coping with drunken husbands who fell asleep immediately afterwards or insisted on going to bed for their weekly romp. Loud singing of Cockney or dirty songs, knees-up dancing and lots of drinking was the order of the day, and if you didn't join in, you were a spoilsport or stuck-up. The louder you were, the drunker you got, and the more underwear you showed when you kicked your knees up, the more life-and-soul-of-the-party you were.

I liked the abandonment of these usually hard-working women; I was one of them, and I threw myself into the wild and tipsy dances on the way there, and into the drunken ones coming back. I wasn't going to be called a spoilsport. My repertoire of Cockney songs was learnt on those crazy journeys – 'Barefoot Days', 'Any Old Iron', 'My Old Dutch', and the like. The thought often crossed my mind as that coach sped through the country lanes on the way home, looking like the film *The Snake Pit* on wheels: if anything went wrong and the charabanc crashed, the mothers, wives, grannies and girlfriends of a whole district of Croydon would be lost in one fell swoop. The coach driver always stayed sober, thank goodness.

Those trips, no matter how much I enjoyed them at the time, couldn't keep my spirits up for a whole year; the music didn't satisfy my soul and I grew more and more discontented. To my in-laws I guess I seemed stand-offish. I liked music they didn't like, and when anything came on the radio that seemed interesting to me but wasn't to their taste, it was switched off. The visit of the singer Benjamino Gigli to Croydon was a wonderful release – I booked a seat and went by myself – as no one was interested in coming with me. I often went, alone, to the large cinema to see an artist or act; it was a place I hoped one day I might appear myself (and I did).

Meanwhile I was feeling more and more isolated and despondent. I couldn't pretend any longer, and asked George to take me back to Southall, forfeiting our place on the Crydon housing list.

Teenage Marriage

One month after my nineteenth birthday I became pregnant. It was 1945, and we lived at my mother's house for the nine months. The local midwife visited me regularly. I had an issue of orange juice, cod-liver oil, and vitamin tablets; pregnant women were looked after extremely well then, and we could go to the head of any queue as long as we had our green ration book or looked unbalanced and liable to tip over.

When the time came Mother put me to bed: I wasn't in too much pain as yet, but I was ready. After eight hours of bloody hard labour, which they all said was an easy time for a first baby, my first boy-child was in my arms and I was content. I sang to him a lot and I and the household adored him. He was quite a new experience for me, although I had been around babies for as long as I could remember.

Baby Stuart was mine and I enjoyed him, but at times I forgot I had a new baby. When I was allowed out of bed for the first time, I went shopping, proudly pushing my new baby in my new pram down the high street, accepting all the compliments with a big silly grin on my face, hoping that I looked slimmer after several months of heavyweight duty. Shop-window glances told me the truth, but I kept on smiling. After all I had never been sylph-like – what did the shop windows expect?

I parked the pram outside the greengrocer's to make my purchases, and went through the happy ritual: 'Yes my life will certainly be different, sleepless and very messy, but oh! so wonderful and changed for the better'; bought my potatoes and said my goodbyes, then started to walk home, leaving the pram, with my beautiful newborn son contentedly cooing inside it, outside the shop. It wasn't until I was halfway home that I realized something was missing. When it dawned on me what it was, the about turn was made at the speed of light and I was certainly a pound or two slimmer when I got back to the shop.

The lonely, shiny new pram was still where I'd left it but just in case anyone had noticed, I pretended that I had just come out of the shop next door. Stuart was oblivious of his mother's neglectful memory and gave me a windy smile. I walked home ashamed, but with a good story to tell mother and everyone else at 48 Orchard Avenue.

8

A Kick-Start

It's hard to pinpoint the reasons why a relationship breaks down – how or when it starts to collapse. I think, in retrospect, that George and I were simply cruising along together, with no place else to go. The added strain of coming to terms with a lack of a home of our own didn't help and nor did we ever discuss each other's problems, but it's obvious now that George had many that an older, less ambitious (though this hadn't surfaced quite yet) woman would at least have been aware of. I was the wrong first wife for him: I didn't comfort, I wasn't happy with my lot and I was always searching for ways out, while George had a happy-go-lucky nature that tended to conceal worries he could do little about.

We continually moved back and forth from Southall to Croydon, hoping that one day, one of them would come up with a house or flat, and in the meantime we lived with mother-in-laws, in one room. We were not the only ones: my sister Sylvia, who had two babies by now, was living in a freezing community house in Southall, one grotty step nearer to getting an equally grotty home of her own. George's sisters were also on waiting lists, so there was a lot of shared discontent and misery.

I decided that what George and I needed was a holiday by the sea when the winter was over. How we were going to pay for it I hadn't worked out, but that was never a hindrance to me once I'd made up my mind. First I gave up smoking, putting what I might have spent in a tin marked 'holiday money'. I wasn't smoking very heavily so it was pretty meagre, but it was a help, along with some home work, and making my own and the baby's clothes.

For some reason, probably because it was the cheapest deal we could find, we went to Hastings. We went to a show at the White Rock Pavilion and although it wasn't a particularly good show I remember getting all the old feelings that I had when I was a child: I wanted to be up on that stage. I came out extremely despondent. At first I thought it was because we hadn't brought Stuart, and it's true I was missing him, but the more shows we saw the worse I felt. Eventually I realized that it wasn't so much maternal feelings that were ruining the holiday for us, as my childhood dreams surfacing again and the fact that I could see no way of doing anything about them.

I was a misery to be with. Nat King Cole had a big song out at the time called 'Nature Boy'. The lyrics, the melody and the way that he sang it, moved me immensely, but George wasn't all that keen. I learnt it and would sing it to him at the top of my voice and argue its case, while we sat together on the rocky beach, which seemed just the right setting for it, or as we walked the ancient fishing town and sloping lanes.

There was a boy.
A very strange enchanted boy –
they say he wandered very far very far, over land and sea;
a little shy and sad of eye
– but very wise was he.

The song and my singing of it became the reason for dissension between us on that holiday – I couldn't convince him it had any worth. When I grew angry George said it wasn't his idea of a holiday song, it was too melancholy. I guess he was right, but that wasn't the point: it was different, and beautifully sung and played, which was something he couldn't grasp. But it was also highlighting the mood I was in, and the start of change in the relationship between me and George.

When we returned home from Hastings things continued much as before, but my musical ambition had been reawakened and when I took young Stuart for walks in the park, I would sit on a park bench lost in secret day-dreams once again, about how I would be discovered.

Then something happened that started to make my daydreams come true. I found myself at a party with my brother, George and others: it was a local musicians' party, so there was playing and singing. I can't recall why I was invited: they were my brother Alec's friends and I didn't feel completely at home, so when someone asked me to sing I declined, but Alec kept on insisting that I get up to sing.

In the end it was easier to give in. I sang my song and a couple of other popular songs of the time without creating a great stir, but people were appreciative, and we went home at the end of the party having had a pretty good time. A couple of days later one of the musicians, a drummer who was at the party, called round to offer me my first semi-professional gig. It was a dance for the Labour Party in my old school hall at Mellow Lane, Hayes End, with a big band; the drummer was the leader, and he offered me the going minimum union rate for my services: thirty-two shillings and sixpence.

I accepted, and I was on my way. I was cool to him, but when he left, with fat little Stuart in my arms, I whizzed around the kitchen singing the silly song of the time: 'We don't want her, you can have her, she's too fat for me.' Stuart always liked to be sung to and it could have been any song as long as he was jiggled at the same time, but for fun I would change the words to '*he*'s too fat', and away we'd go. He laughed a lot and I danced a lot, to the consternation of whoever was living in that household at the time.

On this occasion it was my mother's lodgers who had to put up with it: my mother was used to these outbursts from her children when something had gone right for them, and she was happy for me. I think she knew that all was not as it should be between George and me – she was keeping an eye on us, but saying nothing.

Saturday, my big evening, finally arrived. The energy and excitement the family radiated on my behalf was so wonderful, you would have thought it was their début. They all rallied round to soothe my nervousness. The girls helped me with my makeup and clothes, I'm not sure that they made me exactly glamorous, in fact I know they didn't, unless you think a Christmas-tree fairy look-a-like glamorous, but they tried, and a little of their glitz rubbed off me.

Everything seemed so big-time to me. Until then I had only been involved in amateur performances with just a piano, but to me this was like Hollywood: even the way the people talked was different. They had a language of their own that I longed to learn; I longed to belong, to be one of the boys. A big disappointment of course was not having the big band back me: had I exercised common sense I would have known that it would be impossible, unless I had brought with me the arrangements for the songs that I was going to sing. I didn't even know what an arrangement was, leave alone have one to hand out. Here was one naïve, pretty dumb singer, who didn't even know what key she sang the songs in; all she knew was that she was going to earn the grand sum of one pound twelve shillings and sixpence.

The drummer band leader told me to get together with the pianist to sort out the keys of the songs before the public came in and started writhing. I could not believe my luck: here I was standing on the stage sorting out keys for songs that would eventually unlock the door to my future, in the place where, what seemed only a couple of beats ago, I had played 'Wall' in the school production of *A Midsummer Night's Dream*. It was an entirely new experience, this process of finding a comfortable register, in a leisurely, civilized fashion, for songs I was going to perform the same night.

When I'd sung in a pub, a talent contest or an audition, I was inevitably chucked on, out of pressure of time, ending in an embarrassing struggle to pitch the song by guesswork, while the eyes of other hopeful performers, also waiting to be thrown into the same hell, pierced my uptight back. While my heart beat loud enough to be in a rhythm section – if it would only do the right beat and stop missing them. On these occasions, only faith, hope and a little charity could help me out: faith in my ear, hope that it hadn't let me down, and a little charitable understanding if I had started too high, I would eventually hit the highest note in the song. Meanwhile the pianist generally floundered around behind me trying to find, by ear, if he had one, the key I had just picked out of the blue. Lack of time or the inability of the pianist to play in any other key than the song was written in didn't help, but more than anything it was the sheer amateurishness of the singer that was at fault.

I blush with shame when I think of what those poor musicians had to go through and why so few vocalists earned their respect. But here I was at last being treated seriously with a concern to get it right. It was the rhythm section who accompanied me from the big band: I remember only the bass player's name from that date, Ossie Newman, because he became a close friend of the family and was the musician who pushed me further towards my childhood dreams.

The dance hall began to fill up with supporters of the Labour Party determined to have a good time, and they did, carried away by the energetic, high-spirited music. Because it was in Hayes End and virtually across the road from our last home with Pa, who was still in residence there, I invited him to come to the dance and hear me sing. I think he appreciated the thought, as all his attempts to come back into the fold alongside Mother had failed, and he had to rely on his children to include him in the happenings in their lives.

The earth didn't move and bells didn't ring as they did in the pictures, as I expected – in fact I doubt if many people actually heard me as I stood trying to make an impression, with my strangely madeup face and yet another attempt to bring my rebellious hair to heel. I found out later the only reason they had a singer was because the booker insisted on one; but Pa stood listening, obviously very proud, in front of the bandstand, beaming up at me when I sang (a story he was to repeat several times with as much pride, as the years passed by and my success grew). Every now and again he'd disappear to go a-wooing, and reappear whizzing around, as best he could under such crowded circumstances, performing his favourite dance, the tango, clutching a nubile blonde or brunette.

There was another person who listened and liked what he heard enough to say he would like me to sing in a group he played in, and that was Ossie Newman. He had only to convince the trumpet-playing leader, Stan, who had had a much more glamorous singer in mind, that I was a better singer.

I continued with the talent contests, one of which solidified the date with Ossie's small band. As usual I failed to win. I had decided to sing the 'Tennessee Waltz', a popular country and western song of the day. Why I had chosen this, when there were so many better songs more suitable for my voice, I have never fathomed – maybe it was because the pianist knew it with his eyes shut or because it only had an octave and a bit to cope with, so I was fairly safe with the key, and wouldn't have to go through the miserable rigmarole that showed me up to be the ignoramus that I was. Well, the song did nothing for me and I did nothing for the song. My track-record remained unbroken – I didn't get to take home the trophy – but these appearances were beginning to become my hobby, so losing didn't upset me that much.

I was not aware that in the wings Ossie, with great faith in my untutored musicality, had made Stan listen to me. His glamorous girl singer lost the job, and I achieved a second much-needed kick-start towards the future.

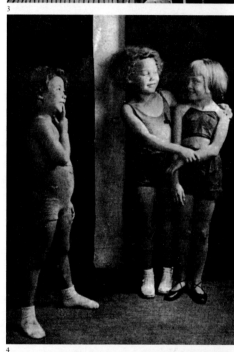

My mother, my father and
amaican grandmother.

dancing class – (l to r)
, Clemmie and friend
ine

e Campbell children –
r) Alec, Sylvia, Clemmie

1 One of the first groups I worked with in Southall – at t[he]
back bass player Ossie, brother Alec and me

2 An evening in Southall – (l to r) bandleader Stan, Beryl
(Alec's wife), Alec, Sylvia, Ossie

3 George and me on holiday in Hastings in 1948

4 The Dankworth Seven in 1952

5 J.D. with Ronnie Scott, 1949

6,7 Me – in wig – with John; and in my dreaded first dres[s]
(with cut ribbons)

6

7

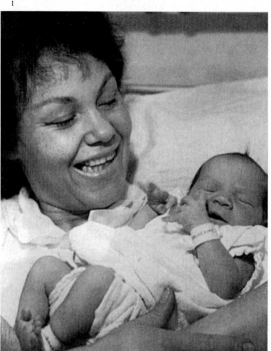

1,2 With baby Jackie and toddlers Alec and Jackie
3 Alec in a daisy chain listens – (l to r) John
Williams, J.D., me, Richard Rodney Bennett

4

5
6

4,5 The family growing up
6 Ma Dankworth
7 7 Jackie

John and me (at the top relaxing in the Dead Sea) and our two much loved houses – in Wavendon, near Milton Keynes (facing page) and in Sonoma, California (right)

1 Our California family – (l to r) Sharon, Stuart, Thomas, Christopher, me and John
2 Son Alec, me and granddaughter Michele
3 Granddaughter Emily at the piano

9

Audition in a Cellar

Now came some of the the happiest days of my life, seedling days that instinctively I knew would grow, if I tended them carefully, into healthy weeks, months and years. I didn't say much to anybody about what was going on in my heart, having been so often laughed at in the past. Surprisingly my brother became an enthusiastic ally: we went to rehearsals together, and met the other musicians in the area, some of whom have since climbed the ladder of success, like Jim Marshall, founder and head of 'Marshall-Amplification'. In those days Jim was a singer/drummer. The amplification idea germinated along with his paradiddles, then developed into a multi-million international concern, but at heart he is still a performer.

My brother and I sang duets. He understood the ambitions and swirling undercurrents of discontent that made people difficult and angry to live with; he was sympathetic and made no disparaging comments. He was also artistically ambitious, eventually realizing these ambitions in several ways, after our paths went in different directions. Meanwhile we both loved music enough to pursue it for fun with all the other Southall musicians, but with hope for the future.

My other confidant at that time was baby Stuart, whom I could sing to and talk to, knowing that he would agree, and chuckle at my silly joys, loves, hates and miseries, without passing judgement. There was nobody else who could have coped with me, at this disintegrating rebirth that was going on. There were so many tidal emotions to sort out, and I knew that somebody would be hurt if I ever found calm.

Ossie Newman now took me under his wing, searching out bands in London who were advertising for a singer. There was a snag to his interest in me: though he did genuinely admire my singing and thought that I could go far with the right handling, he had also become fond of me, and I realized he was starting to think of me as a potential lover. My inborn survival kit told me that I should not get involved in this way. If he was going to be my manager, that's what it should be, period.

Apart from odd gigs with the band and rehearsals, he managed to get auditions for me in and about London. One was an all-girl band whose leader was named Blanche Coleman. She had been looking for a singer for some time, but with strings attached. Bass strings. When I sang for her she quite liked my voice, but then asked if I could play the bass. 'Sorry, no,' I replied and added, 'I wish I could.' I saw an oh-not-another-one look on her face, which meant this was a replay of what the poor woman had sat through for several days. I should have said yes, and figured out how later, with lessons from Ossie. In those days bass players could get away with murder and often did, because they couldn't be heard too well, but I had to own up, so I didn't get to be a singing bass player.

Later I auditioned for Scots trumpeter Duncan Whyte, who had a band in the Astoria Ballroom, Charing Cross Road. When he had heard me sing, his only comment was, 'She's got good pipes.' His look was pretty obvious: pipes I had, but where were the other endowments a band-singer had to have – big boobs or long shapely legs, long blonde or black swinging hair? There was no way I could supply or fake these requirements, so I went my way, and he stayed where he was. Other auditions were no more successful, but I had to keep on doing them, whether they were dignified or not (mostly they were not).

I couldn't let Ossie down, but I could see he was getting dangerously more infatuated, as we spent more and more time together dashing from one audition to another. I didn't feel that we would be right together, so when he pressured me for a response, my excuse was always, 'I can't let anything come between me and my family – I would rather give up all my ambitions and desires.' I must have just seen a Bette Davis tragic film at the time, it rings so false. But I believed what I was saying at the time; I didn't love Ossie or anyone else and I didn't want to be involved with anything but music.

I was once again having a wonderful dramatic lesson, but this time it wasn't make-believe, and I had to be careful to control not only my emotions, but another's too. I was stupid, naïve, and cocky enough to think that because I was married, Ossie would not pursue this side of his interest in me, flattering though I found it. I should have brought the relationship to an end: after all I wasn't getting any work, I was just enjoying myself.

Ossie was acquainted with an important publicity man, Kenneth Pitt, who lived in Southall, though his office was in London. Ossie invited him to places where we might be performing in the area, to get him interested enough to work on Harold Davison, *the* band agent of the day, who had offices in the same building in Shaftesbury Avenue. We managed to impress him enough for him to convince Harold Davison I was worth talking to, and an appointment was made.

Ossie was terribly excited about this opportunity and impressed on me its importance – compared with the other things that had happened so far, this was my real chance. But I had to play my part well by tarting myself up for it. Looking through my rather meagre wardrobe didn't fill me with confidence – I could see nothing that would bring about a job-winning transformation, so once again I put myself in the hands of the girls. My brother's wife, Beryl, loaned me her fur coat, shoes I got from my sister, and others in the house also contributed one way or another. I went through a general tidy-up of hair and face as I had on previous occasions. Once they considered me right for the job, they passed me down the line to Ossie, who nodded approval, and we set out together for Shaftesbury Avenue, and the afternoon date with the agent who had most of the big-name bands as his clients.

We arrived early and had the usual fidgety wait in the outer office, reading the posters, being impressed with all the famous names on the walls, talking to each other in whispers outside the big man's door. Then the call to enter came: he was ready to see me. The coat was making me hot, and I was scared. Ossie wished me good luck. I entered the inner sanctum.

Sitting behind a large desk, the cigar-smoking mogul greeted me, then invited me to sit down, still in my hot fur coat. It started to be a very uncomfortable experience. I wasn't used to being scrutinized so closely. I knew that perspiration was gathering all over my top lip and melting the makeup job so carefully achieved, but I didn't dare lick my lips for fear of smudging my perfectly painted lipstick – which was going to run anyway because of the sweat. Inwardly I was in as much turmoil as outwardly. Nothing would stay still or quiet.

Davison asked me what experience I had and who with. I could only say local dances and talent contests – oh God, not very impressive, and on top of it, all this sweat. But Ken Pitt had done a good deal of talking to get me this far, so I knew I had to go through with it. It was beginning to feel like a scene from one of the many musical films I had grown up believing would one day be my fate too, so I decided to act the part.

When Davison said that there was no one at the moment who wanted a singer on his books except a jazz combination led by John Dankworth, I got the feeling he was giving me the option to say that that was not my domain, and thank you very much for affording me so much of his extremely busy time. I think it was quite a surprise to him when I showed a smiling enthusiasm for more detailed information. So, without much optimism in his voice for my success, he went on to tell me that the band was rehearsing right now at the 51 Club in Great Newport Street: if

I was prepared to go along there, he would ring in advance to let them know I was on my way.

His second surprise, I'm sure, was when I agreed to this hurriedly arranged audition. I didn't know where it was but I managed to conceal my lack of knowledge of London's night life. I stood up, glad to be able to vacate the high office at last and cool off, but expressing my appreciation of his efforts on my behalf in the best Hollywood tradition.

Ossie was waiting for the verdict outside. When I told him where and who I was going to audition for, he was more ecstatic than I was, as this group was apparently the crème de la crème of British modern jazz. On the way from Shaftesbury Avenue to the 51 Club he gave me an eager tutorial on the Johnny Dankworth Seven, with a run down on all the members and what they played. I had been well and truly thrown in at the deep end, and any moment now I had to prove I could swim.

The club was in the cellar of a building on the corner of Charing Cross Road and Great Newport Street. I had never been to a jazz club in my life before, so it was an exciting as well as frightening experience. By now I was sure I was disintegrating into my normal scruffy self, what with my perspiration, my ignorance of the art of makeup and, of course, my accursed hair untameable by any product on the market.

I didn't feel that I was going to make a good impression, but I took a deep breath, thought of the future and sprinted down the dark stairs into an unknown world. It was a long, low-ceilinged room and very unglamorous; there were no decorations or furniture apart from some posters of past and coming events, a few chairs, and at one end – more brightly lit than the rest of the cellar – an upright piano.

Seated at the piano was Bill Le Sage and standing nearby was John Dankworth. My heart was pounding with the fear that I would screw up this golden opportunity if I didn't get myself under control. As I was introduced to both of them I tried to act worldly and sophisticated. In fact I don't think they cared one iota about my knowledge of the world or how I went about living in it; all they wanted was a singer good enough to be in their band. They had evidently spent the whole morning listening to girl singers and now they were well into the afternoon.

I was asked what I was going to sing and I gave them a number of choices. They picked 'Embraceable You', 'Orange-Coloured Sky' and 'Paper Moon' – Nat King Cole was very big at the time and was singing good swinging songs. Bill played for me and it was a revelation to be accompanied right away so sympathetically without a rehearsal. Once I knew he was going to support me in a way that had never been supported before, my fears dropped away: I would have gone on singing until I was given the sisterly hook.

Three numbers seemed to be enough to convince them that I had something to offer. John asked if I could sing in the club that night, as they were a co-operative band, and although he and Bill were quite impressed, the other five would have to like me too, and they wouldn't be around until tonight. I didn't hesitate – of course I would! What time did they want me to return? The club opened at eight: they would leave my name at the door to allow me and Ossie in any time after the opening.

The sensational turmoil in my stomach, breathing apparatus and heart took a considerable effort to overcome, just so that I could appear relaxed and in command. I felt quite weak, but I had to get myself together to face the next new hurdle: singing with a professional band in a London jazz club. Ossie was of course elated, and we whiled away the time talking about the prospects, walking and having a meal – during which he told me he was in love with me and that he would like to guide my future, in other words be my manager too.

It was the wrong time, the wrong place and, to carry on with the words of the song, the wrong face. He knew I was having difficulties with my marriage, but I said I would not be disloyal to George and my young son, and for the moment all my emotional energy had to be invested into getting this singing position.

I had phoned home earlier to tell them what had happened and that I would be late. They wished me luck, and I was on my way.

Audition in a Cellar

The club was crowded, hot and full of strange smells, a mixture of the strong fumes of Gauloise cigarettes, sweat and body heat of the jiving dancers and a smell quite alien to my nostrils then, but I was later to learn was marijuana. The Dankworth Seven were not on when we arrived; another group was holding the fort until the star attraction later in the evening. John and I spotted each other from across the dance floor; he was talking to his girlfriend, a tall blonde from Canada. He crossed the floor with her to tell me that he would introduce me before I came up to sing. We worked out the order of the songs and he was gone.

I started to see him for the first time, now that my fear was beginning to subside. Tall, attractively gaunt, with a strong nose and a full-lipped, large mouth, he looked very boyish and had great charm. I sat down, watching and listening to the music that I liked but knew little about, then heard my name and realized it was now up to me to prove myself to the other musicians who had not heard me. I was petrified.

I walked to the stand literally quaking from head to toe. This was real stage-fright, and I had to control it before I started to sing, or I was doomed. My love of singing and natural talent came to the rescue: when I had to do it and there was an audience in front of me, I performed. 'Paper Moon', with bass, drums, and interjections by the other musicians swung around me and lifted me into musical heaven. I could not believe what was happening to me – I had found my place at last – please God make them like me! The other two songs were just as strong as far as the backing was concerned, so how could I go wrong? Until now I had always had to contend with pub musicians who couldn't play in my key or didn't know the song, or audition pianists who could not swing.

The audience clapped politely; they obviously hadn't felt what I had, and I left the stand more or less sure that like all the other auditions I had attended, I wouldn't pass. (I wasn't a good auditioner.) John came up to me after his set finished and asked if I could hang on while he talked to the others; he'd see me in the office around the corner, which was the local pub. We all gathered eventually, me to hear the outcome of their decision about me, them to quench their thirst after a hard blow in a hot cellar. They were all very nice to me, and asked me where I had been hiding all this time as they hadn't heard of me. Then John dropped the bombshell: 'We would all like you to be our vocalist.' It was unanimous! I started shaking hands with all of them, Don Rendell, Jimmy Deuchar, Tony Kinsey, Eddie Harvey, Eric Dawson. My wish had been granted, my prayer answered.

They offered me six pounds a week, more than I had ever earned before, but for some reason I have never been able to fathom I asked for seven, and got it. I giggle inwardly at my cheek even today. It was my first ambitious move in the business, small but effective. The next question was, 'Can you start right away?' I said 'yes' without thinking how I was going to handle my domestic affairs. I was going to be what I had dreamed of and worked towards all my life, and my family were going to be happy for me. I had arrived.

The next hurdle I had to jump was arranging with George, my mother and sister Sylvia how Stuart would be looked after while I was away on tour. As we were all living together anyway, they already did the baby-sitting, so it wasn't going to be hard to sort out, as long as they would agree to take on more of the responsibility. I was able to help financially now, and even though it was a small amount, it was still a help.

I didn't have too much persuading to do: they were all so happy for me, to have got this far towards a goal they knew I had been pursuing from childhood. All, that is, except George, who naturally had reservations, but was carried along with everyone else. So it was settled. Mother and Sylvia together would take over care of Stuart while I was on tour, so that I could go journeying without worrying about him – he would be as well looked after as if I were there, probably better.

My next problem was a working outfit, something to impress the band and the audience while I sat and sang on the stand. I went to Oxford Street to buy my first working dress, where my inexperience in the art of buying evening wear first raised its silly head. The lady assistants were out to makeup their commissions for the day, not to give advice on what was the best buy for a girl who would only have one dress, which she would have to wear constantly, night after night, until she had saved enough money to come back for a second one.

The shop I chose was at the Tottenham Court Road end of Oxford Street, not considered the ritziest end even then. Like most of the shops in the street it was run by two or three Jewish ladies who had the sales formula off pat. First I was put into a dress that was obviously a couple of sizes too big for me. Standing behind me, the assistant took into her hands all the slack, pulling and tugging till the front of the dress looked like the models in windows (till you look at all the pinning at the back), then, still clutching for grim death, called out to someone at the back of the shop: 'Come over here and have a look at this! She looks wonderful, don't she look wonderful? Just look at the fit, perfect, a little tuck here and there, perfect, she couldn't get a better bargain anywhere, now could she?' 'Or a better fit,' adds her number two. 'Just look at the fit!' This routine would carry on, with number two not in the least bit interested but occasionally muttering, fag in mouth, 'Yea, oh yea, mmm, true' in response to my lady's chatter.

Nothing original was coming out of her mouth: it was the sales pitch for anyone who was in the least bit indecisive, and they certainly had a beauty in their hands with me. How I was there by myself in the first place was a mystery, but I certainly must have been, as nobody in their right mind would have chosen the dress that I stepped out of that shop with, unless she was a débutante with a lady's maid – but a deb would not have been at that end or any end of Oxford Street.

The dress was white – which was the first and most important mistake. Two, it was lace, or lace-like organza, material that needed a lady's maid to keep its crispness. Three, the design was more suitable for an ingenue soprano with the Palm Court Strings than for a contralto with a modern jazz band.

At the time I was quite proud that I had picked out this reasonably priced dress all by myself, till I took it along to the first rehearsal with all the musicians present, hoping to get a reaction. They were not in the least bit interested in my eventual white nightmare, and not until I got on the coach for the first date out of town did I get a sense of their non-approval. Frank was the first to ask, in a very friendly manner, 'Let's have a look at the new dress!' I brought it out and held it up, proud of my buy. He gazed at it for some time, assessing its beauty, I assumed, for it had a red cabbage rose at the bosom, with two long red ribbons hanging from the rose to the hem of the ankle-length dress. After Frank and the other boys had had a long hard look, Frank produced a pair of scissors from somewhere, and cut the red ribbons to above the waist. 'What did you do that for?' I asked grumpily. 'Because it looks a bit snappier,' was the reply, and the rest of the band agreed.

I knew from that little incident that if I didn't start standing up for myself with this group, they would be a difficult lot to handle. Of course the dress never survived the rigours of touring: over the next six months or so it got yellower and yellower, then greyer and greyer. There were no one-day cleaners on the road in those days, so its crispness as well as its colour wilted drastically. I was eventually christened 'Scruff', a rather unkind if accurately observed nickname.

It wasn't easy to keep tidy on the road, and mastering the packing, makeup, hair and clothes was difficult without the girls lending me a hand. Often, because of the rotten roads of the day, we'd arrive at a dance hall so late that I had only a short time to put on the dress, and makeup over stale makeup, because there was no warm water to wash off the old stuff. Then I had get on the bandstand and try to look as if I had been to a beauty shop. Glamorous was not what I felt or could ever have been called.

I loved one-night stands, because I was seeing the British Isles for the first time and the tour was revelation of its beauty, the variety of its landscapes and its inhabitants. The other advantage of one-nighters is that if you hate a place you're not going to be there for a lifetime, but there were very few places where I couldn't find something to interest me.

I was experiencing all this with a group of musicians who were wonderful companions to work and travel with. Bill Le Sage was not only the pianist, he was also the manager, who looked after me on the road, along with Frank Holder the singer and Latin American percussionist. They both saw to it that I was never left by myself for want of company. Generally it was the three of us who sat together when, after a long spell on the road, the coach pulled in at a truckers' café. The others took a little longer to get close to, but by the time the Seven broke up, we were all close friends.

My first date with the band was a dance in the north of England, shared with the Tito Burns Sextet. Tito was a jazz accordion player married to a singer called Terry Devon – they did vocalese duets, like an American couple, Jackie and Roy who were singing at the time with a bandleader called Charlie Ventura. Terry also sang solo. I was a fan of this band, as Tito and the band had a regular radio programme that I liked to listen to, called the *Accordion Club*. The accordion was not a favourite instrument of mine, but I did like the music played on this programme. I was thrown into a world that to me was the height of worldly sophistication.

Terry was in a beaded, strapless creation with a full skirt, not an Oxford Street buy and not white. This gown had been made by someone who knew the band-singers' uniform of the day, something that I had to wait a while to achieve. The musicians had uniforms which made life a lot easier for them than for the girl singers. Terry impressed me, not only as a singer, but as a devoted wife, when I saw her in the dressing room sewing dress shields under the arms of Tito's band jacket. She confided in me that she had to do this straight away as Tito perspired so much that the coat would be ruined otherwise. I thought to myself, 'Wow! Fancy her telling me these personal details about someone I listen to on the radio!' Terry was of course talking to me as a sister singer who, like her, knew about the difficulties of the road, working in hot conditions that ruined clothes if they were not protected. She was his lady's maid. As she looked at my crisp, brand spanking new, white lace creation, Terry must have thought I was a genius of the road, knowing all the wrinkles, or how to get them out of white dresses. I liked being accepted as an equal and didn't put her wise.

On that first date I also became aware that I was reasonably attractive on stage. I had a habit – still do – of continually licking my lips, which removes any trace of lipstick. I am not aware that I do it, only the absence of lipstick lets me know. One of the musicians in Tito's band found this and me appealing as he watched and listened. When our set finished he cornered me as I came off the bandstand and made advances, saying he liked the way I licked my lips. I didn't know what he was talking about, but he obviously thought it was some seductive message I was sending out. I should have made a with-it, flippant remark, but that would have been beyond me at that time, so I weakly fled to the safety of Frank and Bill.

The fans had their favourite bands, and they loved the music those bands played, so they would stand around the bandstand, looking up wide-eyed, listening adoringly to their favourite instrumentalist or singer, while the jitterbuggers jittered away in the background, taking over the floor, while some persevering dance patrons tried to quick-step or fox-trot it to a music patently unsuited to the art of ballroom dancing. Frank and I sat side by side on the stand, watching the gyrating couples, sometimes commenting on a particular pair who could really swing, and knew each other's hand-holds and turns by instinct or hours of practice. Something I never learnt, what hand to grasp when I swivelled around, but most musicians and singers watch dancing rather than participating.

Jitterbugging, for which modern jazz was ideal, was a style of dancing that became so popular it just took over the dance halls, to the chagrin of a lot of the older promoters, who roped them off at the back of the hall. Gerry Cohen, a highly respected Northern promoter, would have no truck with them – he was a back-of-the-hall roper until it became quite apparent that the gyraters were going to be his bread and butter. Before that came about, if he saw any of them creeping past the rope, lacking the space to do the intricate twists, turns and throws, he would come on to the stand, stop the music and in a commanding Northern accent, berate the offenders over the microphone: 'That pair that has broken the cordon can just get back behind yon rope, I'll not stand gyrating on't dance floor.' He finally lost the battle, as the rope gradually crept up the ballroom before the jitterbugging hordes, eventually to disappear for ever.

10

On the Road with the Dankworth Seven

There was always a sense of uncertainty and challenge on the bandstand: the singers had to be awake, alert and ready to jump up to the microphone to sing when the introduction of one of their songs was played. John never told his singers when or what they were going to sing on the stand (we were only programmed for concerts), so we had to commit to memory all the musical introductions to the songs that were arranged for us. At first this was a trial for me, and if it hadn't been for Frank, who gave me little pushes or jabs if he spotted me dreaming, I would have been in a lot of trouble.

Frank, the experienced one, was beginning to discover that this new young singer was not a sophisticated London jazz-club habituée, and that he'd better guide her or she would not last in the cynical world of jazz musicians, who could be extremely cruel to singers they didn't respect. I learned quickly: my ears were being trained and they were receptive to everything that was going on around me. I was a student in one of the best on-the-job travelling musical schools of modern jazz in Britain; touring along with searchers and learners who were also movers and shakers of a like mind, how could I not learn?

'The Dankworth Seven' had employed several girl singers before me, one of whom had not had their unanimous approval, so she had suffered, as I heard, after a gig. They had conceived a practical joke they would play on her after she had retired for the night. One of them knocked on her door saying he wanted to speak to her urgently, and once he was in the room, sat on her bed and declared his undying love for her. Within seconds came another knock on the door, and another request to speak. The musician already in the room dived under the bed when the next entered. This continued until several bodies were under and the laughter couldn't be controlled any more by bods beneath or above. She must have been a good sport even if not such a great singer.

The singer they had employed before me was someone they all admired very much: Marian Williams, a tall, young, handsome, well-endowed English/African, a Londoner with a Cockney accent, who sang like a dream and adored jazz (which Frank took pains to point out to me). The reason she had left was more concerned with practical finances than with practical joking. Being a cooperative band, whatever was earned they shared out between them, all except Marian, to whom they paid a salary of ten pounds a week. Evidently, they got behind with the wages one week, and her father, who was a very large wrestler or boxer, came to the club asking for her wages – no please or thank you, just, I'll take them if you don't mind. She left because they couldn't afford her or a punch-up.

Such stories as those were circulated with relish to counter the tedium of the road. I'm sure I was told some of them to put me on guard for anything that might occur, but the Dankworth Seven were considered the gentlemen of the road compared with some. There was a band at the time who initiated a new girl singer by continually saying 'F..k, f..k, f..k' one after the other into her face. This would put her into a state of shock, after which they'd say: 'We are getting you used to the word, because you're going to hear it a lot in this band.' There were many expletives that are in common usage today that shocked most people then, and certainly girls – me for one. My family didn't swear, so it wasn't part of my vocabulary: I would have been slapped if I had.

As indeed I was, when I called my mother a berk. This word

came out of Cockney rhyming slang and was used a lot by musicians if anyone did anything stupid; not knowing the secret language all that well, I merrily put it to use myself if anything daft was done by anybody, innocently showing off my new hip word, without knowing it was the unrhyming part of 'Berkshire Hunt' that was being used. My mother did something silly and innocuous which amused me and I said 'You silly berk!' She clouted me (aged twenty-four), then gave me a lesson in Cockney rhyming slang. The word is still used, innocently divorced from the original meaning. And I can still feel the sting of that slap.

The 'Seven' were having a problem renaming me. My given name Clementine Campbell was too cumbersome for posters, and my nickname Clem made me sound like a cowboy. My married name, Langridge, didn't roll off the tongue well for a supposedly up-and-coming glamorous jazz singer.

Astonishingly, I had no say in the matter at all. One day I went to a rehearsal in the basement of a Frith Street café in Soho, next door to where Ronnie Scott's Jazz Club is now. I arrived eager to rehearse, so that I could commit the introductions of my songs to memory; instead, I was handed my new name. They kept my initials but that's about all. I must have liked it to accept it without much comment, or maybe I really wanted to be renamed so as to be able to say: 'This is not really Clemmie singing, this is Cleo Laine, it's a part.' The boys still called me Clemmie though – some of them still do even today. The story is that they put surnames and first names into separate hats, pulled out one and then the other and that's how I became Cleo Laine, the name that everyone knows me as today. I'm so used to it now that when anyone calls me Clem or Clemmie (apart from family or musicians from those days) I am amused and curious; did they know me when it belonged to me, once upon a time? 'Cleo Laine' certainly looked good on the posters and programmes, and it soon became a part of me that I loved, but for some it was a problem – those who wanted me to remain for ever Clemmie.

I was growing up fast. A few months after joining the band John and Bill Le Sage took me aside and said there was a possibility of a radio series, which they hoped I would be part of, but the BBC would want to audition me; they couldn't just give me the job. It was a bit of a blow to my ego; it seemed I was good enough to sing with the band everywhere and anywhere except on the air – but this was BBC policy so I had no option but to agree. Once again I would have to go through what I had thought had come to an end. I was terribly scared that if I didn't pass it would be the last of my band-singing days. And if I did pass I would have a considerable rise in pay. So I worked hard rehearsing with the band, and getting my nerves under control.

When the day finally came for the audition, the hard work paid off. We all passed with flying colours, resulting in a regular weekly broadcast that turned out to be very popular. John wrote a theme song, words as well, which Frank, I and some of the boys sang jollily. I can't remember much of it except the ending, which went like this: 'Whether you're in Glamorgan or Todmorden, Aberdeen or Glorious Devon, we hope you like the Johnny Dankworth Seven.' Not the greatest of lyrics, but it did the trick when we eventually visited any of the places mentioned.

The Dankworth Seven was influenced stylistically by the Miles Davis 'Birth of the Cool' band, and they played the great tunes of Charlie Parker, Thelonius Monk, Dizzy Gillespie and Miles Davis, but what gave the band a distinctive sound of its own were John's writing for it, and also the 'head arrangements'. These were tunes played at rehearsals where all the Seven would contribute ideas, occasionally composing tunes on the spot, harmonizing, orchestrating and ending the day with a new repertoire.

John D. and Ronnie Scott were two of the first who became band musicians on the *Queen Mary*, their only aim being to get to New York to devour the music being played by men like Lester Young, Lee Konitz, Max Roach, Coleman Hawkins and Billie Holiday – along with, of course, Charlie Parker, their god. But I won't go into John's story. I was not there, and he will tell it himself one day. For myself, unlike those lucky ships' musicians, I didn't hear these great jazz musicians performing in person until the Musicians Union lifted the ban on American bands performing in Britain.

As the Seven became more and more popular through our BBC programme, the pace of touring picked up, so that often I was away from home for a week at a time. Sometimes I arrived home to find that something important had happened without my knowledge. One event turned all our lives around, and in retrospect I can trace the cause of later incidents back to this last and, as it turned out, sad move for Mother and me. Returning home tired but very happy, the wind was knocked out of my free-wheeling sails when Mother announced she was going into the catering business again, that she had acquired another café, in Hanwell, a few miles away from Southall. She would be moving (Mother had done it again) to where Ben's Café was situated. Once again she was cutting ties with Pa, who was getting dangerously close to infiltrating himself back into the fold via his children and grandchildren, whom he loved and spoiled so shamelessly that it annoyed Mother. Sylvia and Geoff, her husband, would be going with her, to help set it up and work alongside her, as there were living quarters big enough for my sister, her two children and of course Stuart; but not for George and me.

It was a blow that I was not prepared for, and I felt extremely hurt at being excluded from this family move, but realized at the same time that I couldn't rely on the family for my comforts and needs all my life. I had to grow up and start thinking for myself and how to tackle the change it would obviously bring about for George and me. I also had to think about how I could remain close to Stuart. Apart from Stuart, selfishly, I was not thinking of anybody but myself and how I was going to get around this problem, which made me angry with my mother. As anger always made me get off my backside and be doing, I started by showing I was unconcerned – I understood, I said, and oh, she was not to worry about me.

A place had to be found somewhere in the same area – well, that was one problem solved immediately – Hanwell. Although I was earning more than seven pounds a week now, it was still not enough, with payments for Stuart, road expenses, and the erratic work of George in the building trade, to buy anything, or to get anything other than a rented room or rooms. The housing shortage was still disastrous for us young married couples, especially if you had parents with enough room to accommodate you or if you didn't have several children or a returning husband who had fought in France or the Middle East. After weeks of searching and rejection, I eventually found an unsatisfactory bedsitter for myself and George in the same street as the café, which enabled me to see Stuart and the family as often as possible when I was home, and for a while it worked. But I was always happy when a reasonably long tour came about, which took me away from the problems I knew I would eventually have to face.

In the meantime I got back to the music and the travelling. I was starting to understand and love the music that I sat listening to nightly on the stand, realizing at the same time how inadequate my equipment for the job really was. Here I was, a contralto with a very limited range, who would never consider a song with a large span, although John edged me up by doing arrangements of songs in higher keys unbeknown to me, keys I would never have picked for myself at the time. Or he'd do a modulation to a higher key within a song, which I was able to cope with, proving that it was often mind over matter. If I was told something was difficult, I couldn't do it, so he hid it from me until I did it naturally, not only testing out my range, but my ear, widening my musical knowledge and my musical vocabulary with terms like Modulation, Coda, Back to sign, Segue – an endless list, quite unknown to me before. I was a student, and these musicians became my tutors.

I realized how lucky I was starting my career alongside musicians of such integrity, so I was determined to improve on my few assets. Hanwell, not being the musical centre of the country, was not going to show me the way, but I thought if I searched out a local piano teacher it would do me no harm, so I browsed through the local papers and found an ad for 'PianoForte: All grades taught for Associated Board Examinations', with an address not far from the bedsitter. It turned out to be an unsuccessful venture.

The teacher's house was reminiscent of my aunt's house in Penge – dark, heavy and with a musty smell of antiquity, polish and cooking. The hall was long, narrow and dark, a feature of Victorian houses, with rooms leading off, one of which was where the teacher gave his lessons. There was a line of chairs against the wall of the hall for waiting, in case he got behind or someone coming late caused him to jump ahead. It was there that I sat and waited on my first visit. All his qualifications, which seemed impressive, were hanging on the wall opposite me, so I had no option but to read them over and over and over again, building up my confidence in my decision.

He was very formal: everything about him was so headmasterish that I instinctively bridled with rebellion in his presence, asking him if he could teach me songs that I knew he wouldn't know, and I knew was not his method of teaching. It was obvious that neither of us liked each other much, but I needed him more than he needed me, so I smiled and made the best of it – until one day I asked him about chords. He was certainly not interested in jazz and didn't know what I was asking him to show me. I probably didn't know how to explain what I wanted with any confidence, so to save face he replied, 'All you people want to know or play is spirituals or jazz.'

I couldn't believe what I was hearing. It made me so furious that all the latent influence of my father's lectures came to the fore and I spat out with as much dignity as I could muster: 'That's a rather sweeping generalization from someone with such limited musical interests!' and flounced out – out of his stuffy music room, with its stiff upright piano, leaving the severe music teacher to mutilate his next victim, a reluctant small child (not one of 'us people').

I went back to listening and imbibing as much as I could from the musicians I toured with. On tour there were always fans or musicians who would invite the whole band, vocalists as well, to come back to their homes for a blow or a listening session of the latest records in their collection. They ranged from an Edinburgh lawyer, Pat Smythe, who played wonderful piano and eventually gave up legal work to become a highly respected professional pianist in London, to George Scott Henderson, a Glaswegian pawnbroker who also played excellent piano and should have given up broking to be a musician, but didn't. Then way down in Torquay there were Charles and Audrey Gean, a couple of eccentric music-lovers and dress-shopowners. Their hospitality was legendary to every band who visited that seaside town: after a gig the bands would all converge to listen to the Geans' fine record collection, and drink, talk and play the night away.

Most of the bands on the road who played modern jazz were part of this fraternity, so we occasionally met up at these oases on the road, which included Indian and Chinese restaurants, musicians' watering holes, even today. They were open at ridiculous hours in cities as diverse as Manchester, where the Indian food was amazing, to Liverpool, where the Chinese food couldn't be bettered anywhere in the world. Combined with the music, these were enriching experiences for a suburban bumpkin like me.

All the musicians in the Seven had widely different characters that over months and years I got to fathom out. Bill Le Sage to me was the most uncomplicated of them: he was a warm, caring man whom you took your problems to. He hung about with Eric Dawson, the bass player, a childlike Harpo Marx type, who needed Bill's fatherly nature on the road. Eric at one time turned vegetarian: the only one in a bunch of carnivores, he chose to eat his vegetable sandwich on the coach on his own, while the rest of us ate our usual unhealthy fry-ups. When he had finished his meal he would come to the café in search of company, sit at one of our tables and stare long and hard at the obnoxious food we were eating and proclaim just one word over and over again, every few seconds – 'toxic . . . toxic . . . toxic' – until someone in the party said, 'Piss off Eric!' Then he'd get up, quite unconcerned about the sudden blast of humorous profanity, and go back to the coach. When we returned, all ready to depart, he would be sitting there alone, sadly determined, and we greeted him as if nothing had happened.

On the Road with the Dankworth Seven

It certainly wasn't easy being a vegetarian on the road in those days, as I was to find out for myself several years later when I became one. It was considerd a cranky thing to be, and it was virtually impossible to find places to eat outside London. Eric didn't fare well trying to be a travelling vegetarian bass player, which is heavy manual work. Once, to the consternation of us all, he collapsed, but then quite determinedly carried on, Eric laughingly told us what his father-in-law said when he heard of his collapse: 'What you need, my boy, is a damn good steak inside you.'

Wonderful Don Rendell, who was educated at Marlborough College and was the only one in the band who had been to boarding school, didn't care what he ate – he was called the dustbin of the band, bolting his food down voraciously. We came to the conclusion that he ate like that because his mother wasn't there to box his ear for eating sloppily and that all public schoolboys were messy eaters. The rest of us were pleb eaters and fairly average, depending on the amount of time we had to linger. John was always a bit of a gobbler, food being secondary to more important things.

I never got to know very well either Tony Kinsey, the first drummer with the Seven, or trumpet player Jimmy Deuchar, since they left the band not long after I joined, when Eddie Taylor and Eddie Blair replaced them. Eddie Harvey the trombonist was always charming, calling people he liked 'Nut' – it was a term of endearment to him, and meant that he had accepted you as a friend, so I was pleased when he started to say to me, 'How are you, Nut?'

Though sometimes sarcastic and cynical, they were all gentle men, and they all had a sense of humour that pre-dated many current comedy teams in its wackiness and imagination. It certainly combated the tedium of the coach. As on those ladies' day outings there were many sing-songs and I started to learn what the men might have sung on their outings, such as 'There was an old monk of great reknown' and various other army versions of popular songs and marches; it seems that coaches bring out

all the vulgar doggerel and ribaldry known to man. I was quite
familiar with most of it, enjoying the bawdiness, as indeed I had
on the Croydon outings.

It wasn't all coarse banter – games were invented too, such as
'Newts' and 'Boat Race Snap'. John D. was fascinated by the
way newts walked unconcernedly all over each other in their
tanks and here we all were, in a coach-shaped tank, and the
idea took shape. One person would silently and jerkily place a
hand or foot anywhere on the body of a seated companion, then
keep perfectly still. The companion must remain impervious and
quite still, then another from behind moves on to the top of the
first two, dispassionately placing any part of his body anywhere he
thinks fit. This silently continued until the bodies in the pile could
contain themselves no longer, collapsing into a heap of laughter all
over the coach.

Boat Race Snap ('Face Snap', 'boat race' being Cockney rhyming
slang for 'face') only involved two at a time – the others were judges
or cheerers. The two players had a choice of four faces: a big grin,
a scowl, a stuck-out tongue and crossed eyes. You sat back to back
and got your chosen face ready, and when the referee said 'go', you
both turned round. If both players had the same face, the first to call
out 'snap!' won the round. This game too usually deteriorated into
hysterical laughter on my part, whether I was playing or watching.
Oh how I loved some of those dreadful journeys.

Although I was having the time of my life when I was on the
road, at home things were pretty shaky. The bedsitter wasn't
working and George and I were having a hard time seeing eye
to eye. Things were moving at such a pace with the Seven –
our first television appearance, a tour of Germany, broadcasts
and concerts as well as the dances all over the country – and
that was where I wanted to be.

I had discovered a hair conditioner by now called Countess that got
my hair under control and reasonably tamed if I applied it and didn't
wash it all out, then put my hair in very large rollers. It came out
almost straight and manageable, and if it didn't rain or the weather

wasn't humid, for a while the bush was under control; I started to look fairly tidy. 'Countess', although not going so far as to make me look the part, was a blessing at the time. It was in an extremely small tube and the amount I had to use cost me the earth.

Eventually, however, it disappeared from the market, and I had to go searching once again – so the saga of my woolly head continued. Meanwhile it was the joy of my, and the television studio's existence, as my hair was primped and cajoled for its first television appearance without my having to go through a lot of misery and pain.

We were booked as part of a variety show at the Nuffield Centre in central London. The other artists appearing for the first time on television in this show were Benny Hill and the singer Shirley Abicair. Shirley was an attractive folk singer who accompanied herself on the zither, an instrument made popular at the time by the picture *The Third Man* and the Harry Lime theme. It was unusual and it brought her considerable fame. Benny Hill came from out of the blue as far as we were concerned. Whoever put the show together in the first place had an eye and ear for up-and-coming talent. Benny compèred and also had his own spot, which marked the beginning of his astronomical career on television first in Britain, Europe, eventually crossing the Atlantic to become the darling of the USA. Later, long before colour television, when he had his own shows, I did a few guest appearances on them, but I never got to know him well: he was always an extremely private man.

11

Falling in Love

This first television appearance was in black and white – colour had not hit Britain yet – and it brought about my first lesson in TV makeup (it was a long time before I knew enough about it to be able to do it for myself). I'm sure it was the makeup girls' first appearance too: they had a whale of a time redesigning the map of my phiz. What was a large square-jawed face they attempted to make into a pixi-ish oval with a gruesome paint job – the standard TV face taught at the time in the colleges for cosmetics: whatever kind of face you had they aimed at giving you the oval. My jaw was shaded dark brown and away, an attempt was made to make my nose look long and aquiline, my eyebrows were given a look of complete surprise, and my lips became ox-blood red. The eyes for some strange reason had very little done to them and after a massive powdering job they looked like two little black holes in the snow.

I stared at this face in the mirror with dumb amazement. My unfamiliar lips could not form the words of revulsion that were being formed in my head as my eyes roamed over the face that had disappeared into a clown, and what eventually came out of my mouth was nothing whatsoever to do with what was in my mind and what I wanted to say, which would have made everyone unhappy. Instead I said, 'Well! Won't everyone be surprised?' As

I recall I was the butt of a lot of unkind jokes and merry quips. 'I see you've been playing with that flour bag again, Clee,' and 'Hey, Lainey, didn't you tell the surgeon you wanted to keep your eyes?'

When colour television arrived, yet another regulation face map was drawn, but it was easier to live with than black and white. I now look more or less like me on TV, the result depending a lot more on the amount of time given to it and the skill of the lighting technician. I have sometimes looked very glamorous, but mostly I look like normal old me. On occasions people have stopped me in the street to say, 'Oh! you look much nicer than you do on the telly!'

On my days off I spent most of my time at the café, helping or hindering Mother. Waitressing was a job I soon found I had no talent for. People are so indecisive about their food; a waitress has to have the patience of Job. If the cook gets it wrong, it's the waiter who gets the full-throttle abuse, so I didn't volunteer my services for out front too often. I kept Mother amused with my touring adventures and she heard all my current tales of woe, such as the bedsitter situation, which was beginning to irritate George and me: we couldn't have a good row, and we couldn't make love because of the close proximity of the landlady, so we were both in an unhappy state of mind.

Mother listened sympathetically and, as she had always done, came to the rescue. Over the shop were a couple of storage rooms, not really habitable, but I promised to work on them on my free days if she would let us take them over. Mother caved in pretty easily: I think she liked my company and felt a little guilty about excluding me when they moved. Her motherly instincts never ever left her. So, I scrubbed, swept, repaired cracks in walls, replaced broken floorboards, whitewashed, papered and furnished. I was pleased with my efforts, and for a while I was content to be back with the family and closer to Stuart, who was growing into an independent, strong-willed little boy, with manageable curls and a happy disposition. He was liked by all the tradesmen and customers of the café, often having treats that other children wouldn't have had.

Stuart and the milkman became firm friends and he would have a regular ride in his electric milkcart after the deliveries were over and the milkman had had his cuppa and his chat with Mother. On one occasion Stuart was sitting impatiently outside at the wheel of the cart, eager to get started on his ride around the square. He was pretending he was the driver, making unelectric milkcart noises, simulating instead the noise that Sterling Moss's racing machine might make on its way to the finishing line. Almost everyone thought this was highly amusing, until the observant four-year-old discovered the trick of making the machine actually move. To his innocent delight away he and the cart went, slowly but inevitably towards traffic lights that were signalling red. Once started, however, Stuart was not about to stop for anyone or anything until he had gone right around the square. Fortunately, the cafe's next-door neighbour was the barracks of the Territorial Army. Just as Stuart was about to jump the lights, a Sergeant Philips was marching round the corner on his way to the café. He spotted the runaway and stopped him just in time, hauling the driver, kicking and squawking his head off, from his seat.

The inhabitants of the café were jump-started from their tranquillity into a state of panic by the entrance of the incredulous soldier carrying the protesting infant in his arms. The inquisition started there and then: 'How?', 'When?' 'Why?' Wonderment, explanations and excuses. The whole shop was exhilarated by the exploits of the four-year-old racing driver of Hanwell Road.

On another occasion the army saved my bacon when I missed a train that would have got me to London and the Savoy Hotel, where we had been hired to perform for a débutante who had specially asked for 'The Johnny Dankworth Seven', I suspect much to the dismay of her parents and the resident society bandleader Carol Gibbons. I had got the time and the train completely muddled. I had made preparation beforehand for this classy date by having a new dress made especially for the occasion by a well-meaning local dressmaker who copied a design from the

Vogue pattern book: a black, strapless, very simple design, with a few silver sequins placed tastefully about. My dress was ready but here I was, stuck in Hanwell, with a large cardboard box, a makeup case, a place to go, but no way to get there.

Time was running out and I had almost given up when Mother told the sad story to one of the soldiers, who promised to come to my rescue and drive me to London. I gathered up my belongings and made ready to get into a car, when he suggested that I might like to put on something a little warmer, as motor bikes could be a bit chilly. I really had no choice. With scarf tied firmly under chin to protect the newly coiffed hair, skirt tucked well up around my knees and wearing a fashionable duffle coat with hood up, I climbed aboard, looking more like a monk on a spree than a glam song-bird.

I hung on like grim death as we whizzed up the Uxbridge Road towards the metropolis. The soldier (whose name, unforgivably, I've forgotten) tried to hold a conversation with me along the way, but hollering above the rushing wind and traffic would not have improved my vocal ability for the night, and given the uncomfortable proximity of my mouth to his back, and the attention I had to give to the box with my little black dress in it, I did very little batting of the ball back. Eventually, however, we arrived.

The commissionaire hovered, suspiciously waiting to see what might transpire, but then wandered over to give us a hand with our luggage. Neither the soldier nor I had a clue about the correct procedure of entry for the lower ranks in orchestras or combos playing at the Savoy, and innocently we enlisted his help. When he discovered that my position was that of a lowly band crooner, his attitude changed, so much so that we felt we should stand to attention whilst receiving our instructions – which were to remove ourselves and our tackle forthwith from the exclusive façade, and direct ourselves to the service entrance. After finding my way through the back-doubles, the kitchen (the first of many) eventually led to the band room for non-permanent musicians.

In fact, grand hotels all over the world quite often overlook the needs of entertainers: only if you are a star performer can you enter by the front, be greeted by the doorman and have a suite for a dressing room. But I wasn't to learn about that till much later. For now I was in with the boys, changing behind a temporary screen in a corner. We all felt out of place, as we were not sure what was expected of us. We had been asked for, but to do what? To play jazz, as in a club, or play commercial music for dancing? This was John's and the boys' dilemma, and one that they had to solve before going on. Frank and I had our repertoire of fairly well-known standards: Frank was not only a singer of Latin American music, he was also an expert at playing congo drums, bongos and all the percussive Latin instruments, some of which he taught me to play for the Latin section of dances.

It was an exclusive and smallish party in one of the many smaller function rooms. The time came when we had to sidle in and pretend we were invisible until ready to play, which went according to plan – except that the play was not exactly what was required by the Hooray Henrys prancing around the dance floor. Word was somehow maydayed to Carol Gibbons that all was not well in one of his rooms and he came and sat down at the piano to give a demonstration to Bill and John of what was required by these dancing fools. He played a few socially accepted tunes in the style he was well known for, hoped he would be copied, and vanished.

Instead, as soon as he had gone, Frank decided to do his manic bongo act. This really got things going, and the debs began to let their hair down with a vengeance. It was at this point that my black strapless dress came down too. I was required to play the congo drum, which I slung over my shoulder, but it was all too frenetic for the slender foundation that was supposedly supporting my little black number, and halfway through a Samba the top half started to slither down to my waist. Luckily the lights were low and I had a black strapless bra on underneath, so few noticed, and those who did were probably tipsy enough to think 'Whoopee! an orgy at last'. My embarrassment was such that the evening was ruined for me: all I wanted was a place to hide. I don't know

115

how I got home – I think Frank must have given me a bed for the night.

At the end of 1952, the band was booked to play in an American camp somewhere in the north for the New Year celebrations.

As midnight struck, the group, Frank and I played and sang the traditional 'Auld Lang Syne' to ourselves, as the room suddenly became full of manic, hail-fellow-whoever-you-are bonhomie, and we joined in with the fun of blowing paper trumpets, wearing funny hats, popping champagne corks and drinking the contents, throwing streamers, and kissing. Kissing everyone in sight, first the one on your left, then right, behind you and in front of you – mustn't miss anyone out.

As the only girl on the stand I was having a beanfeast. I turned, looking for my next New Year peck, and saw that oh! it was the boss. We embraced, kissed, kissed and kissed and although it was well past the witching hour I was hearing Big Ben all over again – this was not a New Year's peck, at least not for me. I didn't know where to look to hide what I had just felt: I just hoped that what was going on inside me was not written on my face. There was no point thinking that it was the champagne playing games with me, because in my heart of hearts I knew I was in trouble. I had never felt anything quite so passionately before, ever. I must have covered up the amazement I felt, somehow, as the night's merry-making continued normally into the drunken morning, and nothing was said. But I was changed.

I didn't find it difficult later to be in John's company, in fact I loved it, and back on the road, we seemed to gravitate towards each other more often than we had before. One afternoon in Edinburgh, where we had a week's engagement at a restaurant called The West End Café, John suggested that we use the piano they had in the basement to routine some new songs for the week, so that we didn't get stale. I expected Bill would be there to play the piano, but it was John who sat down to play – we were alone. I stood behind him to sing. Reading the lyrics over his shoulders, I had to stare at the back of his boyish head and back as he played the songs that he thought might work, making suggestions and asking how I felt about them. As the afternoon went on I knew I had fallen in love. I was deeply affected by his presence and secretly hoped that one day I would affect him in the same way. I had to wait quite a while before it did, for him to make any advances in my direction that one could say were more than friendship.

In the meantime I was happy to be his friend, and he seemed fond of me. Edinburgh remains one of my favourite cities, and during that one week I learnt more about Scotland than I had in all the schools I'd attended in my childhood. As I discovered, along with the others, its history, castles, avenues, back lanes and mounds, I fell in love for the second time that week, in both cases discovering new things to admire, love, and get angry about. It was in Edinburgh that I first played (well, played at playing) golf; Pat Smythe, along with all his other considerable talents, was expert at the game, and didn't seemed to mind an idiot tagging along, smashing up the hallowed grounds. With Don Rendell, I climbed 'Arthur's Seat', not the normal, sensible way but up the side, which was more like climbing Everest, as there were no paths, but a lot of grappling to do.

Every day was a new adventure. How we had the energy for work as well as all this fun and discovery can only be put down to youthful ignorance of the possible consequences. Yet we seemed to survive it unscathed.

A trip to Germany was imminent and Bill had to get my passport and all the details sorted out. I had a tremendous shock when he told me that the Passport Office had me registered in the name of Hitching, rather than Campbell. I told him they must have made a mistake or to stop messing around, but he was deadly serious. I was so stunned by his news; all I wanted to do was to throw the passport away from me as far as I possibly could. What did it all mean? Here I was, a twenty-six-year-old married woman with a small son, and someone was telling me I wasn't who I thought I was. I couldn't wait to get back home to Ben's Café, to confront my mother with this passport and ask her what the hell it all meant.

Up until that moment I had always thought I was a Campbell, the legitimate daughter of Sylvan Alexander Campbell and Minnie Blanche Hitching.

Throwing the passport in front of Mother in the Kitchen of Ben's Café, I asked her to explain it.

I was then to hear from my mother what I had not heard when the door closed on me that day so long ago in Penge. 'What about the children, Minnie?' was asked because Mother and Pa were not married, and because Mother was still married to someone else. Not surprising that the door was closed.

Mother of course was as distraught as I was, but tried to explain, as I yelled angrily at her 'Why didn't you tell me long ago, rather than me finding out for myself in this embarrassing way, at the age of twenty-six?' She had no real reason for not telling me, unless she thought that of all her children I would be the last to understand.

After I had calmed down enough to listen, she explained. Evidently not long after I was born they had had one of their ugly rows, in which Father threatened to leave her, then she threatened to leave him – so to add insult to injury, she registered me in her maiden name instead of his (unlike my brother and sister, who were down as Campbells). When I heard this I blew up again in such a thunderous way that she must have thought, 'I really should have given this one the Campbell name.' I told her it wasn't her and Pa's past that angered me, or the fact that I had been born out of wedlock, so much as the realization that I wouldn't have known at all if I had not needed a passport. It took a long time for me to forgive my mother for this.

We made two trips in Germany, one to the American zone, the other to the British. The first was just to entertain the American forces, but the trip to the British zone was commercial, and for the benefit of German civilians. The US camps were virtually towns in themselves, isolated from the German community, with all the amenities and luxuries that hadn't been seen in Europe for many years, if ever. We were all given passes to visit the PX wherever we played, which to us were like Aladdin's caves. Everyday things were so inexpensive and plentiful compared with at home, luxury items too, so you can imagine how we made the most of our visits to them, with purchases galore for our loved ones at home. Stuart and my nephew Callum had some silly and extraordinary gifts brought back for them, like lederhosen, which I don't think either of them dared wear in Hanwell. However, a beautifully made miniature copy of a Mercedes Benz was Stuart's idea of heaven, and would be a collector's item if he still had it today.

Although I knew that Germany had been badly bombed during the war I wasn't prepared for some of the devastation that was still apparent in the early fifties; the country had certainly taken a pounding and, because of this, hotel accommodation was at times hard to find. I remember in Hamburg some of the lads had to be housed on barges.

The boys decided that as they were in Hamburg they should pay a visit to the Reeperbahn, the famous red-light district, but they were lumbered with me, and didn't know how I would react to the suggestion. They didn't like to send me back to the hotel to be on my own, so they just said we're all going in together, but we'd have to chose a good show. That entailed walking the whole length of the street, being exhorted to enter and review the mysteries of the female body in every club we passed. I can't say that the prospect thrilled me but I was as curious as the lads, on my first visit to such blatant, licensed, open sex. I had no say in the final choice, which I thought fairly weak in the event. A beautiful young girl in a bubble bath gradually exposed her limbs, very artistically, in a titillating way, but when the crucial full frontal exposure was about to be revealed they dimmed the lights to such an extent that the lads might as well have stayed in the hotel, used their imagination and saved their money. Our visit to the red light district was not considered a huge success. Of course some of them may have paid another visit and chosen something more explicit without me along to spoil the fun, but I never heard of it.

Another time we all went out to eat together. The restaurant we picked wasn't doing great business – I think at one point we were the only customers – but they did have a small combination playing, for dancing, not very hip music, mainly polkas, tangos and waltzes. I was eventually invited to dance a waltz with Billy, which I accepted. We moved to the postage-stamp dance floor and it soon became evident to me that Billy was no expert at the waltz. We stumbled around for a while, trying to get our feet coordinated, when Eddie Taylor came over to us, I thought to my rescue. He said 'Excuse me,' and I hoped he was going to ask to take over the dance from Billy. Instead, when Bill and I parted, Eddie took Bill in his arms and started dancing with him. A little while later Eric Dawson excused Bill and danced away with Eddie. We of course fell about laughing, but the head waiter was not amused. Walking on to the dance floor he tapped them on the shoulder and in the best English he could muster, said, 'Germany, man, lady dance. Lady, lady dance. Man, man, not dance.' By then the joke was over and they retreated, giggling with glee.

For me the German tours will remain in my memory as the start of romance between John and me. We got closer than ever before and, on the second long trip, became lovers. It was on that tour that John confided to me that he was going to give up the small group and form a big band. He hadn't decided what its forces would be, only that they were going to be large. I wasn't sure whether I was to be included and I must admit I was inwardly disturbed by the news. I liked things as they were: the plans seemed a threat to our new relationship.

John had never declared his love for me or expressed any wish that I should end my marriage. I don't think he even thought of ending his bachelor state at that time. I knew, however, that my marriage was ended, whether or not my future was going to be with John, and I would have to leave George. When I told my mother she wasn't surprised, but said, 'Are you sure you know what you are doing?' I replied, 'Never surer.'

I went on holiday on my own to the south of France, to a camp site near Valerise, a few miles from Cannes, where I hoped to sort out the tangled mess of decisions I had to make: how and when I was going to tell George; where I would go when I left; if I did, what I would do about Stuart; whether George would let me keep him; whether to ask for a divorce. It wasn't going to be easy to explain that I was leaving him because I didn't love him any more. He would know there was more to it than that, but I didn't see why I should have to explain that John was the eventual catalyst of my making up my mind to do what after all had been brewing inside me for a year or two. The relationship had come to an end, that was all, and I felt it immoral to keep up the pretence any longer.

So I went my solitary way with the intention of trying to sort out all these problems. I slept in a tent, showered every morning under cold water, helped wash up the tin plates that we ate our food off, which was very Spartan fare, and made friends with a lot of nice people, some of whom who I have bumped into again over the years. I had a great time and came back refreshed and ready for work, funking the reason for wanting to get away to be on my own.

12

Lone Girl with the Big Band

During all this emotional upheaval I had made my first recording for Esquire Records, I'd begun to be recognized in the *Melody Maker* polls and I'd appeared at the Albert Hall in The Jazz Jamboree with all the other top bands, singers and musicians of the country: Ted Heath, Kenny Baker's Dozen, Tito Burns, Ronnie Scott, Lita Rosa and so on.

The dream that John had of forming a big band was materializing quickly in his mind, and it was not long, once it had all come together to his satisfaction, before he let everyone in the Seven know of his plans, telling them also that he would like them to be involved. Tenor player Don Rendell declined, and so did drummer Eddie Taylor. Frank and I accepted, along with Ed Harvey trombone, Eric Dawson bass, Bill Le Sage piano, and Eddie Blair trumpet. John also recruited a new male singer, Tony Mansell, as it was the style for big bands to have a male ballad singer, a rhythm singer (Frank) and a girl singer who sang both (me). For some reason I was required to be under contract for this band, unlike the Seven. I'm not aware if the other singers had to be; I'm sure the musicians weren't.

Anyway, I was asked to visit the Harold Davison office again. This time I felt more at ease and on more equal terms than on my first visit; this time he was asking me if I would like to sign a contract as they would like me to stay with the band. I of course wanted very much to stay singing with the band, and I am sure I didn't put on a poker face when he expressed that wish. He didn't have to work very hard persuading me, knowing from the start I wouldn't be hard to bargain with. So on 4 January 1954 I signed a contract as singer with the Johnny Dankworth Big Band for a minimum of a year, with an option of a further two years on their side. My wages would be eighteen pounds a week for three dates. Any extra date in the week would bring me in a further four pounds but broadcasts or recordings would be separate. On top of that, if we did a summer season, or one week in the same place, there would be a flat wage of twenty-five pounds. I wasn't to be paid for holidays. It was a very one-sided deal even for that period, but I didn't object. My original business chutzpah had flown away on the wings of a dove, with the advent of love.

The time leading up to the launch of the orchestra was so hectic that very little thought was given to anything (not even love), apart from how to give it a good send-off. Not a stone was left unturned in the interests of getting it as right as it could be. Les Perrin, the doyen of publicity men, was hired to blow our trumpet to the press, and sisters Kitty and Chippy Grimes came in to the fold too, Kitty to write the brochure and Chippy to design and make dresses for me, also to create a new look for the band. They came up with the great idea of putting each section into different coloured jackets: orange for the trumpets, pale blue for the rhythm section, green trombones, and the saxes a citreous yellow. Kitty interviewed everyone in the band and wrote capsulated biographies of us all, making each of us feel crucial to the success of the venture. This was a good bit of psychology, because we all put ourselves out to make it a success.

What with daily rehearsals, interviews and fittings for dresses and jackets, our time was well and truly occupied. John was working flat out, twenty-four hours of the day, up all night, doing most of the writing for the band, then straight on to rehearsals in the morning, ink often still wet on the orchestrations and parts. Or else the copyist would follow him on to rehearsal to continue copying the parts, so that as he finished each one, he could pass it on to the musician or instrument in question. I had the greatest admiration for the way that John seemed able to take command, apparently inexhaustibly, of every situation or problem that came up, whilst juggling with ten jobs at a time.

It wasn't until we were about to burst on to the public scene that I noticed that the naturally gaunt look that I found so attractive was beginning to look like fatigue and worn-through overwork. These concentrated periods of work and no sleep eventually landed John with a migraine attack, turning his face the colour of stone with patches of moss that hadn't made contact with the light for a season or two. I was to become familiar with that sad countenance in time, but I thought then he was on the verge of collapse and was very worried. Somehow he was able to work through it.

We opened in Nottingham in October 1953 at the Astoria Ballroom in an atmosphere of great excitement and anticipation. We didn't disappoint the fans – they loved everything about us, the showmanship that was incorporated into the playing of music considered uncommercial, the new and familiar faces. But most of all they loved the young, slim, newly suited leader, who sprang on to the stage, saxophone ready to join in the play, after the colourful, twenty-piece-strong ensemble had got themselves settled in their sections, and then exploded into the first bars of the signature tune. And there was I, the lone girl, sitting on that stage between Tony and Frank, surrounded by seventeen other musicians who, during the weeks of laborious work rehearsing together, became kin, sharing the fruits of this moment with them all.

Not long into 1954 I made up my mind to come clean with George and tell him what I intended to do. My state of mind when I was at home must have given him a clue that all was not well between us, and that things were about to come to a head in some form or another. It didn't happen the way I had planned, which was just to tell him; it came about unexpectedly. While I was at home for a short period, the territorial barracks had organized a dance to which we were all invited – evidently they happened regularly when I was not there, and George, Geoff and Sylvia would go together. This time I went along with them, and during the course of the evening I noticed George paying a little too much attention to a pretty young woman who obviously knew him well enough to come over, throw her arm around his neck and sit on his lap without him or her showing any embarrassment, or him any objection, in front of his wife.

Ordinarily I would have taken it with a pinch of salt, but for some reason I became quite irate and walked out. George didn't follow me home immediately, so I had to sit, seethe, and nurse my pride at what I thought was a humiliating scene. When he at last returned, a little the worse for a spot of imbibing, I let all my frustrations and anger boil over on to the poor man. We were alone, so I was able to become a fish-wife with impunity. We ended up on the floor, after getting into a scuffle, with the anger suddenly turning to tears. I declared that I was not staying a moment longer and would be leaving as soon as I possibly could. I don't think George believed me; but I had said it at last, and immediately I felt the weight of my own deception lift. I hadn't wanted it to happen in this way, but at least he would soon know what the weeks of tension that had grown between us had been about. Luckily I had to go on tour the following day, so I didn't have to live in the uncomfortable atmosphere I had brought about.

Whilst on the road I'd become friends with Dorothy, the girlfriend of Eddie Harvey, and she told me she was thinking of moving to London as soon as she could find a place and someone to share expenses with. She was living with her family in Edinburgh, and I think they were concerned for her welfare if she came to London to live by herself. So together we found two furnished rooms in a house in Holland Park. They were large and spacious and the landlady was sweet and eccentric, either concerned about us or nosy, whichever way you look at it, but harmless. When I got back from the last date out of town, I told George what I had done, then Sylvia and Mother, explained that I would keep in close touch with them and Stuart, and left.

The next four years were a mixture of extreme happiness and turmoil, as I attempted to sort out the conflicts that one after the other I had to face up to, brought about by my action. I wanted Stuart to live with me, but George refused even to consider it. When I visited he was always kind, thinking it was a phase that would pass and we would be back together soon, as we got on fine. But he was adamant about Stuart.

At that time I never really knew what I meant to John; I never asked him and he never said. Frankly, he was committed to only one thing, and that was music and the band. We both had other boyfriends and girlfriends. John, who was always interested in languages, invariably had a girlfriend who spoke the language he was interested in at the time. I became close to an air steward who drove an extremely large, black, old American car, which had a blow-out one night on the way back from a performance, smashing into a telegraph pole, with me and the manager of the band, Don Read, as passengers. Everyone said that if it had not been for the car's sturdy, elephantine proportions we would not have got away with just shock, as was the case. The car was a write-off. I also had a boyfriend who was a policeman, who I met in Torquay during a week's engagement.

For me, these other men were very good friends, nothing more. By now John and I were seeing much more of each other out of work hours and I was quite crazy about him. We spent a lot of time together at a flat that belonged to a friend of Pat Smythe's and John's, an architect called Martin Richmond, who played the bass and like Pat was an jazz aficionado. Although Martin only lived around the corner, walking distance away from me in Holland Park, we often went back to his place after spending the evening at The Studio Club in Swallow Street.

The Studio Club was a social meeting and eating club which

was originally intended for painters and writers but which musicians infiltrated because of the stylish jazz pianist, Alan Clare. We'd stay there till the early hours of the morning, playing, talking, listening, joking.

Often we left a club at dawn, unwashed or brushed, to jump on to the coach parked at the pick-up in Allsop Place, a little street off Marylebone Road near Madame Tussaud's. Once on the road, we'd catch up on sleep on the way to our next date.

We were burning the candle at both ends and in the middle and it was beginning to tell on me. I found that with the late nights, travel and drinking my voice was beginning to suffer: I had to do something about it fast. In fact I didn't give up all that activity until much later. I had found long ago I could drink most of the boys under the table, when I was with the Seven. Originally I had been a moderate drinker of brown ale only – I couldn't afford anything else – but I learnt to keep up with them after they told me they didn't think a lady should drink brown ale. I was then introduced to gin and tonic, which never became my drink, but I found it didn't affect me any more than brown ale, and if, like smoking, it was the thing to do, I would have a go. So I drank and smoked because all the others did, not because I wanted or needed to.

As for my voice problem, I had a stroke of good luck. I had noticed, while out walking, a school of music, conveniently very close to where I was living, called The Holland Park School of Music. One day I went inside and asked to see the singing teacher. I hadn't thought ahead about this or made any enquiries, contrary to everything I had vowed after my piano fiasco. I didn't even know if the teacher was a he or a she. She saw me right away – if I had had to make an appointment I think I might not have gone back. Madame Ertle was fresh-faced and small of stature, with a fullish figure, and spoke with an attractive European accent, which I later learnt was Hungarian. I liked her at once, and she seemed to like me. I told her what I wanted, which was of course singing lessons, but that I was not a classical singer; I did not want to be one or to be turned into one. Would she take me on to improve what I had? She made no comment at first on what I had said, but eventually volunteered: 'Vuld you like to sinc somsinc for me?' For some reason a spiritual came to mind (which was a laugh after my last encounter with a music teacher) and I sang 'Steal Away'. She listened attentively, then played some scales, which she asked me to sing along with. And so I became Madame Ertle's student. She never told me why she took me under her wing, but she became my mentor, guiding me in good directions. Because of her my breathing improved, with notes added to my range that I had been unable to touch before, and in time, as we got to know each other better, our relationship changed from student/teacher to friend/teacher.

We did more talking about singing than the singing of scales. Often she would stop in the middle of one to say, 'Sit down and let's talk.' If there was a note difficult to achieve, she would say, 'It is all in your mind Cleo, think it and it will come in the end, it is there already.' So we would then sit talking of ways to overcome my vocal problems.

Her history was quite tragic: she'd lost all her family during the war, escaping death herself when she was recruited to work as a labourer in factories in occupied Europe. Surviving near starvation, she came to England after the war with her husband, who then died. She became deeply involved and interested in Buddhism and yoga, which helped to bring her peace in her distress. It was Madame Ertle who introduced me to the two philosophies and gave me books to read on the subject. I was later to find them of considerable help to me also, when I was sorting out the mess I had got myself into.

At the same school I found another piano teacher, whose company and teaching I found a little more attractive than the Hanwell fiasco. I must have been a great disappointment to him: I wasn't able to do much practice, and when I'd go back for the next lesson there'd be little or no improvement. He also gave me oral lessons, which I liked, and set me tasks that I had to work out and put down on paper for him. But without a piano to practise on, it became a waste of my money and his time.

I didn't give up until I moved from Holland Park to Abbey

129

Gardens, St John's Wood. When Dorothy and Eddie got married, I had to look for a less expensive place, or else share with another girl. I struck lucky, finding a basement flat in that classy area of London, a short walk from Abbey Road Studios, where I was later to record with the band under the direction of the band's producer, George Martin. Two girls shared with me in this two-room, one-kitchen, basement flat, in a three-storey house above us, all owned by an excitable Frenchwoman. One of the girls was John's secretary Dell Milton, the other a young girl called Carol, who came from Coventry. It was not the grandest of flats, and we had our work cut out to make it into a reasonably comfortable living quarter, but it was cheap, we had a lot of girlish fun and made friends with the other tenants.

At the very top of the house were a couple who were aspiring actors, but they aspired much more than they acted, and one of the ways they earned a living was ushering at Covent Garden Opera House. I remember seeing *Der Rosenkavalier* there for the first time, under their auspices. They were a sweet couple, but very narrow-minded in their choice of music. The rest of us enjoyed and appreciated other styles of well-sung or well-played music, but they refused even to contemplate anything else. So we argued.

Sharing beneath them, which on some occasions must have been hell for the top couple, were Don Read, the manager of the band and an avid jazz record buyer, and Les Williams, a classically trained, talented composer and orchestrator, who had to earn his living in all fields of music, so listened to it all happily. On the ground floor, in the grandest of the flats, lived the amazingly beautiful daughter of our French landlady. Her mother had worked hard to educate her in Swiss finishing schools, then posed as her daughter's lady's maid to help her break into high society and find a rich husband. I benefited from her stay, and her clear-out of end-of-season, beautiful handmade clothes.

Maurice Clark was a song plugger for Chappell's Music Publishers, who also lived in that flat for a time: he was a fun-loving party-giver, and he enjoyed cooking for his friends, more often than not feeding the whole household. Because of Maurice's warm social nature he was taken advantage of by some of his boyfriends, and he would turn to us girls for comfort. Several of his friends were American service men, who were as gay as an old boot. Which makes me hoot with laughter when I think about them, and the controversy going on today about letting gays into the military. They have always been there, doing a great silent job, in both the US and the British forces.

As a song plugger, Maurice's music was the top ten, as well as the standards we were all fond of, except on the top floor. This house was to be one of the first since my childhood containing so many diverse people under the same roof, that was made to work through music.

It was Maurice who introduced me to Frankie Howerd, the extraordinary comedian, who at the time was not being appreciated as he should have been, and was going through one of his many gloomy patches. On that first occasion we discovered that we shared a common love of Sarah Vaughan's singing; he especially liked the recorded version of her singing the 'Lord's Prayer'. I preferred other things she had done, but it was the introduction to our long, passing-like-ships-in-the-night friendship in the business.

Some time during my stay at Abbey Gardens John acquired an orchestrator named David Lindup. David was eventually to become to John what Billy Strayhorn was to Duke Ellington, doing many of the orchestrations for his film and TV scores, compositions and recordings, working in close collaboration with John. David was one of the kindest and most thoughtful men I had ever met, listening to people's troubles with great concern, when he had many of his own. Within the musicians' fraternity he had a lot of friends. Musicians always have a tale of woe to tell at some point in their lives and David became the 'Joe' of the 'Set 'em up Joe, I got a little story' song. He would have made a great listening barman. He was very short-sighted, slight of physique and had bones that were so brittle that if you shook his hand too warmly it was liable to break into bits. That, combined with the state of his eyes, made him very vulnerable. There never seemed a time when David didn't have an arm or leg in plaster, or when he wasn't walking on crutches.

Starting as a tenor player, doing one-night stands, as we all were, David's eyesight and breakages had got the better of him, and he retired himself from the road to concentrate on writing music for a living. Appearing slow and Mr Magoo-ish on first meeting him, he would surprise one with the quick wit and thoughtful intelligence that marked everything he did. Because of his obvious physical problems, rather than having to go through constant sympathy, he became a clown, whom everyone loved and invited to the party. John and David were a double act who kept me sewn up with love and laughter. We became known as 'The Three Musketeers' as we went everywhere together.

Meanwhile my voice was getting stronger and my reputation was growing as a stylish interpreter of songs. I was asked to do the occasional television appearance too, by myself. I wrote my first song at Abbey Gardens, an attempt at lyrics and music; Les Williams orchestrated it for me. It was a waltz called 'While We Dance' – very unmemorable, but I got a chance to sing it on a broadcast, so my efforts were not in vain. It was to be many years before I made a fool of myself in public again, but I had secretly started to write lyrics and poems.

After a youth-hostelling holiday with another couple in France, John and I had fallen into the habit of being together: if he didn't ring I became miserable, and if he did ring and I was out, he'd ask where I had been.

It was time to ask George for a divorce. After many discussions I managed to convince him I was serious and he reluctantly filed for desertion against me. When I told John what I had done, his attitude changed. He realized that I hadn't been playing around and introduced me to his lawyer, Bernard Sheriden, to look after my interests. Although I wanted this divorce and the end to my marriage, it was the start of much gloom and doom, as our lawyers went back and forth arguing on our behalf. It wasn't an angry spiteful procedure, as most divorces are. My sister and mother got custody of Stuart, which I agreed to as they had looked after him all this time anyhow, but now it became a legal affair it took me quite a while to face up to and accept it. Even though I was keeping up my visiting and financial responsibilities, I felt extremely guilty.

Stuart came on tour with me whenever we had a resident summer date, and he also came to visit me in London regularly. I'm sure that it was harder for me than it was for him, even though I was getting what I wanted, my freedom from George. But who can ever tell? I used to spend many hours alone, browsing in the bookshops of Charing Cross Road. I would pick up something to read to do with whatever I was taking part in, seeing or hearing at the time: ballet, paintings, opera, jazz, poetry. I was never sure if the books were good on the subjects that I selected to read in this *ad hoc* fashion. I bought some because I loved the feel or look of them, and I'd often strike lucky, discovering for myself artists that I had never heard of but who appealed to me through their work and style.

In an American paperback called *The Seven Arts* (which I still possess) there was a poetry section that contained a poem by e.e. cummings. I was impressed by the way he worked with words, and the way they were printed on the page intrigued me. I of course thought I had discovered someone new, along with Frank Lloyd Wright, who was also included in the book. I told Pat Smythe and Martin Richmond about my wonderful finds, and they immediately put me straight. I started to buy everything I could find or afford about them. The more I read about e. e. cummings, the more I liked both the man and his writing. It was his influence that led to my tentative writing of poetry, some of which I later turned into lyrics for songs. I also came to sing a setting of a cummings poem.

John now had an office in Denmark Street, the Tin Pan Alley of London. Dell Milton was his loyal secretary, and later a writer, David Dearlove, became manager. David wrote lyrics for songs and vetted any material sent to the office by other composers in the hope of getting it played by the orchestra, or sung by one of the three singers. He had an acute ear for a good melody. It was David who persuaded John to record *African Waltz*. The recording of this instrumental was tacked on to the end of a session, just to please David. It eventually became one of the biggest big-band hits that John and the band ever had, selling over a million singles.

John and the orchestra were on the crest of a wave. David was also the lyricist of a song called 'Let's Slip Away' that John wrote the music for and I recorded, which managed to get into the hit parade (as they called it in those days). Not very high, but it had a lot of attention and air play, and it brought my singing and image to a wider audience. It was George Martin, who later became known as the 'fifth Beatle' long before the Beatles' astronomical rise, who brought about John's other million seller in 1956. We were broadcasting regularly each week and new musical ideas had to keep flowing. One of them, devised by John, was a different arrangement each week of the nursery ryhme 'Three Blind Mice', played in the styles of various jazz men, from Gerry Mulligan to Stan Kenton, Benny Goodman and others. George thought that a condensed version of this weekly feature could be a smash hit, and he was right – it soared.

The band was far more successful than the singers, but we rode along with its glory, and were happy to do so. John had pointed out to Frank, Tony and me at the very beginning that it would never be a singers' band and it was certainly working out that way. John had such a sure instinct for that band, it just couldn't go wrong.

13

Secret Marriage

No matter how I assessed the years before 1958, one thing was certain: I could not have been chosen as a leading lady at The Royal Court Theatre if I had not joined the Dankworth Seven or stayed in Hanwell. So when some people say that John Dankworth is my Svengali, in that respect they are quite correct. Before the Seven experience I hardly knew how to walk on to a stage.

In fact I had once been told by some fellow singers: 'You know, when you get to the microphone you know exactly what to do, the song is sold, but you walk on like a rhino and back off like a goat, when you should walk on and off like a queen.' I practised that advice.

After those years I never had any difficulty in looking an audience in the eye and saying confidently to myself, if you could do it, you'd be up here too. Music was my life blood. I had been singing songs all these years, but now I realized that the lyrics needed interpretation too, I was beginning to fall in love with the words and the art of expressing them.

But I knew that I was not going to remain a band singer. Luck struck unexpectedly, as luck does, in 1958, when I made one decision and received two resounding telephone calls that changed all the signposts around for the next few years or so.

Cleo

I was temporarily living in Southwark as David Lindup's lodger, in a house where he and John and their copyist Ken Williams burnt a lot of midnight oil, orchestrating and arranging.

David, John and I did some very wild, spur-of-the-moment things together in the early sixties. One day we heard through the musical grapevine that Miles Davis, the Modern Jazz Quartet, Bud Powell and other American jazz luminaries were appearing for one night only in Paris, at the Salle Pleyel. On the day of the concert we decided to get into the car there and then and drive to France. Not only did we not have tickets for the concert but when we got to the other side of the Channel we realized we didn't know the route to Paris. We had no maps in the car, so we had to rely on the only directional tool we possessed; David's pocket diary, which handily had a map of Europe in it. The journey took longer than we had expected. We arrived just in time to see the 'Sold Out' sign go up, with masses of milling people hoping like us for a last-minute count that would unearth that extra seat. Then, across the barrier, John spotted a music critic from the *Melody Maker*. The critic called out a friendly 'Hello John!' When John told him our plight the critic pulled strings for us, and we were in. The concert was a once-in-a-lifetime event – such a wonderful experience for me, hearing American musicians in the flesh for the first time, since they were still banned in the UK. After the concert we sat in a bar and talked reverently about what we had just heard. It had been so refreshing to see and hear such wonderful innovative music being played with dignity and balls. Bud Powell was a sick man and sadly it affected his music, but that night the audience showed their respect for the great jazz musician he was.

When I left David's to live on Kilburn High Road, the flat was mine. It was the top flat of three, all occupied by musicians. I lived alone, with my own front door, my own furniture, with a sitting room, bedroom, bathroom and kitchen, the very top floor. It had no lift, so I walked up and down the three flights of stairs happily singing, from top to bottom, bottom to top, daily, just like a bird. The acoustics of that staircase were perfect for singing – I sang at the top of my lungs, full out, up and down. There wasn't a soul to disturb. On my right going up was a stone wall, and on the other side of the stone wall was the Westminster Bank; our staircase rose above it. On my left going up were the flats of the other tenants. Dennis Ackerman, the tenor player, and his wife Jackie (who later became Stan Tracey's wife); above them were singer Jean Tracey with her pianist husband Stan; and on the top branch my nest. The habitat was a place to live, create, rehearse and party.

It was during the Kilburn period that we got to know the members of the Count Basie Band and Duke Ellington Band quite well, Clark Terry, Frank Wess, Jimmy Hamilton, Thad Jones, Cat Anderson among them.

Jimmy Hamilton, Duke's clarinet player, came to the flat for a meal with his wife Vivienne, and I served them apple pie and ice-cream at the end of it. Jimmy was very impressed with the pie and said, 'That was good Cleo, ya know,' settling himself comfortably in the chair and sucking his teeth, preparing us and himself for what was about to be a profound dissertation on food; 'England don't have too many pie shops, matter of fact they don't have none, if you opinned a pie shop Cleo, you would cleeen up Cleo, you would cleeen up!' 'Ain't that the truth?' echoed Vivienne. Jimmy ignored the interjection and continued, as we waited patiently for the explanation on how we could achieve the cleeen-up. He continued in his slow steady drawl: 'You could sell your apple pie, then some blueberry pie, strawberry pie, gooseberry pie, peach pie, blackberry pie . . .' We waited all eyes and ears for him to come to the end of this list of goodies with the magic solution, whereupon he paused, took a deep breath and dived in again with 'or a combination of apple pie and blackberries, blueberries and . . .', and finished by going through the whole list again in combinations of two, salivating at the very thought of what he'd just bored us stiff with.

The Kilburn Empire, the large cinema down the high street, was where we did our *Melody Maker* Jazz Poll concerts; visiting bands such as Ellington, Basie, Buddy Rich played there too, and Norman Granz presented his jazz at the Philharmonic concerts there. It was there I saw Miles Davis for the second time, by which time he had decided to turn his back on his adoring audience. I thought it was a hoot, but preferred to watch his beautiful face while he was playing rather than his backside.

Norman introduced us to Oscar Peterson, Ella Fitzgerald, Lester Young, Dizzy Gillespie and many more, some of whom became friends, others acquaintances. At that time jazz writer Sinclair Traill was co-owner, along with the Queen's cousin the Hon. Gerald Lascelles, of a magazine called *Jazz Journal*. John and I became friends with them through their love of jazz as we met at various concerts all over London. Sinclair and his wife, Mipsy, invited us to dinner at their small, beautifully furnished London home. The Lascelles, who were also expected, were a little late and when Gerald came in he apologized and then said, as he sniffed the air, 'Hmm! Mipsy! you got the Johnson's Polish out for me, eh!' She was terribly embarrassed, trying to brush it off with 'Well, you are our Queen's cousin,' or words to that effect. We all laughed uncomfortably and got on with the evening. I vowed after that I'd never polish up for anyone special, not on the day, that is.

That evening Gerald invited us to a dinner in honour of Duke Ellington at his home in Virginia Water, once the home of his uncle Edward, the Prince of Wales. It was my first encounter with such an assortment of cutlery, and feeling very nervous that I might do somthing daft enough to provoke Gerald's amused comment, I did an Eliza Doolittle and watched our hostess like a hawk. Ellington in his elegant way had no problems; he ate like an American, with one fork.

I watched and listened, then Ellington sat at the piano to play. I had recorded a song written by Billy Strayhorn called 'Lush Life' and when he asked me what I would like to hear, he played it for me. Thankfully he didn't ask me to sing it, I would have fainted away if he had. John and Ellington got on famously, while I looked on in admiration. After 'Lush Life' John was able to show the Duke how the middle eight of his tune 'Morning Glory' went. Ellington, who by then we were calling Edward, started to play the tune, got to the middle and faltered. 'You know, I can't remember how it goes,' he said, and was about to leave the piano seat when J.D. stepped in. Edward was happy to be reminded, and the author and John finished the tune as a duet.

Sinclair asked Ellington the question he must have been asked umpteen times, judging by the slick speed of the reply: 'Edward, how do you keep that band so together and so loyal to you?' 'You've got to have a gimmick, Sinclair, and mine is money. I pay them Money.'

John came to the flat sometimes to practise all day, or write all night. As did Stan Tracey in the flat underneath. I often lay awake nights listening to the faint music seeping through the almost soundproof floors and walls, before I dropped contentedly asleep.

Weekends the street became a market place. All the tenants knew the street traders and the traders knew the tenants. Especially the one who plied his wares outside our front door. 'Mornin Clee, mind if I park the toms inside over nite, girl, save me old back wone it, eh!?' I agreed it would, saying I didn't mind, nor did the others apparently, so he'd stack his goods overnight just inside the front door that led on to the pavement, to sell on Saturday. If anything was left over we benefited from doing the favour. It was only very occasionally an embarrassment, when we had posh guests.

As when Joe Losey, the film director, whom John was collaborating with on *The Criminal*, came to call to hear the theme he had written for the film. John and Joe arrived together – John had not told me anyone was coming, I guess it was a spur-of-the-moment decision. I had got into the habit when I heard the bell ring of looking out of the window and if it was someone I knew, throwing the keys down to them; it saved me having to climb up and down unnecessarily. I threw the key down, narrowly missing Joe – embarrassment number one. The second was the climb over orange and tomato boxes to start the four-flight ascent, which for an American film director, especially one with breathing problems like Joe, must have been tantamount to climbing Mount Everest.

Well, he made it to the top, wisecracking when he arrived, about an elevator installation if the film was a smash hit. But after that climb he'd love a drink! A long pause as John looked at me, knowingly, and I looked back at him, unknowingly. I went to the kitchen to see if we had anything to offer; the cupboard was bare. John decided to own up, but said he would dash across the road to the pub, and be back in a jiff. The jiff seemed interminable, while I tried to make small talk with a man who wasn't keen on it. At last John returned, the drinks were poured and they were ready to settle down to listen to the music.

Joe sat down on our sofa bed (that we hadn't quite put back together properly), leant back and went, drink in hand, heels over head backwards, when the back collapsed. He didn't spill a drop; it was one of the greatest prattfalls I'd ever seen. The ice was broken between us for ever, as we couldn't restrain ourselves at the sight of his struggle to save his much-wanted drink, and his dignity.

He liked the theme John had written, I was booked to sing it over the titles, and John went on to work with Joe on several more of his wonderful films. We remained friends until his death.

From my top window to the right was the Irish Bamba Dance Club, which provided me with non-stop entertainment, especially on the weekends when I wasn't working. A Black Maria was always parked on the opposite side of the road at the ready, waiting for the gigs and reels to come to an end, when the Irish dancing community lurched out on to the street, their farewells and last jokes rising up just high enough for me to hear the soft accents of the south, and the harder ones of the north, dancing and mingling together, taking me right back to my childhood. It was always a mystery to me how the fights began, but invariably there was one, and they seemed to enjoy them.

While I was living in Kilburn my divorce became final, and I learnt how to drive too. I needed a car to reduce my dependence on John; when we went out anywhere, if I wanted to leave I didn't have much hope of achieving it until the early hours. Dennis Ackerman, my neighbour on the first floor, went with me to help choose a second-hand car. I bought a Ford Anglia, and although nothing grand it became my pride and joy.

The evening before my test, John accompanied me for a brush-up on the rules of the road. I did everything wrong, giving John a poor demonstration of the likelihood of my getting a driving licence, and a near heart attack. I didn't feel very confident myself when I drove around Hendon the next morning, trying to remember how to pat my head and rub my tummy at the same time. But the examiner passed me, saying only, 'Use the hand signal to slow down more at roundabouts, that's all'. I came back to the flat with the largest grin John had seen on my face since I passed the audition for the Seven, and the commiseration gift that he had bought to console me instantly became a congratulation present.

Now I had a licence I was a free spirit, able to go anywhere and everywhere in my little cream Ford. The best part was being able to visit Stuart, who was living in Stevenage with Sylvia and Mother. The housing list had come up for her at last, and as mother's health wasn't good and the café wasn't doing too well, they moved to Stevenage. This – final – move also brought Pa back into our lives; healthy and still irascible, he visited weekends to see the grandchildren he loved, bringing them gifts and amusing them (as he had done their parents) with his outrageous stories. He'd also go drinking in the local with Geoff and George; anything for a sing-song.

Pa looked at me with suspicion for a while at what I had done but I took no notice of him or of anyone else who disapproved. But I still had a lot of sorting out to do for myself. If I had time on my hands during the day I would visit the church on the high street, not to relive the smells (although they still affected me) or contemplate becoming a nun, but to sit in its calm and peaceful atmosphere, so that undisturbed by callers or telephones I could think through my problems and try to come to terms with what I had to do in order to grow up – yes, grow up. I was determined to be as independent and self-sufficient as I possibly could, and to achieve that I had to be on my own, for the first time in my life, and learn to enjoy it.

For the first time I was able to visit people who lived a distance from me without thinking – I could just pick up and go. I started visiting Madame Ertle, who had left the Holland Park School to teach at her home in Barnes, and was my other source of peace and calm. I was getting around a lot in London as well, discovering the city.

My new-found freedom had given me a dog as well as a car. Candy was a Sealyham, a bit like the white dog on the whisky bottle. He looked adorable, but he turned out to have the most neurotic character I've ever come across in a four-legged animal. He was a spur-of-the moment buy that I never regreted, though he might have done if he'd had a choice. John and David were not in favour and should have talked me out of it. Candy hated everyone except me, who fed and watered him, and John as long as he didn't play the saxophone. He hated anything that had a ringing high pitch: telephones, doorbells, music and especially the saxophone. In an attempt to cure him of this inconvenient trait, John decided to practise all day with the dog in the room. The howling was so pitiful he had to leave; John gave up before Candy. Eventually we palmed him off on Sylvia, as Stuart was fond of him and they had a garden, but it turned out that poor Candy had a disintegrating liver, even though he had never touched a drop as far as I knew, and he was put out of his misery.

I now made another big decision: I was going to leave the band. To do what? That was in the lap of the gods. I had had a long and enjoyable run, made a lot of valuable friends and learnt a great deal, but it was not where I belonged. When I told John he would have to look for another singer, he didn't say very much at the time, just, 'Oh! all right. You won't leave right away, will you? You'll give me time to find someone?' 'Of course,' I replied. And that was that.

Secret Marriage

Weeks went by. I was getting odd solo engagements on television, travelling to Manchester a lot to do a religious show that musicians found so incongruous and laughable, they called it 'Jumping with Jesus'. It was while I was there recording a TV show that I received a message that I was wanted on the phone – a public phone in a corridor of the studio. I wondered who it could be: Stuart? Had he hurt himself? I knew mother wasn't well, could it be Sylvia? All possible disasters flashed on to the screen. I hadn't anticipated any good news: long-distance phone calls were like telegrams to me, bad news.

I arrived at the phone in an irritable mood.

'Hello, Cleo Laine here,' I grumbled.

'Will you marry me?' said a voice I recognized as John's.

At first I couldn't believe what he'd said, but he affirmed it and I said, 'Yes, of course I will.'

Even though I had said yes, and put the receiver down, I still could not believe it. I had no expectations from John, no reason to believe that marriage would be the outcome of our relationship; I was quite resigned to sharing my pebble with other seekers. Why would such an elegant, available bachelor want to marry me?

And if John thought that marrying me would make me stay with the band, I thought, he had miscalculated, badly. I had no intention of staying. I didn't know what I was going to do but I had made up my mind. It became a joke that we told against ourselves: 'He thought he was going to get a cheap singer, but he what he got was an expensive wife.'

John and I married secretly, the day after St Patrick's Day 1958, telling no one but David Lindup, whom we wouldn't allow home the night before in case he let the cat out of the bag accidentally. So we watched the shenanigans of the Bamba Club from my top window. John hadn't got a ring and I hadn't bought anything new to wear. In the morning, as soon as the shops opened, John dashed across the street to the jeweller's opposite, and bought a cheap ring. (I still wear the same ring, but with the pretty pattern now worn away.) We then phoned a few more of our friends and told them: Ken Moule the pianist and his first wife, a close friend

143

of John's, Pat Smythe and David were the only ones who could make it. No family; neither of us had told them. They learnt about our marriage the day after, when someone told them it was in the newspapers. John's mother took it very badly, mine philosophically. It was quite some time before we were back in his mother's good books. In retrospect we understood her anger: it was inconsiderate on our part.

After the ceremony at the register office, we booked a table at a fairly smart restaurant in St John's Wood, then finished the day at a jazz club in Soho to hear Alan Clare play the piano. And I was now Mrs Dankworth. I didn't have any fears about it, or any doubts in my mind, unlike my first marriage. It felt wonderful. We were both thirty-one; it was John's first marriage, and it felt like the first for me. It was now time I grew up and acted responsibly. I had always thought that when I reached thirty, overnight I would act in an adult and sensible way. I would look elegant, in black from head to toe, finished off with pearls. I'm still waiting.

14

The Royal Court

Soon after the wedding I had a phone call – from the Royal Court Theatre. Would I be interested in reading for a role in a play that they were putting on? I didn't stop to think whether I was even capable of 'reading' for a part, I just said yes. They were, apparently, in a dilemma about a production they were putting on: they had seen a hundred or so girls for the leading role. The play, which was by Barry Reckord, had won a *Sunday Telegraph* award, and part of the prize was a production at the Royal Court. But they were having trouble casting, and I was something of a last resort. They wanted a West Indian girl really, but at that time in the English theatre black actresses were in short supply.

The script of *Flesh to a Tiger* eventually arrived, and the role appeared to be quite a dramatic one, but being inexperienced about such matters I didn't think this would be the part intended for me; it was merely there to test me. I didn't have to work hard to affect a West Indian accent. Although I had always thought my father never had one, I found my ear was suddenly picking up the musical sounds and nuances of his voice as I read and re-read the part. John helped me learn the lines for the audition.

The day came at last. Here I was again: would I never stop auditioning? John drove me to the theatre. It was a warm day and we had the window of the car open wide. 'Try it again once more,' he said. Some of the language in the play was riper than Gorgonzola, and when we stopped at the lights, with my voice in full throttle, the driver in the car next to us appeared aghast at the way I was berating the poor man at the wheel. He gave John a look of great brotherly sympathy as he drove away, deeply embarrassed.

The Royal Court Theatre was the centre of new modern plays, introducing to London playwrights like Ionesco, Osborne, Wesker, Simpson, Beckett and Genet, as well as actors who are now household names in the theatre. The guiding light of the theatre was George Devine, who was its inspired founder and artistic director. He sought out and nurtured young, up-and-coming directors who had the same passion for the theatre that he did. One of his stage directors at that time was a young man called Tony Richardson, who had won great acclaim for his productions. However, I didn't know anything about him or his reputation and he didn't know anything about mine, so neither one of us was impressed by celebrity or reputation. He wanted an actress and I wanted a change.

I couldn't see him in the dark anyway. I arrived at the stage door and announced myself, and was taken to the side of the little Court stage until they were ready for me. Then I was told to walk on to read the part. Luckily stages make me perform and I performed; to the dark, where out in the auditorium Tony Richardson, Barry Reckord and George Devine watched and assessed. There was an uncomfortable silence for a while after I had finished, then I heard mutterings in the dark. The stage manager had come to my side while all this was going on and kindly said, 'That was very good, Miss Laine,' while the mutters continued. Then suddenly a voice from the dark, that I was hearing for the first time said, with the distinguished sound that he made when he spoke: a petulantly plummy, hoity-toity sound, ripe for the imitators in the theatre world. 'I sey, ahnt we lacky to hev a *name*, too!'

That's how it came across to me, my first introduction to Tony Richardson.

Still in the dark, he asked, 'Could you sing a sorng?'

146

I thought I'd better oblige him, whoever he was, and so I *a-capella*'d 'Stormy Weather'. They were impressed enough to give me the part right away. I'd thought this would be a mere walk-on-and-off start to my acting career, but to my complete surprise it turned out to be the lead, in a prestigious play and theatre, with a prestigious director.

It was a non-singing role that called for a young Jamaican woman to make a choice between modern medicine and a voodoo practice called Obeiha, to cure her young child of an illness, which her friends in the village thought had been brought about by her Obeiha lover, who didn't like the way she was becoming influenced by western ways and ideas. It had added romantic conflicts between the white doctor (played by Edgar Wreford) and the black Obeiha man.

It proved to be an extremely taxing role, that was constantly being rewritten on the road, right up to the London opening, when the stage manager came to me and said he didn't approve of the way I was being treated, and if I didn't think I could cope he would speak to management on my behalf. He didn't think a more experienced actress would have stood for it. But the afternoon of the opening night I learned and rehearsed the new words as well as a completely fresh scene.

I had to darken my skin for the role, although there were West Indians in the cast lighter than I was. Of course my hair came in handy – they actually wanted me that way. In any case I had given up the fight by now; I had gone *au naturel*, long before it became the fashion. All I had to do was to put my head under the shower and I was ready.

It was a great company of relaxed, natural performers. When we were on the road our musical evenings were unforgettable; Tony Richardson lapped them up. Although he was still having problems with the play itself, he adored the company, and often joined the evenings of Caribbean music-making after rehearsals. Several of the cast became close friends, one handsome lady in particular. Pearl Prescott was a Trinidadian, almost six foot, and with her generous body was a combination of earth mother and child. She possessed the most powerful voice I had ever heard, but she didn't know how to control it, so she stuck out like a fistful of sore thumbs when any chorus work had to be done, making Tony cross, because he had to tell her so many times to 'pawul back a bit Pourrl, pawul back!' But even her whisper was louder than the rest of us speaking at the top of our voices, all at once.

She was given a couple of solo lines in the play. One of them sticks in my memory as she had to say it to me every night, and as the weeks went by she got louder and more hysterical, but the audience loved her, and I tried not to giggle when she screamed at me, 'Sympatee, I caint help sympatee.' Actually she couldn't: she sympathized and comforted everyone who had a problem and she was a great cook.

I met Sir Laurence Olivier for the first time after the first-night performance, when he came to my dressing room to congratulate me. Also Peggy Ashcroft, who enquired if I was going to do the matinees. It was such a demanding role – I never seemed to be off the stage – she said she wouldn't do them; but I didn't have her clout. There was a first-night party afterwards, with celebrities having the time of their lives dancing and singing, and the cast in full flight on stage. That night David Lindup met his future first wife, Nadia Cattouse, a cast member.

I had been thrown into the deep end of a new world and I was learning to swim daily. Sometimes I felt I was on the verge of drowning, but my built-in survival kit always came to the rescue, and I'd get away without egg on my face.

When the play finished I thought my acting career was set to go full speed ahead for all time, but it was very slow. I found it was not easy for singers to cross over, unless they gave up singing completely for a few years. Then, once an established actor, you can sing your heart out. I did get a call from George Devine to come in and see him about a proposed production of Genet's *The Blacks* (it had had a successful run in Paris). George had recommended me to the director and wanted me to meet him. The director was a taciturn man, saying hardly a word.

He was very still, with, I thought, a constant twinkle in his eyes as if he found everything that was being said amusing. That was my impression at the time, and I wasn't very comfortable. George asked me all the pertinent questions, which I don't think I answered in an impressive manner; I turned out to be too white for the role anyway, even though the cast wears white masks for most of the time.

After the interview had come to an end, I went on chatting to George Devine and mentioned that I was a bit despondent about my future as an actress. He was very encouraging, saying I shouldn't give up. When I miserably replied, 'Ah well! I'm happily married now, I think I'll become a mother instead,' he didn't approve at all, saying I shouldn't waste my great talent. I felt extremely chuffed and promised him I wouldn't. I left that interview a lot happier than when it began. But for two years I sat by the telephone waiting for the offers to roll in before I decided I had to go back to singing.

I did in fact return to the Royal Court twice. On the first occasion I was introduced to the poetry of black American writers, by the American actor/folk singer Gordon Heath, the Dutch writer/poet Dr Rosey E. Pool and the poet/publisher Erica Marx, owner of the Hand and Flower Press. The performance was called *Black and Unknown Bards*. It was a remarkable evening of caustic, funny, hip and religious poetry, by black American poets such as Margaret Walker, Countee Cullen, Sterling Brown, William Brown, Langston Hughes, Waring Cuney and many more. An album evolved from the stage production, and a book called *Beyond the Blues*, which I was also a part of, along with Brock Peters, Vinette Carroll, and Gordon. I was deeply moved by the whole experience, and by the dedication of the two women who organized it all.

My second appearance at the Court was when Albert Finney arranged an evening to raise money to repair the roof of the theatre which was crumbling, so a little bit of me caps the roof of the theatre that helped send me down a new avenue of learning.

I had been typecast as a West Indian actress by my first play, and there weren't too many West Indian plays about at the time, although I played Yerma on the radio in a transposition of Lorca's play into a West Indian setting. I had to play the waiting game until a director came along who wanted me as any other nationality – except, of course, an English rosebud.

15

America: A New World

John had a date at an Oxford Commemoration Ball at Exeter College. They were always fun to do so I went along with the band to sing; we, like everyone else, were appearing in a tent on the college lawn. We had finished our part so we strolled around listening to the bands that had taken over the last stint. Breakfast was being served in another tent so we decided to go and eat. A scattering of couples were not paying too much attention to the breakfast music being provided for their enjoyment, but between mouthfuls of egg, toast and champagne, the music began to infiltrate and creep into our heads. We started to listen properly.

The untuned piano was fluently speaking to us even with all its faults, reminding us a little of the style of the jazz pianist Erroll Garner. We went over to congratulate the musician and to see who it was. Well, he was short, that being the reason we couldn't see anything of him from behind the back of the upright piano; and he had dark hair and eyes, giving a charming, immediately friendly response to our 'Hello!' with an impish smile. 'Dudley Moore,' he replied, when we asked who he was. He said he was about to leave University to start a musical career, he knew not how. 'If', he said to John, 'you ever want a piano player, I'm available.' We exchanged addresses and said we would keep in touch.

Dudley joined John's band towards the end of 1959, replacing

Dave Lee, and was the pianist on John's hit record *African Waltz*. Meanwhile I hung about, waiting for anything that might turn up. During these periods of waiting, I sang with the band on and off, and did television, cabaret and variety, biding my time for any more exciting work that might come my way.

While I was doing that, J.D. had an invitation to perform at The Newport Jazz Festival in the US with his band, but they did not ask for a singer. By now the Musicians Union ban had been lifted, allowing American bands into the UK, and John and I travelled all over Britain to see and hear any of the visiting US bands. We travelled to Nottingham to hear the first: Stan Kenton, with his ultra modern big band sound. Kenton was extremely tall and unjazz-like in appearance, but he impressed me not only with his music, but with his knowledge of British musicians and their careers, talking about them at great length, with admiration and respect for their contribution to jazz.

The visits of these bands should have been on a reciprocal basis, with British bands visiting the US – but this didn't last for long. English bands visiting the US had to be able to make money for the promoters, just as the American bands must have done for the first spellbinding years in Britain, but there was only a handful of bands remotely in that class – notably Ted Heath's. Both his and John's bands' records had been issued there, and jazz buffs are avid collectors.

This was John's first and only visit with his big band; I went along as a guest and as John's wife. It was my first experience of the USA.

I had to be vaccinated for the trip, as mother had never agreed to any of us being done as children. I chose to have it done on my leg, because I didn't want that ugly mark that so many of my friends had on their arms.

I managed to buy more for that trip than I did for my wedding. As I wasn't booked to sing, I didn't have to go through that depressing process of looking for work clothes: I could and did buy just for my delight.

The journey was my first long-distance flight, and in those

days planes had a stop-over for refuelling at Gander airport in Newfoundland. I had never seen a duty-free shop before, so I spent most of the long spell of waiting there, before embarking again. It was all wonderment, not only for me but for the boys too, since most of them had never been to America, or on such a long flight.

When the US pilot welcomed us or had to give any information about the flight, the boys thought we had George Raft flying the plane. Every American sounded like a film star or the most undiscovered wisecracking comedian in the world. We landed in New York in a heat wave such as I had never experienced before: it was extremely humid and desperately enervating.

My energy level for several days was almost nil. None of us were prepared for this, both clothes-wise or physically. The plane had arrived early enough for us to get to a hotel, refresh ourselves and go out on the town, which I overdid, as my vaccinated leg rebelled against the heat and too much walking, so I had a swollen log of a leg to haul about and, unusual for me, a splitting headache. But I wouldn't be left behind. It was like stepping into another world, a fairground that had deep canyons lit with fairy lights, peopled with some very weird sleepless walkers battling the heat and humidity, in the middle of the night, dressed in the craziest get-ups in the hope of combating the stultifying atmosphere.

And it all seemed to me to be swamped in music, music that flowed from every corner, lifting your spirit above the oppressive weight of the damp, hot night: not canned musak, but live, swinging, thrilling sounds. Name big bands were playing on ledges, lined up at the back of a bar, blowing right above the bartender's head, into the ears of the jazz-loving customers he was serving. There were famous small groups too, whose music enhanced a meal, or a drink in a bar.

And then there was Birdland, the Mecca we immediately headed for, and where we were also to play on that visit.

The boys didn't have as much time off as I did for sightseeing, and so I was taken to places of interest by our friend Chippy Grimes, now living in New York with her first husband, who

153

was an ardent disciple of Lennie Tristano, the pianist. Chippy was now working as a dress designer for a clothes manufacturer. She took me to all the sights, the Empire State Building and the Museum of Modern Art.

With Chippy, and her husband, John and I spent one evening listening to Lennie Tristano and his group. John sat in with them on a couple of numbers, which he said he enjoyed doing, but I knew he had qualms beforehand. I thought he held his own admirably.

One day Zoot Sims's girlfriend Casey took me to Harlem. She was black and a song writer, and was trying to get off the ground with her material, so she did her pitch with me. I'm ashamed to admit it, but when in Harlem you just had to have your hair straightened by an expert – and I capitulated. It looked great – but how would it stay that way, with all that humidity? And what did you do at night to protect it when your head hit the pillow?

John suggested that I put a shower cap over it to keep it in place; thinking he knew what he was talking about I complied. When I woke up the next morning, I took the shower cap off my head and looked in the mirror. There I faced the horror and destruction of my beautifully styled hair of the night before. It had turned into a magnificent fully grown copy of a Bride of Frankenstein nightmare. Of course, the plastic cap had created heat and humidity, making the head sweat. The struggle between the straightened hair and the plastic during the night must have been obscene.

Angry with myself for not using *my* common sense, instead of asking John, I called John (with my limited knowledge of the vocabulary on the subject) all the variations on mother's sons I could think of. I did look a pitiful mess compared with the night before, so it was live with it or get the rollers out again. I spent a miserable day on Jones Beach being nonchalant about it, with pianist Derek Smith and his wife, but a whole day went by before I could own up to it really being my responsibility to take care of the finished product.

When we had to travel to Newport, Rhode Island, for the band's first performance, the boys' spirits were high. They were full of good expectations when they jumped on to the bus, not only about their own music, but about all the music they were going to hear. We had to make a stop on the way out of the city, to pick up a couple more musicians at another hotel. We hadn't been told who they were, and the out-of-town driver had no idea either. Driving down the street where the hotel was situated, a driver coming in the opposite direction rolled his window down and yelled at our driver, 'Heh! man, it's a one way!' Our driver, ignoring his obvious concern and anger, coolly shouted back, 'Heh! I'm only going one way.' Parking the bus, happily oblivious of the irate driver, he opened the door for the new arrivals.

The musicians standing outside the hotel waiting to be picked up caught this speedy New York lipping back incident, and as they clambered on to the bus Dizzy Gillespie and pianist Junior Mance, highly amused at the cheek of the bus driver, commented on it for the whole trip. Of course Dizzy had his little peace pipe lit up, which he was smoking when he got on and for best part of the ride, and this might have made the simple wisecracking a little larger than life. Whatever it was that was tickling his fancy, it made it a fun journey for everyone and an easy social experience.

Dizzy was a happy-go-lucky man, who loved clowning around, some say to the detriment of his music making. But I think anyone who has the ability to laugh at life's inequity, as he must have had to, and make others join in, as well as being an innovator at an important stage in the history of the music he played should, be excused his eccentricities.

Two or so hours later our bus arrived in the delightfully old seaport town of Newport, so different from the ever-changing concrete canyons and cluttered chaos of New York. Newport retained its colourful charm, with clapboard houses and tree-lined streets and lanes, some with the original cobblestones. There was an extremely gracious atmosphere; the town adopted by the wealthy for vacational yacht sailing. The weekend we arrived, the peace and quiet of the leisurely town was being disrupted by the influx of fans

155

to the festival of all jazz festivals, eager to enjoy the get-together of musicians and friends with a like mind.

As I was a guest, I was guided to a large house that fed and housed fans, stars and newsmen who were staying for the whole festival. Our stay was only for that one day's appearance, and it was a broiler. Most sensible people were in shorts and thin T-shirts, or next to nothing with big hats; an informal, anything goes feeling, but with an expectant buzz in the air for the solo of the moment, the inspired creativeness that top jazz musicians are capable of producing when everything is in their favour. It was bound to come from someone that afternoon in such illustrious company, in such a charged atmosphere.

I was being taken care of by Willis Conover, a voice well known in broadcasting for 'Voice of America'. He introduced me to whoever he bumped into that he knew, who were most of the jazz fraternity. It was my first meeting with Quincy Jones, Jimmy Rushing and Johnny Griffin, all of whom, except Quincy, who was there to hear his charts played by the Basie Band that night, were going to play that day along with The Dankworth Big Band. The crowd was not disappointed by any of the artists, from John's big swinging band, holding its own for Britain, to Jimmy Rushing laying down the blues, to Dizzy being his inimitable self. Finally, in a blast of glory, Basie's magnificently controlled power-house ended the day, with the public getting up on to their feet to jitterbug the night's finale.

The band climbed on board the bus back to Manhattan with a warm glow of achievement, although they could not resist holding inquests, dissecting their own and others' solos; owning up to little goofs that they had disguised by quickly turning their solos in a different direction. I always enjoy listening to these inquests after a performance; no one is ever satisfied.

Although I was not billed or hired to sing for any of the US engagements, I did sing on two occasions, of which Birdland was probably the most frightening. John asked me if I would sing a couple of numbers with the band on that date, and I didn't say no, although I would have liked to have done. When I was announced, and was making my way through the crowd to get on to the bandstand, my mind went back to 1951 and my first jazz club appearance in London. My feelings and thoughts were almost identical: 'What the hell am I doing here?' – but I also felt inner terror, with hopes that it would all disappear once I got in front of the band and microphone.

I sang 'Old Devil Moon' and 'Embraceable You'. I didn't know at the time, and I'm thankful that I didn't, but Ella Fitzgerald was in the audience that night: when I had finished my two songs I dashed to the ladies' and we collided there. Ella sweetly congratulated me on my performance, but what stuck in my memory more than anything else she said was, 'You've got good legs, haven't you?' I personally would not have given my legs more than a rating of three out of ten, but Ella approved. Someone else told me that I should keep my English accent; he'd noticed, he said, in 'Old Devil', that I'd slipped into an American accent at the point where the lyric went, 'You and your glance make this romance to hot to handle'. I had sung 'romance' as one normally pronounces it in England, but he thought the British pronounced it 'romunce'. I explained that it then would not rhyme with the way Americans pronounced glance, and that it was one of those rare times in an American lyric when the two accents clashed. To make it sound sensible some adjusting had to be done, and I had sung 'glance' with a Scots accent to make it work. That really confused him.

The other occasion when I sang was at an amusement park called Palisades Park, on the other side of the George Washington Bridge, a vast outdoor area where hardly anyone turned up except Benny Goodman, George Shearing, Bill Finnigan and Leonard Feather: a command performance for a tiny but illustrious audience.

For the other two historic dates all I had to do was look, listen and enjoy. The first one was at the Lewisohn Stadium in New York. Once again the weather was brilliantly hot, the place packed with enthusiastic jazz fans enjoying their idols playing on the high and unglamorous stage. While John's band was playing (once again it was an afternoon concert) a little ripple went through the audience, an excited buzz that Louis Armstrong was in the stadium. As he was just recovering from a heart attack it seemed unlikely, but the buzz got stronger, louder and more and more forceful, until it burst into wild cheers whoops and hollas, then sustained applause, as the master walked on to the stage. The crowd rose as one at the sight of this legendary figure standing there amongst them.

To stop the applause and cries of 'Welcome home, Louis!', he borrowed the trumpet from Stan Palmer, one of the boys in John's brass section, and started to play. Well, the first few bars he could have mimed. The crowd could not contain their joy at seeing a trumpet touch his lips again, and once more a whoosh of cheering applause rose into the hot air, and died as suddenly as it had started. It was a silence of pure reverence for this statesman of jazz and his music. As he played 'When the Saints Go Marching In' with our rhythm section, David Lee, Eric Dawson and Kenny Clare, he gave the crowd what they wanted: a classic Louis performance, bringing the stadium to its feet once more.

Lambertville, New Jersey, was the scene of more historic music making for a week, in a tent with Duke Ellington and his band. John's band did the opening hour of music, and Duke finished the evening with his amazing complex swinging sounds. The drummer on this date had replaced his usual drummer, Sam Woodyard, who had been with him for a considerable time, and I don't think the Duke or the rest of the band were completely happy with him.

There were two shows on Saturdays, one a matinee, which the new drummer wasn't aware of and so didn't turn up for. Our Kenny Clare (sadly no longer with us) knew, through listening over the years to the music of Ellington on record, everything that was being played without having to read a drum book – if one had ever existed. He was asked to come to the rescue and he did, living up to his reputation as a big-band drummer.

John asked the Duke after the show how Kenny had done.

'Wonderful,' he replied. 'I'd trade him for my guy any time.' Kenny Clare became one of the world's great big-band drummers, playing all over the world with a list of stars too numerous to mention.

On that tour we visited a lot of homes of friends, such as Clark Terry, George Shearing, Leonard Feather, Jimmie Hamilton and Cat Anderson, and we had some wild evenings with Thad Jones and his wife. We also spent a day at George Shearing's home, with a Hollywood-style swimming pool in a garden, which was a sight for sore eyes after the heat of the city. George had a collection of glass that gave him great pleasure. Although blind, he had such deep insight into the beauty and quality of each piece, simply by running his hands over it and feeling the contours and texture. I watched his sensitive hands caress the glass and listened to each explanation with admiration. Much later I realized what a fine lesson on art appreciation I had been given that afternoon, hands being just as important as eyes.

The home of Duke Ellington's clarinet player, Jimmy Hamilton, and his wife Vivienne was a handsome brownstone in Upper Manhattan. We were invited, along with other members of both bands, Ellington's and John's, to an evening of good Southern food, music and yarns. But the main object for Jimmie was to show his slides, and none of us could escape the dreaded moment when he announced, 'Folks, come on in now, I got it all set up.' We had to gather in a room where chairs had been set out in front of a screen ready for the presentation. John and I were guests of honour so we were given two extremely comfy recliners to view the collection, and told to stretch out and relax.

Jimmy did the narrating, which turned out to be very similar to his extravagant improvisations on pies. It could have been very exhilarating, except that he had taken the pictures as well. They had been taken at a film studio location for an Otto Preminger film which Duke Ellington had done the music for, and was currently recording. Jimmy, in his laid-back laconic way, slowly announced every character by name, every time they appeared, whether we knew them or not, and if, by accident or lack of skill with the camera, someone's arm, leg or backside was the only thing visible, he explained: 'You see that leg there, in the corner, way up in the back, well that's Duke, he didn't know I was taking it, an I jest missed him.' He missed Lee Remick and Duke Ellington several times and Otto Preminger most times and a lot of the band, but kept the slides and explained the reasons why they were missed every time. Because of the good food and drink, the extreme heat, the comfortable chairs and the darkness of the room, John and I eventually found ourselves nodding off.

Cat Anderson, the lead trumpet player with the Ellington band, lived in Philadelphia, a short drive away from Lambertville, and he and his wife invited us to drive back with them and stay overnight after the show, which we did. The morning presented a bit of a problem when, at breakfast, Cat asked John to bless the table. I looked up at John, wondering how he was going to get out of that little difficulty. I didn't have to wonder for long, because he sweetly smiled his charming smile and said, 'Oh! I think Cleo is much better at that sort of thing than I am.' There was a long silent pause, a deep slow breath from me, as a silly grin spread over my face, tinged with disgust, aimed in the direction of John Dankworth. I groped around in my head trying to remember a short grace I must have learnt and tucked away for a situation just like this from one of the childhood Bible classes I had attended. Thankfully, just as I was about to decline I found the simple 'For what we are about to receive, may the good lord make us truly thankful, Amen.' And kicked John under the table as hard as I possibly could.

Our trip to the United States made us both many new and lasting friends. One was Phil Moore, an arranger and vocal coach for many actresses who had to sing in films (Lena Horne was one of the first singers he worked with). He lived in an apartment in Carnegie Hall, which at that time was dangerously near to being demolished. There was a radio talk show in New York at the time with a host by the name of Long John. Artists, writers, musicians would just drop in unannounced and talk about anything that they felt strongly about. Because of this casual approach it didn't always come off, but sometimes it was exciting. Phil was a regular dropper-inner, and brought any visiting friends along with him to ring the changes.

That is how John and I came to be on the air in July 1959, when the sad news was announced that Billie Holiday had died that day, in a New York hospital. We were all stunned by the news, even though we knew her health and body had been taxed over the years by a drug habit she found hard to control, but the rumour was that she was at that time 'clean' (a euphemism for 'drug free'). They asked us all to talk about her contribution to jazz, and how much she would be missed. The lady influenced and continues to influence jazz singers all over the world. Thankfully, there is a large collection of her recordings always available, keeping the memory of her alive.

I returned to Britain sad at having had to leave the vitality of New York behind, but glad to be home, exhausted, renewed, uplifted, and ready for work.

16

Valmouth

Plays or musicals that shock the social mores of the time very rarely go into later eras holding on to that reputation, except sometimes as a history lesson, to show how theatre has advanced, or occasionally that it has gone full circle and that nothing changes. Sandy Wilson's risqué musical of the late fifties, *Valmouth*, never succeeded in shocking again when a revival was mounted, because it is almost impossible to shock anyone today in the theatre.

When I was called to take over from Bertice Reading, who could not do the 1959 London run, *Valmouth* already had a growing reputation for titillating audiences both on tour and at the Lyric Theatre Hammersmith.

The cast that I joined for the run at the Saville Theatre included Dorothy Cooper, Fenella Fielding, Doris Hare and Peter Gilmore, and was directed by Vida Hope, who was highly thought of in the theatre. I had to inherit the costumes designed for Bertice, whose figure you could honestly describe as roly-poly. Although no sylph, I hardly fit the mantle comfortably, and Tony Walton, the set and costume designer, had to insert a few strategic pads and tucks. It was my first musical and my first comedy role, and it would have helped to be roly-poly and have a lot of chutzpah.

Valmouth was based on the writings of Ronald Firbank. Sandy

Wilson took characters from Firbank's other books and placed them all together in the 1918 novel, *Valmouth* – a clever idea, and to my mind the best musical score Sandy Wilson wrote. It was considered rather daring in part, because of the outrageous performances by some of the actors, and because of the outrageous characters who inhabited Valmouth. The hundred-year-old lady, Mrs Took, and her buddy Mrs Yajnarvalkya, the masseuse and procurist of young men for aging women or nymphomaniacs, were played by Doris Hare and me; the two whacky old ladies who took the waters and hopefully men, by Dorothy Cooper and Betty Hardy. The nun who sang her head off on her only speaking day was Marcia Ashton, and the country lass who lay on her back with her legs in the air singing a love song to a fish clasped between her toes was Patsy Rowlands. The fish and song was considered so suggestive that when the Lord Chamberlain's office came to inspect, before royalty was about to visit us in the shape of Princess Margaret, it had to be cut (this was in the days of censorship).

The show gathered a cult following: people came to see it over and over again, and still talk about their favourite character, how wonderfully naughty it was, and how they wish it would be brought back. My part, Mrs Yaj, needed experience in the art of delivering a comic line, which I didn't have, but under the careful guidance of my good buddy, Doris, I had daily lessons on how to counteract the upstagers, how not to kill my laugh line and not to be despondent when the laugh didn't come – it happened to the best of them.

Once again the company was a joy, each one giving me a lesson in stagecraft. Fenella Fielding was the scene-stealer of all time, making her name in the role of the nymphomaniac. Her delivery was worth watching every night, and it was Fenella you went to for the latest stage gossip and makeup. I was told, go see Fenella, when Vida said I must wear false eyelashes for the part. She also pointed me in the direction of the shop which was the cheapest supplier of yet another dark body makeup to cover my too-light-for-the-part skin.

Doris Hare's reputation in the theatre is legendary, and her stories were endless. I was depressed by a note I had been given telling me to do something in a song that seemed all wrong to me. She told, to console me, a story about herself and Noël Coward when she appeared in his 1932 revue, *Words and Music*. He had written a song for four different characters, called 'Mad about the Boy', and Doris was to sing the Charlady version. 'I worked hard on the song, alone,' she said, 'with the pianist, working out a pretty good interpretation. I was really pleased with myself. We were eventually called to the stage to rehearse, and perform each version for the master himself. Cleo darling,' she said, 'I gave my all; and an inspired thought came to me when I was in the throes of it,' she said, reliving the moment. 'I manoeuvred to a position so that if I flung out my arm, a pot on the table would go flying, on the line "I'm fired with cupid's arrow, every Wednesday from four to six". Well, I managed to do it, and the bloody pot went flying! When I'd finished, Noël came over to me and said, "Terribly funny dahling, but I don't think the pot, do you?" Well,' she said, 'I was a bit disappointed at his response to my efforts, but I did it the way he wanted – for a while. But eventually I went back to how I'd done it in rehearsal. When Noël saw it, he admitted, "Dahling, you were right."'

Everyone in a show has a warming-up method: most do the conventional scales, but you get the odd eccentric with their own special prescription. Doris and I had dressing rooms next door to each other, down a long corridor. Her warm-up was to go from the start of the corridor to the door of her room, yelling at the top of her voice greetings to everyone in the other rooms. Mine being the last, she would yell, 'How are you my dear, in good voice?', stick her head in the door to make sure, and that was it. I questioned her about it once: 'It makes me laugh, but doesn't it hurt your voice?' She replied, 'If I can do that, girl, I'm all right. I'm in good voice.' I can't remember her being off any time, for anything, for the whole run. My experience as yet didn't run to any form of pre-preparation, except a prayer, a gargle, fingers crossed, and the occasional Buddhist hum.

Cleo

Every November when the fogs came, I became ill with bronchitis. Stupidly I was still smoking, but not when I was sick. If I could give it up then, why not for ever, I asked myself? But I was a nicotine addict at that time, and apart from the November fogs I survived. Madame Ertle, whom I visited regularly while I was in *Valmouth*, despaired of me, saying that a lot of my vocal problems would vanish if I gave up, but the penny dropped very slowly into the dumb numbskull.

The week before the show closed I had to go to a voice doctor in Harley Street, who was noted for getting performers on if they were having voice trouble. He said he would help me this time, knowing we were due to close, but that when it did, I shouldn't talk for a month or I would end up speaking and singing like Tallulah Bankhead. Much as I admired Miss Bankhead's style and sound, I preferred the noise I was making. So another warning penny was dropped into the maze.

The last week of *Valmouth* was very emotional for all of us, like the end of a mass love affair. As members of the cast passed one another, walking to and from the stage, such sad looks were exchanged, sighs of resignation at our fate, which had been pinned up on the notice board. It was the second taste of this ritual farewell for me, rich in the traditions of the theatre. It is hard to let go, to leave the ordered life the theatre imposes on you, the comfort that you create for yourself in the dressing room (for some, more home than home), your nine-to-five job in reverse; especially if there isn't another on the horizon. The song 'I will miss you', a duet sung by Doris and me, almost collapsed as we both broke down with emotion. Doris loves a good cry and the song often brought tears to her eyes during the run, so the end was just too much for her.

The audience were emotional about the show ending too, adding their immense collective feelings to the cast's; buckets of tears were shed. We kissed, hugged, said we would keep in touch, and passed on to other things. Thank goodness there are those in the theatre who are keepers-in-touch who, once they experience that close relationship, like to hold on to the memory with constant friendship. I bless them.

17

Aspley Guise

In 1954 John had made a solo trip to South Africa, playing with local musicians. The fact that he could not play to black audiences appalled him: his musical mentors were black, he was playing the music created by them, but to white audiences, while his black fans had to sweep the stage, clean the toilets and hear the music in the background.

David Lee, the pianist who accompanied John, knew of the great love some of the black musicians had for John and the music he played, and arranged clandestine meetings between them, so that they could play together and listen too. These were loving gatherings between like souls, but dangerous for all if found out. Later, David left South Africa with his family and became the pianist with John's big band. He also became the band's manager, leaving late in 1959 to go solo; that was when Dudley Moore took over the chair.

John was asked to go back several times after that first visit, with requests that I accompany him. As it was illegal for a white and a person of colour to cohabit, let alone be allowed into a white hotel as a guest, at that time the request for me was made in ignorance of my heritage. J.D. had no desire to return under these circumstances, and he never went there again.

It was John's South African experience that made us aware

of this offensive law and brought us into the Anti-Apartheid movement in England. This was how we met and became friends with Father Trevor Huddleston, Canon Collins, Errol de Burgh Wilmot and others. We had a long and fruitful first meeting with John Neville, the actor, and his family at Canon Collins's home near St Paul's Cathedral. But the main centre of activity was the house of Sylvester and Jenny Stein, in Regent's Park Road opposite Primrose Hill. It was here that we met most of the South African exiles and sympathizers and learnt about the iniquities of that country.

Sylvester Stein had been the editor of the famous South African Magazine *Drum* when, in 1957, Althea Gibson, the black American tennis player, won the Wimbledon Tennis Championship. He wanted to put a picture of her and the white player she had beaten, with their arms around each other, on the front cover. They wouldn't let him do it, so he resigned and came to Britain.

Sylvester was an eccentric, fun-loving, freewheeling adventurer, novelist and magazine editor, whereas Jenny, an artist who exhibited paintings from their home, was the hub of it all and the chief soup cooker, trying to keep it all sane and together and getting cross with us if she failed, which she did from time to time. We were both taken into the bosom of the family, along with all their friends. It was an open house, a London salon, where South African intellectuals hobnobbed with musicians like Jean Hart and Marian Montgomery, painters like Mike and Evie Williams, Jack Smith, writers like Anthony Sampson, Doris Lessing and Eleanor Bron.

Around this time John had a call one day from Winchester Prison to say that they had a young man in custody who had stowed away on a ship from South Africa; he'd given John's name as a possible benefactor. John couldn't think who it could be. 'The name he gives is Pinocchio,' they said, adding, 'He said you would remember that name.' John did: he wasn't a musician, but a fanatical fan, who knew and could scat sing every chorus of any black American musician he had heard on record, all the while playing along with his fingers the imaginary instrument he was imitating. He was tiny – hence his name.

What they wanted to know of course was whether we would sponsor him into the country; if not, he would have to be sent back. We said yes, got in the car and drove to Winchester, where Pinocchio was waiting for us. We brought him home, clothed him, found him a job in Denmark Street, and loaned him an instrument. When he told us that his great desire was to play like Charlie Parker, how could John resist that? The Steins gave a welcoming party for him and he was found a place to stay with a room of his own. He eventually became a face in all the jazz clubs, and everyone got to know him as 'Pesky Pinoch', but he never learnt how to play like Charlie Parker.

In September 1959 I became pregnant. It wasn't a planned pregnancy, but I was happy and contented with the prospect of having John's baby. I intended to work as close to the birth as I could, but I started threatening to miscarry after the third month, so my doctor advised me to stop immediately, and take things very slowly. That part of it wasn't hard, but time did drag.

During this pregnancy we read that a motorway was being built from London to the North. We had friends, TV director Quentin Lawrence (whom we worked with a lot) and his wife Ming, who lived in a village called Blunham, not far from Bedford. We visited and stayed weekends in their spacious Georgian manor house, so large that it had been divided into two. John and I fell in love with the idea of getting something like it for ourselves. Every time we visited we got more and more broody about it, starting to look around the area with the help of Ming and her flock of six children, Stuart making seven from time to time.

They were idyllic days, and I felt ready to live in the country. Eventually we did find a Georgian house in the village of Aspley Guise, not far from an M1 turnoff. It was enormous, with lots of land. Fifteen thousand pounds was the asking price for the house, two cottages and several acres. We asked our married pals Ken Moule and David Lindup (now married to Nadia) to come in with us and split it up, but they didn't feel the way we did about going to the country at that point, and as we couldn't afford it on our own, we didn't pursue the idea.

During this pregnancy David Dearlove, John's publishing manager, was always looking for new songs or thinking up new ideas for us to consider. One of them was a musical for me based on *The Ides of March* and the other *The Day of the Triffids*. J.D. wasn't keen on writing the music for either idea – I think he found the subjects too serious to attempt at the time – so nothing came of those ideas, but he was tempted to collaborate with David and Sylvester Stein on a musical based on Sylvestor's comic novel, *Old Letch*. They renamed the musical *Qwertyuiop*, the top line of course of the typewriter. It was hilarious, and some of the songs were brilliant. Dudley played the piano for the demonstration tape and I sang some of the songs, heaving with child. Tony Mansell, Dudley and John sang the male songs. It was never taken up by anyone at the time, I can never understand why, but I was certainly surrounded by a team with a strong creative force. If it's true that babies take sounds and feelings from the outside into the womb, this baby was doing all right.

David managed to get Dudley and me a film, based on the Caryl Brahms's book, *Bullet in the Ballet*. That was my first encounter with Caryl and Ned Sherrin, that later developed into a close friendship and working relationship. I can vaguely remember David trying to organize Dudley and me into a duo cabaret act, but we did more laughing at ourselves than work. It must have made poor David very despondent, for apart from a few songs and John's hit records, *African Waltz* and *Moanin'*, none of his ideas got off the ground and he eventually gave up the business altogether, moving to the West Country with his family.

I went very upmarket to have my second baby, from the front room of Orchard Avenue to the London Clinic. I started labour nine months to the day (oh yes, I knew the day), which the doctor thought was extraordinary, as there was such a long gap between the two babies. I was whisked into the hospital and gave birth before the doctor arrived, at about 10 p.m. on 14 May 1960, to a young son. It was so easy. I was in the clinic for over a week which was unusual but very restful, getting acquainted with my new son, and receiving visits and good wishes galore.

Karel Reisz, with whom John was working at the time, and the new star of Karel's film *Saturday Night and Sunday Morning*, Albert Finney, came and met the new Dankworth, who had great lungs and greeted everyone with a full chorus. It was also front-page news in the press (this time both families knew about it first).

I felt complete, rounded and fulfilled. I had my career, the man of my dreams, and two sons (my teenage wish for seven might come true). Reality struck when I got home and had to learn all over again how to cope with a wind-filled baby in a two-room flat. John was re-forming his band at about the same time and I began to feel neglected. One day an argument started over something quite trivial and I grew so angry about it that I said, 'Don't you realize I've just had a baby?' He retorted, 'Don't you realize I've just had a band?' The Clemmie of old came to the boil, and over the top of the pan I went, aiming the lightly framed abstract painting (previously on the wall), to frame John's head perfectly. It was an irrational thing to do, because I quite liked the painting. But just recalling it makes me want to go and punch him right now.

How on earth were two very touchy artistic people going to make this marriage work? It was the first of many a spat before we found a way. We went looking for houses again, and ended where we had started. In our search we returned to the first house we looked at in the village of Aspley Guise, now split up. The land had been sold, the two cottages also, but the large main house was yet to go, so we looked at it again, fell in love with it and scraped together seven thousand pounds to make it ours. We moved our bed, a few special bits and pieces and the baby into the empty house in the summer of 1960.

The answer to one of our problems was space, which we had found, together with an escape route from each other's unpredictable temperaments, especially mine. Here in this house our close relationship, brought even closer by marriage but not really tested until now, could survive and grow. We felt happy about our future together, here in the warm inviting house, with its big garden and its two grand redwood trees, trees that I came to love. Outside the window of the main big room was a wide-spreading strawberry tree; the garden was packed with trees and shrubs.

The sun was shining on that first day, and the baby (whom we called Baby because we hadn't named or registered him yet), wiggled his toes in the sun, sleepily contented. This was our first home together.

We had no furniture, and very little money to purchase any, since buying the house had creamed off all available cash. So for the first few weeks we lived mainly in the kitchen, with the table and two or three antique chairs that I had picked up when I was living in Kilburn. There had been a little shop at the back of the High Street, to which I'd paid regular visits. I also bought large vases that I had converted into lamps. Not exactly a pre-thought-out furniture plan for a starter home.

A good friend of ours in the music publishing world, Fred Jackson and his wife Pieter, gave us after our wedding a 1934 Premier Cru Château Latour claret. We took this to Nether Hall on the day we moved in, intending to open it, so that we could drink to our new home, our new two-week-old baby, and our future togetherness. It was all so peaceful, so romantic. As we opened the bottle, and poured out three glasses – two full and a wee symbolic drop for the baby – we heard, 'Anyone at home?' Our romantic moment flew out of the kitchen window as Stan Rudge, a jovial neighbour, burst into the quiet, announcing himself as a welcoming committee for the village.

We could not hide our already poured delight, and as there was a third glass standing waiting, even though it was the baby's, we asked him to join us in a house-warming toast. The glass of much treasured wine was knocked back in one gulp, and another or two. Stan became a part of our village life, he threw himself into everything with much verve, and in small doses, was good to be with, not least for the village gossip. The next, rather more subtle welcome, was from the children of Tom and Jinnie Haynes, who came bearing a posy of flowers and a little frock for the baby.

So, we had settled into country life in a grand Georgian house and I liked the feeling immensely. But our life was not a bed of roses: between us we had no idea how to organize our money, pay bills on time, work, and arrange the house. We started going to house auction sales, which helped fill a few spaces, but still could not afford to buy any comfortable seating for the large and beautiful main room.

Until on the way to Stevenage, baby in the back of the car to see Stuart and the family, I noticed, displayed outside an antique-come-junk shop, an old-fashioned three-piece suite, two large comfortable-looking, bulbous chairs and a sofa to match. I screeched to a halt and left the shop the proud owner of a three-piece suite. I sang all the way to Stevenage. When I arrived home, full of cheer because of my bargain, and told J.D. what I had bought, he almost hit the ceiling at the thought of how we were going to pay for it. He was just starting to give me a lecture on responsibility when I told him the extortionate price we had to pay: 'Three pounds, four with delivery.' The lecture was shelved.

When the furniture arrived, I removed the chintz covers, stuck them in the washing machine, darned a couple of holes and at last we had a presentable seating arrangement. Later I made brand new covers for them, when we decided to have a big party, but that's another story.

Meanwhile, domesticity was coming thick and fast and neither of us really liked it. John found it harder than I did, because he hadn't had to account for his movements to anyone in all seriousness since he'd been a child; and for me, it was not what I'd ever wanted, but until it was sorted out, the responsibility rested on my incompetent shoulders.

One day I had a phone call from an employee of the electricity board, who said, 'I don't want to intrude into your private life,

Miss Laine, but as an admirer of yours, I would hate to think you and Mr Dankworth were working in the dark, which will be the case soon, as they are going to cut off your electricity.' We rummaged through all the final demands, found the offensive bit of paper and rushed it to the electricity office in the nick of time.

We then advertised for a secretary and found Tod Wye – who straightened out our lives, while living in chaos herself. Tod came into our lives when she was most needed. John had interviewed about five women and said she was the most sensible and experienced of them all. For some reason on her first day John put on a business suit and tie, starting off on a good efficient footing, he said, but this didn't last long. On the second day she was late, and full of apologies. John rushed into my room and in a loud whisper said, 'She says one of her unmarried mothers is playing up.'

Todd was living in a rambling old farm house called Tickford Manor, which had once been grand but was now extremely old and tired: no matter how much love they injected into it, they were not able to revive the corpse. She lived there with her three children and her highly intelligent, eccentric, lovable husband, Eric. On the surface she appeared extremely county, cold and stuck-up, but she was the most giving person I'd encountered, since my mother. She was also a little eccentric herself, making her lovable too, once you got to know her. The unmarried mothers were young girls she housed and counselled, until they made up their minds whether they wanted to keep their babies or have them adopted.

Our bills were now getting paid in time and the books were almost in order. An answerphone was also installed – at that time a fairly new machine to have in a home, which some callers liked and others hated. Dudley was one of the latter: when answered by the machine rather than one of us, the message he left was, 'Machines! machines! machines!!!!! They're taking over! Taking over the whole world!!!' Slam!

I was getting itchy to get back to work, while John was starting to work hard on film scores for Joe Losey and Karel Reisz and touring with the band. I discovered that I was very jealous of his good fortune, and wasn't facing up to this fact honestly, so our spats increased, until I realized my attitude would do more harm to our marriage than work or the lack of it on my part. We were getting to know each other, gradually revealing our naked selves as we really were, with all our warts, carbuncles and boils, as well as a lot of amazing discoveries.

John was a kind and thoughtful man who forgave easily, thank goodness, when I said unkind and cruel things in the course of my tempers and frustration at not working. I was lucky too, that he did not want me to give up my work to look after house, home and him. But there was another side of John that was as dark and complex as the other was light and carefree. Complete neglect of everything and everyone, with depressions and upsets about minor things that soon passed, but left others upset.

All of which took me a while to understand and come to terms with. This was always when he was about to work or working. If I had read a poem by James Kirkup called 'The Poet' during the first unsettled months of our marriage, I might have been a more sympathetic creature to live with. I think the sentiments expressed apply to musicians too.

The Poet

Each instant of his life, a task, he never rests,
And works most when he appears to be doing nothing,
The least of it is putting down in words
What usually remains unwritten and unspoken,
And would so often be much better left
Unsaid, for it is really the unspeakable
That he must try to give an ordinary tongue to.

And if, by art and accident,
He utters the unutterable, then
It must appear as natural as a breath,
Yet be an inspiration. And he must go,

175

The lonelier for his unwanted miracle,
His singular way, a gentle lunatic at large
In the societies of cross and reasonable men.

Often John would be ostensibly in repose, but if you looked closer you could see that his eyes were darting violently around in his head, and in another world, which wasn't easy for others to penetrate. To make contact with him, I had to pretend I was a spaceship pilot, 'Tuning in to John Dankworth, Tuning in to John Dankworth, are you receiving me?'

I was learning, and so was he. Kirkup's poem gave me an insight into all creative minds.

We had sensibly decided, even though I still had the lease, not to use the London flat as a pied-à-terre; that if either of us were away, we would do our best to come home, whatever the time. So I acquired a lodger: Dudley Moore took over the flat and stayed there until he could afford a more salubrious address.

18

Sad Times

Slowly but surely my mother was disintegrating before our eyes. Although my sister Sylvia and her husband Geoff, at the end, bore the weight of the decline of this once strong and powerful woman, since she was living with them, we all felt heavy of heart for not having observed the symptoms sooner; we'd dismissed them as stubborn idiosyncrasies. It is only in retrospect, knowing what has come to light medically since, that we can put a name to what was occurring; what she had was Alzheimer's.

I visited her weekly and watched her crumble into that walking death, as she got thinner and thinner and more and more ancient as the weeks passed, becoming aggressive at not being able to understand what was happening to her in the few lucid moments that she had. Most of the time I saw a sweet wayward child, who did not recognize me, Sylvia or anyone else.

I didn't have to contend with the daily detail and upsets as Sylvia had to – I walked in then sadly away from it after each visit – until Sylvia asked if I would have her at Nether Hall for a while, to give her and her family a rest. Luckily she asked me when I was relatively free and could devote my time to Mother, as unlike Sylvia, I had live-in help for baby Alec and twelve-year-old Stuart who had decided he wanted to come and live with us permanently.

Caring for mother on a daily basis was an unnerving experience for me. She was harder to keep safe from harming herself than the small children in the house, as the move from the known to the unknown had disorientated her. A twenty-four-hour watch had to be kept by me and everyone else in the house, after I found her wandering the corridors of the rambling old house one night. These corridors went off in all directions and were a maze of confusion even for a mind that could fathom left and right directions; but for a mind that was on the blink, it must have been a terrifying nightmare. Nightly I found her on landings, at the top of stairs and at the bottom of stairs, or trying to get through doors that we had to lock to restrain her from walking into the street; I would have to talk her calmly back to bed, as I would a child. When being thwarted she often had a tantrum and had to be calmed down, but the most distressing times for me were when she was found in these wandering situations, with her mind switched back to reality, having messed herself and her bed because of her incontinence. Then the battle between mother and child became real and painful, and she underwent a short spell of dreadful, shame-faced embarrassment, because her daughter had to guide her back to her room, clean her and her bed, as if she were a baby, then put her back into bed, tucking her in with pleas to stay put so that she would be safe.

The clear spells never lasted very long, and I was never sure if I liked those moments, for her or me. They were always a challenge, because I was never really certain if she was having one, until I had asked her, in my reversed role, motherly manner, to 'Come along now, it's time to wash for bedtime' in a tone that I would never have normally used, as daughter/friend, only when she was vague and functioning in another dimension. During the clear moments Mother stood up to me and asked very angrily, who the hell did I think I was talking to? Once again she was her old self, which made me want to cry, as I stood and took the old temper with joy and happiness, knowing that in a few seconds she would revert to being a zombie.

There were funny moments, as when the family were all at

Sad Times

supper with John sitting next to Mother having a conversation of sorts with her, she with no recollection of who he was, but being quite the charming hostess, talking to him as she would to a complete stranger. I was sitting at the other end of the table listening, when she said to him, 'Oh so you know my daughter Clemmie do you'? He replied, 'Why, yes of course, I'm married to her, she's my wife,' pointing towards me. This was ignored and so was I, as she continued to tell him that she hadn't seen me for some time, and felt quite cross because I had been neglecting to visit her recently.

Sad moments were when I caught her having an illusary conversation with her brothers, asking them why they had done something which had obviously upset her. I never learnt what it was, but she asked the questions with sadness in her voice.

My sister was thankful for the short rest, which revitalized her to continue looking after Mother for a while longer, until a professional nurse came daily to help lift some of the burden. Mother didn't co-operate at all, but they were skilled enough to handle it.

Eventually she went into hospital with pneumonia. Those visits were the most painful of all. I used to drive first to Stevenage and leave Stuart and the baby with Sylvia. She loved having them, especially the new baby. I always admired Sylvia's love of children and how they were drawn towards her maternal instinct: she had a special gift. Nothing seemed to upset her where children were concerned, unless they started doing damage to each other. She would take Stuart and the baby over while I drove off to Hitchin to visit mother. I wrote in my diary after one visit that she was 'sitting up in bed and looked better than I had seen her for a long time, but her leg was paining her. She didn't seem to know me, her mind wandered and she thought she was home; offering me a cup of tea, and asking me how the cupboard looked that she had scrubbed across the room. She was cheerful enough, but obviously in another world. I was depressed, though happy that she was in hospital where she could be looked after properly.'

179

Mother died in November 1964 aged seventy-five, three years after I wrote that. I was happy that she had been released from the indignity of those last years, also that Sylvia and Geoff could now return to a normal family life. We had been gradually losing her for at least six years and perhaps for much longer. I asked my doctor, who looked after her when she stayed with me, what was it that had happened to her, and he said it was premature senility.

Pa wept when we buried her.

19

Here is the News

Here is the News was a revue devised and developed in Cambridge
for the Cambridge University Footlights Theatre by the brilliant
satirist, John Bird, and performed by, among others, himself
and Eleanor Bron. Someone thought that they had a commercial
property on their hands that should be developed, so John Bird
set about doing it. Willie Donaldson and his partner Albert
Leywood were the impresarios who raised the money to mount
the production and get it on the road for an eventual opening in
London.

It was my first excursion back into the theatre since the birth
of the baby. I was so happy to be working once again, especially
with this exciting group: artists collected together from so many
different theatrical and musical backgrounds. I loved going to
rehearsals and getting back into the swing of it once more. John
Bird directed and Patrick Gowers wrote and arranged the jazz
score, which was played by a ten-piece group consisting of some
of the finest jazz musicians in the country. The writers were
not to be sneezed at either, some of the most avant-garde of
the period: Eugene Ionesco, N.F. Simpson, Andrew Sinclair,
Arthur Clegg, Peter Cook and John Bird. On paper, for a lot
of London theatre-goers and intellectuals, the ingredients spelt
sure-fire success.

Sean Kenny, the whizz-kid of stage design, was brought in, and Sheila Hancock, Valentine Dyall, Lance Percival, Richard Goulden, Robin Ray, Henry McGee, Roddy Maud Roxby, Kathy Keaton added up to a very talented cast, the young mixed in with the more experienced. We opened on a Bank Holiday Monday in one of the biggest theatres in the country, the Coventry Theatre, to an audience expecting a little slap and tickle; what they got, of course, was political satire, commentary on the problems of the day, bombs, vice, red tape, commercialism, racial prejudice, and hypocrisy. We were well before our time, and Coventry wasn't interested in the future of theatre on this opening night.

From the stage, as we performed, we heard seat after seat thud upwards as the occupants vacated them, complaining loud and clear as they walked out, that they hadn't paid good money to sit through a load of rubbish, while on stage actors heaved, pushed and struggled to move one of Sean Kenny's trolleys offstage, so that the next sketch could be got on with. Some of the breakdowns were hilariously funny, but the audience was not in the mood for that kind of under-rehearsed slapstick.

The week in Coventry brought out tensions and insecurities amongst the cast, as daily rehearsals, called to improve the night before's disasters, did nothing of the sort on the night. There was a running gag that I thought hilarious, which brought not a titter from the audience: this was when (as one reviewer described them) 'the wonderful line of toothily-grinning musical-comedy soldiers' with wooden guns would pop up from out of nowhere and shoot whoever was on stage at the time, or just march across the stage – no reason was given for any of this capering about, it just became more threatening and macabre as the show proceeded, making the small Bank Holiday crowd in the oversized theatre uncomfortable and edgy.

One night my solo blues number, 'Rubies for the Queen', which usually got a reasonable amount of attention, failed to register. I battled on, a little baffled, as there was laughter coming from the audience, which was a rare and joyful sound, but this was not a comedy song. I checked quickly to see if anything was exposed that should have been neat, tidy or tucked away, but everything was in order, no zips undone, and the amount of boob on display would have had a hard time disturbing the judgement of a Vatican conference with the Lord Chamberlain in attendance. So I put it down to the perceptiveness of the audience: perhaps it really was a comic song, and my reading of it had been wrong all this time.

It became clear eventually. The sketch before me was an underwater event, an illusion brought about by lighting (when it worked). Robin Ray was suspended Peter-Pan-like by Kirby wires, dressed to look like a diver with snorkel, goggles and flippers. Spying a chest on the sea bed he imitates swimming to get down to it; then the chest opens and out spring the toy soldiers who shoot him. He pretends dead and the soldiers march off (under water) while Robin, in a blackout, is whisked off. Lights up, I am discovered sitting on a couch ready to sing my sad song, but something is not right, and that something is Robin Ray, still hanging uncomfortably above my head. To add to the mayhem, at the end of my song a sheet is thrown over my head by two actors who should then proceed to push me off, but the trolley got stuck and would not move.

By this time I was hysterical with laughter and the sheet, supposedly now covering a statue, came to life with spasmodic judderings that were getting heartier and more violent, as the situation becoming more ludicrous with every moment. The two actors responsible for getting me off, Allen Mitchell and Edwin Finn, tried to remove me and the trolley but finally, utterly exasperated, stage-whispered to me under the sheet, 'Sorry, Clee, we can't move this bloody thing off, we'll have to leave you.' Under my drapery, I then heard them improvise acting, wiping their hands of the whole matter, then still improvising, grumbling as they walked off. Why they thought they could fool the audience at this point I can only put down to professionalism. Meanwhile I waited for the lights to dim so that I could creep off unseen, but they didn't, so I had to walk off with the sheet still over my head in full view of the utterly confused, amazed, but heartily laughing audience. Oh! Robin was hanging through all of this.

Nightly, bizarre occurrences happened that didn't give the cast much confidence that the show would ever transfer to a London stage. Sheila was upset and asked for new sketches to be written, though with the material that she had to work with, she still got good reviews for her marvellous work in the production; but the general consensus was that, although different and offbeat, the point of a lot of the sketches was obscure.

While I was in Nottingham I managed, under threat of prosecution, and the cast, to register our son (he was six months old) as Alexander William Tamba Dankworth. At last he was a recognized citizen of Great Britain.

By the time we got to Oxford the show had changed for the better, considerably, and the reviews bore that out. *Here is the News* was presented several years too early for the time when such a revue could please an audience: *Beyond the Fringe* and *Monty Python* finally broke the mould.

It finished in Oxford with attempts, when John Bird fell ill, by Eleanor Fazan to whip it into West End shape. Money ran out and I remember the cast doing a performance for a Greek financier in the hope of raising money to continue, but it didn't work, and that was the end of the *News*.

While Dudley was with the band, he had asked John for three weeks off to appear at the Edinburgh Festival in a revue that he and a few university colleagues had put together. It was called *Beyond the Fringe*, and the other members of the cast were Alan Bennett, Jonathan Miller and Peter Cook. It was so successful he never came back to the band, and the rest is history. But he did play for me once or twice, in cabaret in London, while he was in the show.

One of these occasions marked my triumphant return to the Savoy Hotel as a headliner. This time I entered by the front door, welcomed by the commissionaire by name, and given a suite to change and rest in. But for me there was still a taste left of 'artiste, know your place' when I read the notice, hanging on the door of the suite, politely requesting artistes not to fraternize with guests in the showroom, before or after the show. Most wouldn't want to anyway, but there are occasions when it can't be avoided.

The show with Dudley caused a bit of a stir, bringing lots of interviews, one of which I did in the cocktail bar, the afternoon of the first night. I can't remember the reporter's name or the paper, but we got on well, and had a few drinks together. After the interview, I felt sleepy, and decided to go to my room and rest until show time.

There are mistakes you make in your career once only, because they are so embarrassing or because you have let people down, and the guilt is unbearable; like missing an entrance, being late for an engagement, forgetting your shoes, jewellery, bra or eyelashes. I now added to that list, don't sleep or drink before a show. It was a combination of four things that did it: smoking, an over-heated room, alcohol and sleep.

John came into the room an hour before I was due on, to see if there was anything he could do for me and to wish me well. He found me curled up on the couch, fast asleep, and it took him quite a while before he was able to wake me up. When he managed it, I found I could hardly speak, let alone sing. It was a singer's worst nightmare, and I was confronting it for the first time. What should have been a leisurely, meditative, thoughtful hour of getting ready turned into one of those classic Hollywood movie scene disasters. If there had been an Eve about, she would have gone on in my place.

In a soporific haze I was dunked under a cold shower; dozens of cups of coffee were poured down my miserable throat, and I was told to keep on my feet and walk around to wake myself up – while I did a lot of pathetic wailing along the lines of 'I can't go on, I can't go on, I've let everybody down!' Well, I was got on and it was one of the most gruesome first nights I have ever experienced; how I managed to get through the

185

evening, I have no idea. I can only put it down to Doctor Stage who, when the chips are down, pumps masses of adrenaline into you.

Not only did that incident cause me extreme embarrassment and guilt, it took the whole season there to live it down. I now turn down all unnecessary heat in a dressing room and never ever sleep or drink on a performance day.

Smoking I gave up completely, after John gave me the Sunday papers' treatment. When I'd been pregnant, I hadn't smoked for the whole nine months – I felt nauseous if I even put an unlit cigarette in my mouth – but as soon as the baby was born, I started lighting up again. My cure took place one Sunday morning at Nether Hall. Strewn all over the floor, papers, coffee cups, me in dressing gown, cigarette dangling from my mouth as I turned over a page, I must have looked a gruesome slut as John came into the room. Obviously disgusted, he said, 'Why don't you give up that nauseating habit?' I replied churlishly, 'Why should I?' knowing of course that I should and also that an answer like that would rile him. 'Because,' he said, 'If you don't, I will keep giving you *The Sunday Times* treatment until you do.' Rolling up all the Sunday papers he gave me my first treatment and hit me on the head with them. As I was well padded, they didn't do much damage, but the message was at last knocked into the dumb brain.

To give up I had to give up drinking and coffee too, as they went along with my smoking habit. Although there wasn't any immediate change in my voice, I did suffer less during the winter, when the fogs hit the country. Gradually a clearer sound developed and my technical ability strengthened, so that my voice could do considerably more than it had in the past without tiring.

For the Savoy date, I had a beaded dress made by Darnell's, the dressmaker of the day to all the singing stars in the country. It was an amazing and quite magnificently structured creation. I'm not sure it was me, but it was a glittering sea green, with white beading dangling from the pelvis to the floor, cut straight and tight, almost impossible to walk in, so I minced on and off as if in dire need of the toilet. The top of the dress was constructed like an iron cage, with a platform on which the boobs rested; the lower part of the top cinched in at the waist, like a vice. It was built like a fortress; altogether a very unsuitable dress for a deep breather.

During my season at the Savoy I lost some weight which I didn't mind, but the dress did. One night, as I stood quite still centre stage, emoting on a slow ballad while trying to take in the whole audience, turning naturally from the waist, first to the right, the top of the dress remained quite firmly pointing to the front. I quickly got myself back to the starting position, wondering (but still emoting) how I was going to cope with this all night. I tried once more to the left, but the absurd picture, which the audience was now viewing, happened again. Undaunted by how my disjointed body was behaving, and how odd it must appear to the elegant socialites in the audience, I finished the performance by shuffling my feet along with my whole body around to the left or right. While everything, except the bosom, remained stock still and firmly stuffed in the mermaid sea-green beaded shell.

20

The Seven Deadly Sins

Cabaret and Sundays concerts kept my vocal and performing skills in trim after the show finished. I now had a manager who was part of the expanding Harold Davison organization in the shape of Dick Katz, jazz pianist, who had been pianist-manager of The Ray Ellington Quartet before turning to full-time artist management. He occasionally played for me, before he found the brilliant accompanist Laurie Holloway to take over the responsibility.

The cabaret scene in Great Britain came into full bloom when the gambling laws were changed, allowing clubs and Bingo halls to open in the most unlikely places. One of my first sorties into the world of club cabaret was in Manchester, working for an ex-wrestler turned club owner named Bill Benny. He had the one classy club in the centre of Manchester and several Bingo halls in the suburbs – generally gutted cinemas, turned into bizarre entertainment centres. The oddness would start at the first band call in the Cabaret Room, where either Dick or the resident pianist ploughed through your music for that night's performance, with a bass player and drummer in attendance. Standing at the back of the good piano player, looking over his shoulder while he played, would be three and sometimes four other men, with their eyes glued to the music being played.

If you'd done the club before, you knew why, but the first time around it was rather off-putting, until they explained that they were the pianists of the other three or four places you would work that night, before coming on to the Cabaret Room.

The most frightening part of the whole procedure was that none of them put their fingers to a keyboard to play your music before the night; they merely watched and listened, while the better piano player deciphered your charts. While you just wished you could go home and end the nightmare.

Before setting off on the marathon run Bill Benny, the owner, would make himself known to the artist of the week. He was a heavily built, hairy man with a lisp, and a tendency to grope young girls: he was well known in Manchester for his little peccadilloes on the side. He introduced himself to me and welcomed me to his posh club, then spat out: 'Shave yourself, shave yourself Clee for the Caburway Womb, the owers don't matter sho much.' Translated, he was saying, 'Save yourself Clee for the Cabaret Room, the others don't matter so much.' I think this speech defect was a hangover from his boxing and wrestling days.

It was quite a gruelling job, even though it was only a twenty-minute performance in each place. Instead of being transported in a bus along with all the other artists who were going to appear at the larger venues, my friend Ernie Garside, whom I stayed with and who occasionally worked as a referee for wrestling bouts at these establishments, drove me in a faster and more comfortable fashion. The evening always started with either Bingo or a wrestling match in the ring in the middle of the flattened floor of the old cinema. When the excitement of these two events had died down, the *Saturday Night Sunday Morning* atmosphere built up, as some of the audience replenished their already over-saturated alcohol level; while others noisily settled themselves in anticipation for the next part of the night's entertainment.

The artists for the night were introduced one by one by the

resident compère, first the magician, then a comic, and a stripper, all giving up trying to entertain as the volley of noise in each hall became more uproarious as the night wore on. Last of the entertaining fiasco was the top of the bill – me – accompanied by an organist whom I had last seen peering over the shoulder of a piano player yet to play for me. It all felt very tacky, after my Johnny Dankworth Seven introduction into the profession, but I was determined to be independent, so it was deep breath time.

I found the organ was a necessary instrument in this situation, as the delicacy of a piano would not have pierced the excited hubbub going on in front of the stage, after the good Bingo win or the bet on the bruiser who had felled his equally hefty opponent. In these caverns, a far cry from the attentive jazz clubs where the only thing I had to do was sing the song good, I did learn how to project my personality. Every night I tried something different, hoping it would make them listen. Although I strengthened my voice by having to sing louder, I discovered that volume was not an attention-getter; in fact it often made the public talk louder and more, because they were not exposed. Sometimes one could, by coming down in volume right at the beginning, embarrass a few moments of silence from them. It was dangerous, but what the hell, I had nothing to lose.

Four of these a night was not a favourite pastime of mine. I was soon to learn what Bill Benny meant by saving myself, as by the time I arrived at the more sophisticated club, my voice often felt shattered.

It was relatively well-paid work, so after the first shock, I did it a few more times, then Laurie Holloway came on the scene and I was saved from that indignity for ever, with a long and happy musical association in slightly better clubs. We worked together up and down the country for several years with and without John, mostly without.

During that time there were many unfounded rumours that John and I had split up, especially when John engaged a new girl singer. The rumours always occurred when we were not in

191

each other's pockets. A couple of times the rumour could have developed into reality, but after a good old Campbell tantrum, we both would see what a stupid mistake it could turn out to be, to break a partnership that worked so beautifully on so many levels – music being the main one.

In 1961 Lotte Lenya, the German singer/actress, had agreed to appear at the Edinburgh Festival in a new mounting of *The Seven Deadly Sins*, a role created for her by her husband, Kurt Weill, and the playwright Bertolt Brecht. The Western Theatre Ballet, a young company, founded by Elizabeth West and Peter Darrell in Bristol, presented and commissioned the choreographer, the late Sir Kenneth Macmillan, to remount it for the Festival. Lenya evidently told Kenneth Macmillan and everyone else concerned with the project to go ahead with the rehearsals without her being present, and she would fit in nearer the opening – she didn't have to learn the music or text as she had, after all, performed it enough times to be able to turn up at the last minute, or so she thought.

I didn't become involved until Lotte Lenya dropped out. The cause given to the press was a broken ankle, but the real reason was the new, involving choreography that Kenneth had done for her and Anya Linden, who was to perform the dancing sister/*alter ego*; both were onstage from start to finish, dancing and/or singing. The original production Lenya had been in with the renowned Berliner Ensemble was stylistically stark and static, and I guess she assumed that Kenneth's approach would be similar. How much pre-production talking was done between them on the style and approach I have no idea, but something obviously went disastrously wrong and Lenya walked out, leaving them high and dry.

The 1961 artistic director and administrator of the festival was Lord Harewood, brother of Sir Gerald Lascelles, who knew me as a jazz singer turned Royal Court actress, so I was approached to see if I would take on the part at the last minute. I asked if I could think about it over the weekend but was told an answer was needed there and then, so I said yes.

The score and a tape of Lotte Lenya singing it in German was sent to me. Until that time I had no idea what I had let myself in for, as I didn't know the opera. I was to soon find out, when I started to work on committing to memory the W.H. Auden translation and the Weill music, so that I would be able to fit into the rehearsals already in progress in Edinburgh for the opening in ten days' time. It was then that I gulped at what I had promised to do, girded my loins, locked myself away and got down to it. I arrived in Edinburgh in less than a week, ready to learn the choreography that would be added, with a pianist, to what I had learnt during my week of purdah.

I was so excited about this new venture: I loved the music, the key written for Lenya sat well in my range, and I was also involved in my other love, dance. I had done my homework well, so I was at least confident that what had been composed would come out of my mouth, and if the gods were kind, with a few more run throughs I might even be inspired on the night.

I only had to do three performances a week (Adrienne Corri was to do the others); the rest of the time I could have an injection of culture. As it was the first time I had been to the Edinburgh Festival, it was quite a heady prospect. First things first though: I had once again to get my head and feet stuck into the unfamiliar world of dance, and minor for me though it was, it became awesome. Costumes had to be fitted, and the unruly hair, now straightened and smoothed, adapted to look like a twenties' bob (in an unsuccessful attempt to match Anya's wig). I was also looking forward to meeting and getting some acting tips from my co-performer, the experienced stage and film actress Adrienne Corri.

We were never to meet. The first day's rehearsal with the full orchestra arrived, an event always full of anticipation, the thrill of hearing for the first time all the sounds that the rehearsal pianist had gallantly struggled with coming to life with a full orchestra. This is an experience I never tire of: there is always something different, such as tempo, or a pause put in or taken out, or a different reading by the conductor. It can throw you – but that first morning everything fell into place for me. Alexander Gibson (now Sir), conductor of the Scottish Symphony Orchestra, was relieved and pleased at the end of the rehearsal – as were the other powers-that-be who had bet on the outsider. They could now breathe easily: the opera could go ahead.

Adrienne Corri was due to rehearse after me in the afternoon, so I thought I would hang around to pick up some tips and learn how an experienced actress was going to set about the role. I went into the auditorium and sat far enough back so that I would not be seen; I had said my goodbyes to everyone, so as far as they were concerned I had left. Miss Corri came to the front of the stage in the black dress that was an exact copy of mine, but she looked beautiful in hers, and if she was going to wear a wig for the part, it wasn't on her head that afternoon. The combination of her glorious auburn mane, slender body, black satin dress and sheer stage presence, as she stood waiting on the edge of the stage for Sir Alexander to start the rehearsal, was quite stunning.

The baton was tapped, the arms raised and the down beat given. The orchestra began to play the solemn, stately intro-duction, and once again I felt that intense excitement, as I sat in the dark empty theatre, waiting for the long introduction to come to the point where it gradually slowed down, for the singer to enter with the first line: 'So my sister and I left Louisiana.' But something was wrong: the words didn't come. The orchestra didn't go right back to the start, but to the vamp which leads the singer in, which is a matter of counting bars until it becomes second nature. Once again no words. Alexander advised her to look at his baton, which would indicate the entrance, and this worked, but in an extremely tentative fashion.

To cut a long story short, Adrienne had no idea what she was doing musically, and it was obvious to everyone, including herself, that she would not get it together in time for the opening. To save herself from this embarrassing situation, she threw a wonderful actressy tantrum, blaming everyone within striking distance for her non-entries. How was she expected to move about the stage and look at a stick? The choreography should be cut out, and this awful dress – did they really expect her to sing properly in such a ghastly creation? Whereupon she ripped it off, dropped it on the floor and stomped off into the wings.

Altogether a very impressive display of stagecraft, had it been in a play. Once again I wondered how the production had come this far without some recognition, by the performer at least, of her musical inadequacy. Anyway I learnt nothing, except how to whip up a good tantrum, and crept out unseen, back to my hotel and a comforting Scots High Tea. The phone call came an hour or so later. Could I meet backstage in an hour's time for a conference on the production? I made my way back to the theatre, where the production team were all gathered, along with the two Kenneths, Elizabeth, Harewood, Ian Spurling, the designer of the sets and the unfortunate frock, which he clasped protectively to his hurt body. To make the chat more convivial, the pub around the corner was suggested, and the number of people attending the conference was cut down to a few.

I was asked, after being told that Miss Corri was indisposed (of course I already knew that – anyone would be after such a histrionic performance, but I didn't let them know I knew), whether I felt able to do all the performances; and if I did, was I prepared to. I had no option but to say yes.

Adrienne got a lot of publicity for her dislike of the production, and for her statement – no animosity felt on any side and so on. It all seemed a bit distasteful to me, but I was new to these theatrical politics that evidently were quite normal practice. I didn't get much thanks for my efforts from the critics, who would have preferred to see the ladies who had deserted the ship. But I got much satisfaction out of the experience.

My weeks in Edinburgh were taken up by visits to all the exhibitions I could fit in during the day, with the evenings filled with the usual social invitations sent to artists performing at the festival. Most times I was accompanied by Ian Spurling, the designer (who had been discovered by Kenneth MacMillan at an end-of-term exhibition at the Slade School of Art and who later lived with us for a while) and Anya Linden, the dancer on loan from the Royal Ballet Company, who was to become Lady Sainsbury. John had an appearance with his big band during the season, and stayed on for a while to be with me. One evening, coming to pick me up soon after the show had finished, as he walked through the theatre to look for me, he heard me singing, at the top of my voice, a song that had nothing to do with the opera. A few seconds later, he heard the flush of a toilet. Arriving backstage he was nonplussed by the absence of a physical Cleo, when her voice was sailing around the theatre in this eerie fashion.

I eventually appeared from the toilet quite oblivious of my ghostly presence filling the airwaves. I had inherited the body mike hired for Lotte Lenya, which was a new experience for me. It was a very early cumbersome model compared to the ones in use today, but I was happy to put it to use, the only trouble with not being familiar with the mechanics of such high-tech equipment (as it was to me then) being that I tended to forget to switch it off. The toilet incident taught me to be on guard.

I got an awful lot of mileage out of the role of Anna: I performed it as a concert piece at the Glasgow Proms, again with Sir Alexander Gibson and the Scottish Symphony Orchestra, and in another production in the US for the Michigan Opera Theatre, whose director, David Dichiera, gave me much early support in America. The more I did the work, the more I loved it, and each time it and I became stronger.

Before I had gone to work on *The Seven Deadlies* I had been in the recording studios and had recorded a song called 'You'll answer to me'. I hadn't liked the song all that much, but to please my recording manager, Jack Baverstock, who was head of Fontana Records (a subsidiary of Philips Records at the time) I agreed to do it, thinking it would be lost in the morass that fails to see the light of day in the record business. While I sang my nightly operatic role in culture-heavy surroundings, this little country and western song that I had covered for the British market – sung in the US by Patti Page but doing nothing there – was oozing its way out of the mire and into the spotlight. I had two important phone calls while I was in bonnie Scotland, one from Jack Baverstock telling me the record was moving, the other from my manager Dick Katz, to say he had got me a *Sunday Night at the London Palladium*, one of the most important television programmes at the time, for plugging a song that was looking healthy, although at the bottom of the charts. I agreed to do it, and when *The Seven Deadly Sins* transferred to the Sadlers Wells Theatre in London, and I was the operatic lead, my simple little single rose to number four in the charts. It was my first and only single to get that high.

The hit record and the opera diva image made me the flavour of the year: I was suddenly invited to do television galore as a guest and eventually I was asked to do a series of my own called *One Man's Music*. This entailed learning the lyrics of ten songs a week, and sometimes the tunes of composers like Gershwin, Jerome Kern, Rogers and Hart, Cole Porter, and Coward. Critics couldn't divorce me from my jazz background, or come to that, the knowledge that I was the outcome of a mixed marriage, and the very thought of me singing 'Don't put your daughter on the stage Mrs Worthington' rather than the blues was too much for them to take, so the more a song or composer lent itself to a jazz rendering, the better the review. In the end I stopped reading them.

The series was an all-consuming period of work for John, David Lindup and myself; John and David did all the orchestrations. Looking back now it was a marathon of music and song that was set for us, much of which was successful. I acquired a repertoire of songs that has given me and audiences huge pleasure over the years.

21

From Cinderella to Lysistrata

While we pitched into all this work our family was growing older in years and stronger in personality. Alec was then two years old, a determined young man with a developing sense of humour that John was beginning to enjoy – or maybe it was John who enjoyed being funny for him. John would pick him up in his arms and carry him around the house pointing to objects a two-year-old would find impossible to name, like 'radiator'; but because Alec had a parrot-like ear, after a couple of promptings he would repeat the word in his high-pitched baby voice. It got so crazy that in the end the baby was prattling out such words as 'anti-disestablishment' with as much pleasure as it gave John to hear him.

Stuart, at sixteen, was catching up on his education at a boarding school in the west of England and growing into a very handsome teenager, with all the problems that go with adolescence. He was also discovering along the way that he had an eye for fine art, passing his exams to go on to further education and the study of graphic design. We had become a strong family unit, with home life and work at last moving along on well-oiled tracks.

We had good local friends, some in the art world, like Derrick Greaves and his wife Johnnie, who lived in Woburn, Tod Wye and her husband Eric, the Hayneses and Mr O'Hara, who walked our dog Ella and her sons Miles and Westbrook almost till the day he died. Our parties were always good fun, pretty loose and easy affairs, and all the above were invited to any gathering, along with next-door neighbour Ted Miller, until we bought his cottage, and could continue into the early hours. Not that Ted cared about our noise.

When I had got through re-covering the three-pound three-piece suite (it didn't bear close inspection), the Nether Hall party scene got into full swing. We had one not long after Ian Spurling came to stay with us, and he artistically tarted up the house for the occasion. We invited everyone we could think of, and most came, from the people I had worked with in the theatre to all the members of John's band, his racing driver friend Les Leston, and cricket player Ted Dexter.

My three-piece suite stood up well to a heavy bashing that night. Towards the end of the evening Ian became emotional about a film star whom he thought had been neglected, and started to cry on her behalf. The scene made our neighbour, who had said goodnight and was on his way out, turn and say in his wonderful, rolling, down-to-earth West Country accent, 'I was going, but I think I'll stay now, it looks like we might have a "Hemingway" ending.' Pa was also back in our midst enjoying all the attention, showing off his singing and what he thought was expert tango dancing: he loved the children and they responded to his obvious childlike delight in them.

My hit record enabled us to make lots of improvements to the house and garden. One of the first buys was a load of gravel to make the paths around the house look handsome. What with painting the outside and decorating the inside, it seemed as if there was an eternal builder in the place. Then, when our neighbour moved, we knocked through into the cottage – yet more building and decorating. The house was also filling up with furniture bought at auctions and antique shops, spotted wherever I was playing on the road. We were settling in, it seemed, for ever.

* * *

The year 1962 brought an amazing variety of music and theatre my way, all of which left me with good friends and memories; some gave me anxieties, but all endowed me with just a little more experience for my next serendipity plunge. The play *A Time to Laugh*, a first play by the American writer Robert Crean, though not a success, brought me to the West End in a straight play with Robert Morley – the supreme prankster, on and offstage. One of the reasons I was given the part was because Robin Fox had seen me at the Royal Court and had recommended me to Tyrone Guthrie as a natural-haired West Indian. For the interview I wore a straight wig, but when I was told the part was to be portrayed by a West Indian girl, I exposed my true colours by removing the unnatural straightness.

It was a United Nations cast headed by Robert and Ruth Gordon, a spiky American actress who had a very strange delivery; then there was the intense British actor Lyndon Brook and equally serious Frances Hyland from Canada. Australian Michael Blakemore was not revealing his directing expertize to us, but was extremely miffed by the constant shortening of the role he had been signed up to play, which was not large to start with; he obviously thought he could do something with it, given the chance, and be noticed if he got it right. He told me he would be on guard in the future, to see that the part he read was the one he was signing the contract for, when it was already so small. He advised me to do the same. The difficulty is always how much weight you have in the first place. Anyway, I noted what he said. And although the play didn't please the critics, it was wonderful to have the experience of being directed by Tyrone Guthrie, the legendary director.

Round about the end of June I was pregnant – and overjoyed. It didn't stop me from performing, continuing up to a few weeks before my daughter was born.

I was three or four months pregnant when I became the subject of a dreadful *This is Your Life* that the BBC perpetrated on me.

The researcher must have had a bad day, when assigned the job. None of my family were invited on, no musicians from the days of The Seven; they just about squeezed John in at the end, and there were many guests who had nothing at all to do with me or my life. I did a lot of play-acting that night.

The next pregnant assignment was the Royal Command Performance, in the presence of the Queen and Prince Philip. Now here was a problem I had to solve quickly, how to look reasonably glamorous with the amount of weight I had started to put on. Tod Wye came to the rescue, recommending a friend of hers who designed a wonderful dress that looked fashionably sexy, yet kept all eyes away from the frontal bump that was starting to assert itself. I felt completely confident and relaxed on that, my first Command Performance, all due I'm sure to my future daughter, who brought me good luck. It was a star-studded cast, shared equally between American and British artists, such as Sir Harry Secombe, Cliff Richard, The Shadows, Frank Ifield, Dickie Henderson, Andy Stewart, Edmundo Ros, John Dankworth for the UK, with Bob Hope, Eartha Kitt, Sophie Tucker, Edie Adams, Rosemary Clooney for the US.

After that experience I was ready to stay at home, taking it easy until the baby was born, which I did for a delectable while, till I got the phone call. Ned Sherrin and Caryl Brahms had written a show based on *Cinderella*, only it was going to be called *Cindy Ella* and take place in the South of the United States. Would I play the part of Cindy Ella? 'You do realize that I am extremely pregnant?' I said. 'Oh, that won't matter,' said Michael Codron, the same man who had presented *Valmouth*. 'You'll be sitting down reading from books, no one will notice. We have Elizabeth Welch, Cy Grant and George Brown, and would love you to join the cast – it will all be very simple and no strain on you.'

I had to think this one over, also to find out if there was any danger involved, as there had been with Alec. I was given the all-clear by my doctor and I agreed. Although I had been told that I would not have to learn the part, because we would be reading, I did commit it to memory as I found reading didn't allow me to get the most out of the parts. I say 'parts' because as well as our main roles, we played other characters as well.

As the rehearsals got underway the director Colin Grahame got more and more ambitious and started to move us around, discarding the idea of book-reading for ever. I managed to get what I hadn't learnt under my belt, but Elizabeth, who had left the learning process a lot later, was having a struggle, so I went to stay with her and between us, working late into the night, we licked the problem and became a moving company. Tony Walton created a dress that entirely hid the Cinderella's eight-month pregnancy and the show opened as a charming matinee-only event at the Garrick Theatre just before Christmas 1962. In the evenings at the same theatre Sheila Hancock and Edward Woodward were performing *The Rattle of a Simple Man* – so Sheila and I were together again, if not in play, at least in spirit.

Caryl and Ned had many performances one way and another with that show. We repeated it at the Arts Theatre, did a television show of it and made a record. Later, with a different cast, they did a larger production.

Early in February, I once again beat the doctor and gave birth, with the help of a student nurse, to my first and only daughter. The young nurse asked me for the name of the baby immediately after her birth. 'I don't have a name for her yet,' I laughed, as I lay in the delivery room, alone with the baby and inexperienced nurse. 'But I must have one, to put a tag around her wrist,' she said. 'What's wrong with Dankworth?' 'Oh that's a surname,' came the reply. 'How many Dankworths have given birth recently?' I asked, after her explanation that surnames only, could, if they were Smith, Brown, Jones, or even Harris, cause a possible mix-up of babies. She was getting so upset, that off the top of my head the baby became Jacqueline, and was tagged there and then by the relieved nurse.

John was once again embroiled with a big band, but this time I held my tongue and picture arm in check. Not long after Jackie's birth I had a call to go to Germany to do some television. I made it an opportunity to take Alec with me so that he could have me to himself for a while. As a rule I didn't like having the children around when I was working – I found that my concentration was divided and both suffered. I would become a nag with the children, get angry with myself for losing my temper, and then I'd not work well. But it was obvious that Alec's nose had been put out of joint by the new arrival and he was feeling neglected. So leaving Jackie at home, I brought along Tod Wye whom he was fond of, and in the snow-bound Strasses of Berlin, the little three-year-old enjoyed the complete attention of us both.

I had put on a tremendous amount of weight carrying Jacqueline and decided I had either to buy a complete new wardrobe or lose it. I was well over twelve stone and at my height it was not healthy. I was recommended to a Harley Street doctor who, with daily injections, soon got my weight down to nine stone. I looked just right and my sea-green mermaid, made for my Savoy date, fitted me once more.

The work of the sixties never let up. John was involved with more and more film writing, which enabled him to subsidize the big band, and keep it on the road, while I became one of the performers in the fantastically popular television series *That Was The Week That Was*. What an amazing show that was: so much talent and Ned Sherrin such a brilliantly imaginative producer/director. He was the commander-in-chief, but allowed the personalities of the actors, singers and commentators to shine through: David Frost, Michael Crawford, John Bird, Millicent Martin, Willie Rushton, Bernard Levin, Eleanor Bron and many more.

My small contribution was to sing solo songs by Caryl Brahms and the occasional jazz duet with the multi-talented Millicent Martin, who was permanently on the show, with a sketch from time to time. I think I missed the opportunity of becoming a regular sketch performer when I messed up a solo piece given to me to do one week, that amazed everyone by my stupidity. I had to talk with a Southern American accent, which was not a problem – that I could do – it was my non-dyslexic delivery of the lines that stunned and amazed. It was one of many in a group of rearranged cliché sayings from films, to be delivered one after the other, in an offhand manner. My contribution was a cynically twisted, maudlin bit from a movie, which I had to read: 'You ain't gonna live and win the Kentucky Derby little fella, you're gonna die.' What came out of my mouth was the original 'You ain't gonna die little fella, you're gonna live and win the Kentucky Derby.' Live on air! David Frost looked at me, slightly bemused, and said, 'Yes! Well, yes!' That was the end of my sketch career. They missed a golden chance, though – they could have built me up as the dim one.

The weekly duets were exciting songs to perform, contributing to improving all the natural assets that I had, while giving me confidence to experiment and uncover the hidden ones. The John Scott tune, with words by Caryl Brahms, called 'Woman Talk', is a classic from the show, written for Millicent and me. I sang the tenor sax part, improvised by Duncan Lamont, while John Scott's alto part was sung by Millicent. It was one of the most successful of that genre performed on the show. I later recorded it as a solo piece, as did Carmen McRae after hearing my version.

When the show ended, not long after, a new one was created called *Not So Much a Programme, More a Way of Life*. In this show I was, along with Annie Ross, part of the regular team. It was yet another controversial and highly stylized show.

During these shows I became aware of fashion being an asset for a performer, when a talented young lady got in touch to ask if she could dress me for the shows. She became my first 'Frockologist', a word I coined for a person who knows your figure so well that you can trust her to create an individual style for you that works. Alice Pollock came along at the right time, to the benefit of both our careers. She had opened a small workroom and had joined forces with a young man who was to become one of the top designers of the sixties and seventies: Ossie Clark. Between them they gave a huge boost to my fashion sense, though later on, when they had expanded out of all proportion, I no longer felt at home when I visited; though Alice was still loyal, she was generally tied up with the model girlfriends of all the current pop groups, so I slowly and quietly tailed off my visits.

Then into my life came Gerry Bedrich, who remained a serious Frockologist for me until he gave up the fashion world in despair, a great loss for me. Gerry and his wife Avril had two shops in Woburn Sands, next to our village of Aspley Guise. When he introduced himself, it transpired that he had worked in the theatre in London, in fact he had worked on the production of *Cindy Ella*, unbeknownst to me, so he had a good theatrical eye. His contacts on my behalf, before they became internationally known, now read like a *Who's Who* of the fashion industry: John Bates, Bill Gibbs, Ian and Marcel, Zandra Rhodes and many more.

During the 1962 Bath Festival John and I were first introduced to Princess Margaret and Lord Snowdon. We were there for the première of a piece of John's that had been commissioned by the festival for the then artistic director, Yehudi Menuhin, and himself, with Maurice Gendron and Raymond Leppard performing it. It was a very special occasion. Ted Leather, who was the Conservative MP for Somerset at the time, planned a party after the concert for the newly married royal couple and the artists involved, along with local dignitaries and other festival performers. The party was highly successful, with a most relaxed atmosphere, due in the main to the jazz musicians who were present – Chris Barber, Ottilie Patterson, John and myself of course, and a few side men, who played into the early hours of the next day, which was a Sunday.

Evidently there was a bishop, the Right Reverend Edward Henderson, at the party. His presence, along with a member of the royal family, at such heathen goings on, upset the Lord's

Day Observance Society, who seemed to have their spies poised to pounce at such events. They told the newspapers they were 'disgusted at a member of the Royal Family and a member of the Bench of Bishops spending the Lord's day in such a fashion, they should have set a better example'. Jeremy Fry and his wife Camilla, with whom the Snowdons were staying at Widcombe Manor while attending the Festival, did not improve the situation by inviting us all to another get-together the next day (Sunday) – though Princess Margaret did go to morning service.

The Frys' party was even better than the first, with Yehudi Menuhin, who was very much involved with Indian music, culture and Yoga, demonstrating his superb calm when he was implored to do a Yoga headstand; without flinching he did a graceful movement into the beneficial pose, after which he was free to enjoy his evening. Princess Margaret became a loyal and good friend from then on, supporting not only our appearances but also the Wavendon Music Centre that we created at the beginning of the 1970s. There was a period when it seemed we met every week, when Quentin and Angela Crewe came to live near us. The Snowdons often came as house guests to Angela's; when they did, we were always part of the small get-togethers, when our sing-song routines were built up, crazy word games played, and early morning scrambled eggs cooked in the large kitchen before the gathering broke up and we drove back to Nether Hall.

Quentin was the restaurant critic for *Queen* magazine and had discovered a place with food that was out of this world but on the wrong side of the tracks. He invited us and Princess Margaret along to sample the fruits of his latest discovery – the 555, in Battersea Park Road. I don't think Quentin informed the owner as to who was in the party he was bringing, as there was a rather rowdy group of young men in the corner when we arrived. The café, because that is what it was, was minuscule, but because of the various write-ups it had had for its exceptional food, it was now the 'in' place.

When we arrived the noisy group was in full swing: it was

a beautifully drunk, before-the-wedding stag party. They took no mind of us and we none of them, until they started singing a rather risqué song, which the men in our party were obviously embarrassed about on the ladies' behalf, but didn't want to be the spoilsports of the men's night of fun. I knew the song was going to get worse, from my Croydon party days, and decided I would start a Cockney piece to counter what was coming up, one that we all could join in and enjoy. So standing up and with the strongest accent I could muster, I let rip with a medley of all the Cockney songs I could remember, starting with 'I'm Henery the Eighth I Am' and finishing with 'There was I waitin' at the Church'. My coach trips were paying off at last.

The stag party tried to out-sing us for a while, but one of the party noticed the young princess and got them to join in with us, eventually coming over to apologize to Tony. From then on it was a combined sing-song, and lots of good luck to the young bridegroom from all for the next day.

We shared with the Snowdons theatre visits, dinners, concerts, New Year celebrations at Kensington Palace; HRH was house guest at Nether Hall, and made many visits to 'The Stables' for fund-raising concerts. When their marriage broke down and they eventually divorced, we remained friends of both, but saw much more of Princess Margaret.

We made a return visit to the Bath festival in 1964, a reunion for me with the Western Theatre Ballet, this time with Peter Darell choreographing a new work for Bath, written by Benny Green and John for me. It was an anti-war, women's rights comic tragedy based on *Lysistrata*, the lady who tried to stop her man endlessly going off to war by refusing him his conjugal rights. The version they wrote was that story through the ages, ending with the atomic bomb. I sang and moved with the dancers, once again enjoying myself immensely. On the same bill was another new work by my former choreographer Kenneth MacMillan, who had done a duo work for Margot Fonteyn and Rudolf Nureyev, with Yehudi Menuhin playing solo violin on the side of the stage.

From Cinderella to Lysistrata

We were all ready and prepared to do our stuff on the first night, when tragedy struck. News came through that Miss Fonteyn's husband had been shot in Panama. She carried on to dance the first night, knowing, as the audience did, what had happened. The theatre was emotionally charged, as we all realized the overwhelming emotional pain and anxiety she must be going through; at the end of the piece the audience rose as one person to salute the courage of Britain's première dancer. She disappeared, never to be seen again. The brilliant, favourite dancer of MacMillan, Lynn Seymour, took over the part; she performed amazingly at such short notice and I became a fan of this most unusual, modern dancer.

It was that year that I became motherless – though because of the nature of her illness my mother would not have been able to appreciate how far her dreams for one of her daughters had materialized.

The record *Shakespeare and all that Jazz* brought me international acclaim when it was voted the best jazz and contemporary record of the year in the magazine *Downbeat*; they gave it a five-star rating, a rare achievement in the record world. It is one of my favourite albums, one that I am most proud of. My voice was coming together and feeling strong, and I had a feeling that I was able to tackle anything that was put in front of me. There was a lot of challenging music, some of which has never been surpassed in my repertoire, combined with some glorious settings of Shakespeare's great words and sonnets. They have never left my programme: they are timeless and a part of me.

Although the record did so well in the United States and Europe, my agency and management did nothing to push me in that direction. The music business was changing with the advent of rock and roll, and they were making more money by fostering artists who were involved with that kind of music. I started to get discontented with them, and John and I began looking for alternative arrangements. It was some time before we made the change but it eventually happened, after twenty-five years or so with the same management. The association had been a good one, but we had become a fixture, and we at least needed a new broom. On a guest appearance on the *Rolf Harris Television Show* I met Phyllis Rounce, Rolf's manager. I was most impressed with the way she was looking after him, and we approached her to see if she was interested. She was, so we joined International Artists in about 1968 and through her we met our new broom and the next manager to guide our careers, Laurie Mansfield, who became the friend and adviser on the next long exciting journey – one which led to international travel at last.

Before this transition I still had two more Edinburgh Festivals to do, acting in *The Trojan Women* and *A Midsummer Night's Dream*. They came about when Frank Dunlop, who was forming his Pop Theatre Group at the time, heard me sing the Weill/Brecht song 'Surabaya Johnnie' at a tribute concert for George Devine in aid of the the Royal Court Theatre. Frank was the first director to ignore the fact that as far as classic plays were concerned, I was thought of as a black actress.

Those two theatre experiences were giant steps in my so far meagre career as an actress. The *Trojan Women* part was another strong dramatic role which obviously suited me, as I received excellent notices, along with a great cast, including Flora Robson, Moira Redman, Jane Asher and Esmond Knight. Our production of *A Midsummer Night's Dream* was, as far as I know, the first in Britain to have one person – me – play the roles of both Titania and Hippolyta. Robin Bailey doubled as Theseus and Oberon.

Frank had also cast live hounds, which ran through the audience at about the same time as the conversation between Theseus and Hippolyta about hunting hounds – 'The confusion of hounds and echo in conjunction' and 'So musical a discord, such sweet thunder'. One evening, when we reached this point, with the hounds bounding purposefully through the auditorium, chaos suddenly reigned, as a woman who had a phobia about dogs went into a screaming hysterical fit. They managed to gather up her limp exhausted body and to expedite her exit, and brought her backstage to sit, while calming hands and water were administered. Unfortunately they forgot that with his silent whistle the dog handler was directing the dogs, as he had done nightly, to rally to him backstage too. This time there was utter mayhem as the woman encountered the dogs for a second time. The hounds were not in the least bit put out, going about their duties in a workmanlike and friendly, doggie way. When the production transferred to London, this part was cut; instead, the dogs stood, obediently doleful, by my side on the stage.

During the same run as *The Dream* Frank asked if I would like to play the maid's part in Ionesco's *The Lesson* with Denise Coffey and Bernard Bresslaw. Once again I trod where angels fear to tread and said yes. I made myself look pretty drab, with a scarf tied around my head and a granny pinny over a shapeless skirt and top. I enjoyed experimenting with the makeup as I knew that if I looked too much like Cleo Laine the critics would have a bean feast. One night I had finished putting the last touches to my face when I was called to the stage to rehearse. On the way, John walked past me in the corridor and asked Denise where I was. 'You've just passed her!' Denise told him. 'That was Cleo? I don't believe it! Phew, that's a grim look into the future.'

With Millicent Martin in
That Was the Week That Was

In Oxford with *Here is the News* with (l to r)
Sheila Hancock, Valentine Dyall, Kathy Kenton,
Richard Goulden and Lance Percival

In Nottingham as Mrs Patrick Campbell in
Dear Liar with Strawberry Jam

With Jan Hunt (top) and Lorna Dallas in
Show Boat

3

4

1 With Dudley Moore
2 In *The Merry Widow*
With:
3 Princess Margaret backstage at *The Mystery of Edwin Drood*
4 Rolling Stones drummer Charlie Watts
5 Clark Terry
6 At a Royal Command Perform[a] with the Queen Mother and (l to Sammy Davis Jr, J.D., Arthur As[h] and Terry Scott

1

He Was Beautiful
(Cavatina)

Music by
STANLEY MYERS

Lyr
CLEO

Recorded by
Cleo
Laine

2

1 The first and only jazz singer
to win a Grammy Award

2 The cover of
'He Was Beautiful'

3 With the Muppets

4 In Las Vegas

1 At a reception for the Wavendon All Music Awards with John and Kiri te Kanawa

With:

2 Chic Corea

3 Stephen Sondheim in New York at the 'Cleo sings Sondheim' recording

4 Frank Sinatra at the Albert Hall

5 Joyce Grenfell

6 Douglas Fairbanks Jr in Los Angeles, fund-raising for Sam Wanamaker's Globe Theater and

7 James Galway

5

6

7

With my current musical supporters
1 in England – (l to r) John Horler (piano), Allan Ganley (drums), J.D. (boss), me, Dave O'Higgins (tenor/flute), Malcolm Creese (bass), Bill Le Sage (vibes/piano)
2 in America – (l to r) Ray Loeckle (tenor/flute), Jim Zimmerman (drums), J.D. (boss), me, Marcus McLaurine (bass), Larry Dunlap (piano)

22

Wavendon

At a T.S. Eliot Tribute Concert in 1965, I shared the stage with another group of stage luminaries: Alec McCowan, Clive Revill, Nicol Williamson, Anna Quayle, John Le Mesurier, Roddy Maud Roxby, when John was asked to set to music for the first performance in its entirety of *Sweeney Agonistes, the Aristophanic Fragment*, which a drama critic of *The Times* said, 'uncannily foreshadows British avant-garde drama of the fifties'. We had a great deal of fun rehearsing it, then performing it on the night. At times it was quite chaotic as different directors, involved elsewhere in the evening, wanted their actors to rehearse with exclusively during the day.

This situation came to a head when Peter Wood, our director, needed and was being deprived of Nicol Williamson (who was reciting a long poem in the first half of the evening) for rehearsal. Sending a young and inexperienced assistant to fetch him several times without any result, Peter, in exasperation, told her to go back and say, 'If you do not come immediately, there will be no Sweeney Agonistes in the programme tonight.' As it was the second half of the evening, the by now cowed, demure young person got to the door to leave yet again, thankful to escape his wrath, when Peter Woods added angrily, 'And use my tone of voice!'. An impossibility, but worth a try. Nicol did eventually come and the memorable cast was able to get on with its business and a successful ending.

It was during these rehearsals that I had my encounter with the great Groucho Marx, who was reciting 'Gus the Theatre Cat' that night. The passage backstage at the old Globe Theatre was long and extremely narrow; it was almost impossible to pass anyone without walking side on. On the way to my dressing room, I saw Groucho approaching in my direction, head on, cigar in mouth, nearly using the recognizable walk. I was going to come face to face with this wonderful raconteur, this legend of my childhood cinema days. How could I let such an opportunity pass without saying how much I admired him? Instead I became a tongue-tied idiot, dumbfounded by the sight and close proximity of the genius. What came out when we reached the impassable moment was 'Mr Marx, er, uhm, can I shake your hand?' Still sucking on his cigar, out of the corner of his mouth came: 'Lady, you can shake anything I got!' After I had shaken his hand we squeezed past each other, never to speak again.

From the early sixties and well into the seventies John was working fulltime on film scores, with top British and American directors. Although he worked from home, our time together was often fleeting, as I was touring the country doing cabaret. His presence at home was a great weight off my mind, because it meant that at least one of us was spending time with the children, as they grew older and more demanding, and that one of us was usually there to cope when tables fell on noses, fingers got stuck in swings and near-drownings occurred.

Which reminds me – the drowning, that is. When John was working on Joe Losey's film *Modesty Blaise*, the children and I accompanied him on a trip to Sicily to work on a song for the stars, Monica Vitti and Terence Stamp. The holiday was not a success, the excessive heat and the luxury five-star hotel making the younger children disgruntled, and as soon as we returned home I took a good look at what we had there, right under our noses. First, we employed a couple who looked after our every need. There was also a beautiful well-kept garden, and the children were fed on the dot at mealtimes. All we lacked to make Nether Hall into a holiday heaven was a swimming pool. That was easy to rectify; I started to dig a hole in the back garden. With my anger level still at bubbling point concerning the Sicily family jaunt, the digging was frenzied enough for a pot hole to blossom in to the shape of a grand piano. Clearly something had to be done with this grave at the bottom of the garden before people began to get suspicious. After much heated discussion about my sudden rush of madness, sensible planning and overseeing were instigated and put into operation by J.D. For my part I conscripted the household, from the eager, hindering tinies to a somewhat reluctant teenager. And our live-in couple helped me finish the digging, rolling up their sleeves and getting down to it as if it were an everyday event. Amused by their lady boss, Sarah wielded the barrow while Andres turned out to be an expert cement spreader.

Eventually, with the extra voluntary help of John's big band, my pothole was turned into a landscaped swimming pool. Where the young Dankworths quickly learnt that if they were going to fall in, it would be pleasanter for them if they knew how to swim, rather than be dragged out by their hair. It was one of the most constructive tempers I ever had, as the whole family and many of our friends benefited from the pool for many seasons.

In 1966, the same year that *Modesty Blaise* hit the screens, a domestic drama hit the Dankworth household that was to last for two unsettled years before it was resolved. Up until then, our household had been ticking along as happily as one could expect, with the ups and downs of touring and the usual run of domestic problems. The early morning post often being the messenger of gloom in the past, I had got out of the habit of opening it before I was ready to face the day, a period of time in the morning which always takes longer than I would like it to. This particular morning in the summer of 1966 it was taking even longer than usual. Undressed, un-madeup, dull of head, I unconcernedly opened the first letter of the pile, with little or no curiosity. John was opposite me doing something early morningish, like reading a paper or eating cornflakes, when I burst into uncontrollable laughter at what I had just read. Pulling myself together at last, I said to John, 'Listen to this,' and read part of the letter to him. He took it from me, to see if I had got it right, and did a good job of falling about laughing himself. We stopped laughing when we realized it was not a joke. This letter from the divorce court meant business, and I was the business; it was frighteningly real. I had been cited in a divorce action.

It was the beginning of a couple of strange years, where the onus was on me to prove that what had been alleged was a lot of rubbish – hard to do, especially when it's made-up rubbish. Once it appeared in the papers our lives were invaded in a way unknown before: pictures were found from newspaper files and printed that I had never even seen before, of me looking like a *femme fatale*, which earned knowing winks for me at airports and anger from the devoted fans of John, while eye avoidance in the local shops was noticeable. Almost everyone thinks that 'cited' means that something has been proved; only a few realize it is just an accusation. Our great friend David Lindup was the gentleman I had been accused of spending a weekend with, and it was painful for him that the collapse of his marriage should involve us. Thankfully I had the support of all my close friends and the most important friend of all, John, who was more angry about it than I was and set about not only presenting facts that made the allegations absurd, but campaigning against an unfair law that allowed anyone to cite anyone they chose, only to drop the case at the last minute – which is what happened with ours.

It was when a new date was alleged, on which David and I had spent time in Holland sharing a hotel room the, number of which was cited, that it all collapsed. I had been to Holland with David on the date, that was a fact: he had agreed to oversee the musical arrangements for a TV appearance of mine. John had not planned to be there, but – a development unknown to the citer – his plans changed at the last moment, and he was able to come with us after all. Our lawyer later went to Holland to look at the register of the hotel to check the date, and found that not only were there three signatures, Mr and Mrs Dankworth and David Lindup, in separate rooms of course, but that the alleged room did not exist. The number given was fictitious.

The manager was willing to come to testify on our behalf, at our expense of course. The day the case came up, two years after that funny breakfast letter, the case against me was dismissed, because all allegations had been withdrawn, and nothing about the hotel or any other proof we had came up in court. We of course were happy it had come to a satisfactory end of sorts, as life could now go on relatively as before. Even though I still got those looks for a while.

In March 1969 we were on the move again, this time to the Old Rectory at Wavendon in Buckinghamshire. John was up to his eyes writing music for yet another film at the time, so all the work fell to me and the young man who worked for us as driver and general factotum, Alan Robson. Together we laboured night and day over eight days, packing and loading a large van and making interminable journeys between the two villages of Aspley Guise and Wavendon, which were luckily only a few miles apart.

We had bought the house over a year before, because we liked the stables and the land behind them, and thought this would be an ideal place to start the venture John and I had been incessantly talking about. After years of working at festivals created by people with outhouses, barns and great halls on their properties we found ourselves guests of Sir Nicholas Sekers, the silk manufacturer, while appearing at Rosehill, the theatre in the grounds of his home. Miki, as he was known, was a fanatical patron of the arts, who with the help of theatre designer Oliver Messel had created a miniature theatre from an ancient barn a stone's throw from his house, presenting to Whitehaven and the area his love of music and theatre.

It was at this theatre that John and I had a simultaneous pipe-dream: 'Wouldn't it be wonderful to have a place like this of our own, one day?' These stables looked ideal.

Cleo

The house itself had looked perfectly livable-in when we first viewed it, but a month later looked as if a bomb had hit the interior, as walls were knocked down to open up the dark claustrophobic Victorian passages and rooms of the old rectory. I had been so fed up with the perpetual coming and going of builders at Nether Hall, I felt this time it should all be done before we moved in.

My resolution to face the move cheerfully weakened with each visit to the site, as we clambered over the daunting obstacle course of collapsed bricks and rubble that left open gaps to scramble through, where windows riddled with dry rot had once overlooked a nicely organized garden, turned now to wilderness. Going back to the ordered and gracious Nether Hall after such visits often made me wonder to myself if our decision had been the right one. We took it in turns to wake each other up in the early hours to ask, 'What the hell have we done?' The one awoken would console and reassure the disturber who, comforted, would then go back to sleep, leaving the disturbed one sitting up wide-awake and disturbed.

It all gradually came together, and with our help the architect solved most of the indoor problems. I made several visits to London to select the wallpapers and colour schemes and I planned where the furniture would go in each room in the new house; I'd read somewhere that was a good thing to do, so I tried to do it by the book. I must say that there was very little sorting out or indecision: as we moved furniture from the old house it was set down in its designated place, in the fresh, decorated room of the new. Friends were really impressed and I let them think that that was the real me.

On Sunday 23 March 1969 we spent our first night at the Old Rectory. It was home; it felt comfortable and friendly immediately, as if I had lived there always, without any disturbing feelings. If you believe, as I do, that a building holds and retains within its walls the history of past occupants and that they exude the atmosphere of love or evil, passing it to the next owner to cope with as best they can, then you will understand how I felt. The house oozed out so much warmth and love that all my previous fears of leaving our first home departed, never to return. I pass by our old house often without a second look of regret or sadness.

Alec was the only one who had doubts about leaving the swimming pool permanently, for someone other than himself to enjoy; at one point he expressed a wish that we should smash it to pieces. I think he was more disturbed by the move than any of us.

Jackie seemed to take it in her stride, until she had to leave her old school to attend the new one in the village. I had enrolled her and seen her happily installed – at least she seemed to be, but there was a slight cloud at meal times that made me ask her if she had any problems at school: was she liking it, what were the teachers like, and the lessons? 'Well,' she said, 'It's all right . . . but it's a bit babyish.' I found this amusing coming from a six-year-old, until she explained that she was in the youngest class, who were having reading lessons. As she had left the other school a good reader and well advanced in her arithmetic lessons it did seem a bit odd. Making enquiries at the school later, I discovered that the cause of Jackie's advanced brainpower, which they were well aware of in the infant class, lay at my hands, and not in my exalted genes; I had inadvertently put the wrong date of birth when I enrolled her, making her almost two years younger than she was. As I was away when all this had to be explained to the headmistress, John took on the duty and got it quickly rectified, returning home with the message from the head that maybe Jacqueline's mother should return to school for arithmetic lessons. I hung my head in shame.

The Old Rectory brought the two families, the Dankworths and the Campbells, together in a way that Nether Hall never quite achieved. I think each family felt more welcome in the Rectory, so that family gatherings became the norm – headed by John's mother and my father, in a musical tradition that I'm sure the old Victorian rectory was no stranger to, at least hymnwise. John and I brought in different sounds, for them there walls to sop up; but the two elders kept up tradition at all the anniversaries and holidays they attended in the long two-pianoed room, with songs like 'Speak to me Thora', 'Smiling Through', 'The Rose of Tralee' and Joyce Kilmer's 'Trees'.

The first Christmases, when my father and Ma Dankworth were alive and literally still kicking, were the real humdinger get-togethers. Starting with the dreaded list-making, for presents, sleeping arrangements, food buying, cooking and oh! everything. I can't believe it's true, it was so long ago, but I did it myself; I didn't like it at the time and I shudder at the thought of it now. John and I always had a good row beforehand. The thought of going through what we considered days wasted on non-musical pursuits was a tug-of-war for us both, between thoughts of utter joy, misery, the call of duty and a rip-roaring two days of joining in with friends and family; we wasted a lot of energy being depressed about what always turned out to be a musical beano anyway. We resisted, but always gave in with a good grace. The children, of course, loved all the preparations and the exciting build-up, being as secretive about their purchases, or lovingly stitched, painted or built hand-mades as I was about my arrangements.

The whole procedure started with Christmas Eve, with most of the family turning up over the next three days: Ma Dankworth, John's sister Avril, Pa, my brother and his wife Beryl, my sister and her husband Geoff and family, together with lots of our friends. The carol-singers would come to the door as we finished supper; the hall table already had a tray set with glasses, wine, sherry, soft drinks and mince-pies awaiting them. We would sit and listen to the distant voices singing their first carol, then we would all leave the table, and greet them at the front door. Off we'd go. The hall of the Old Rectory, much enlarged now, with acoustics to match, would suddenly resound with hearty, full-throated, robust singing, as we all joined in, with harmonies thrown in for good measure by those who knew, or by anyone bold enough to have a go at 'Once in Royal David's City' or 'I Saw Three Ships'.

Once started, there was no turning back, we had begun the three days of a good sing. Pa, the non-believer, was in his element, singing louder than all the rest. When everyone in the house had chosen and heartily participated in their favourite tune, the session finished with the seasonal toast, while the youngsters could at last go over and admire the trimmings on the Christmas tree, simultaneously scoffing mince pies and gulping lemonade. When the carol singers had gone, come what may, we would all, believers and non-believers, walk to Wavendon village church just before midnight to join in another hearty bout of singing. How or why Pa came to join us at this point I didn't dare ask.

After the inexplicable sense of calm and wonder in the church, the short walk back to the Rectory in the invigorating air would bring us back to earth: to the tasks still to be done before bedtime. John and I were the ones who did the stocking-filling, sometimes dressing up as Father Christmas, while the others had last drinks and did last-minute wrapping of gifts.

This was never a problem for Pa; he came with his presents already wrapped, in crumpled, split, brown paper bags. His gifts were always anticipated, for their amusement value alone. All his grandchildren loved him, for his stories, his cheating at cards or any game they talked him into playing, and his eccentric gifts. Watches that didn't go, or had some of the false diamonds missing, paper bags full of chocolates, apples, tangerines and socks the length of which went well past a kneecap and many more completely unsuitable, useless seconds, from a source unknown. I think most of them were left-over goods he couldn't sell from his business on the side, goods we always said had probably fallen off the back of a lorry. He was quite unembarrassed when I told him I knew about him going to the local pub when he visited us, trying to sell watches. Watches that he hid up his arm, eventually to reveal during a chummy drink with the locals. I was so angry with him when I first found out, and told him it had to stop. Some people thought it was very funny, but I didn't.

Christmas Day was like most households, except possibly for

the evening music-making: too much food, too much drink, gifts under the tree, gifts in all the children's pillow cases, visitors popping in, dressing up, crackers, paper hats and arguments. Ma Dankworth loved to sing and play the piano, and Pa loved to sing, dance and show off, so between them they led the musical evening. Pa would pounce on any lady guest at hand to sway her into the tango or a gyrating Charleston, often to the jangle-box sound of the two-piano duetting of Laurie Holloway and John, or Paul Hart and John, or John Taylor or any one of my early pianists; forsaking, for a few moments, their musical esotery to entertain the elders with a medley of tangos and Charlestons, two-steps and waltzes. Everyone had to contribute, playing an instrument, reciting a poem, telling a joke or story.

All this came to an end when my father and Ma Dankworth died within a couple of years of each other at the beginning of the eighties. But the seventies saw many happy parties at the house and we were enjoying the Old Rectory to the full.

We had altered the inside considerably, giving it a much-needed gust of light, while the outside stood, firmly Victorian Gothic, handsomely daring anyone to touch. The house has its history, written about proudly in local pamphlets. It looks extremely impressive and even daunting from the outside, especially to some Americans, who think I live in a castle and have a ghost, neither of which I deny; I cannot be accused of fantasizing, since our music-loving ghost has been sighted by others as well as me.

The real reason for our having moved to the Old Rectory was to some extent being overshadowed by the enjoyment we were deriving from it; our dream could have been forgotten for ever, during the long period of procrastination that attacked us both after each visit to the stables, the proposed theatre site. The place was in a dire state, having functioned as a nut and bolt factory until recently. So thick was the layer of oil, mingled with the dust and dirt of years of neglect, that after the hard work of moving, facing up to the task involved took time. Our inactivity hung about for quite some time before our initial plan was put into operation – eventually with a vigour that surprised even us.

By now our ideas were clearer. What we wanted was a music centre that would present all kinds of music and entertainment, side by side with courses that taught all kinds of music. We wanted to break down barriers and create understanding for different styles of music. It was obviously idealistic, but we knew that there were a lot of artists who already felt the same way as we did, and if we could persuade them to support us, that would be an important start.

Our next move was to get the village on our side, by killing the rumour that it was going to be a swinging night club. We also had to get our freedom from the church, to perform secular music in public on property that had once belonged to the church: a kind of deconsecration. I could never understand why this was necessary, as it hadn't been used as a rectory for years, but we had to get on with our plans or they would never come to fruition.

We needed a launching concert to explain our ideas to everyone, which meant fast work on that filthy stable. All hands were put to the hose: Alan Robson, me, J.D., volunteers from the village, the children and their friends, all laboured to get it clean enough to paint, lay a carpet, dress it up. The village of Wavendon became a beehive of industry, as people came and went, toting paint pots and whitewash, making curtains, building staging. It reminded me of many a film musical I'd seen: 'Heh! let's put on a show!' Once all that energy was mobilized, the bustle and buzz generated towards the opening concert became magnetically powerful; it would have been impossible to stay the momentum if we had had a change of heart. I, an inveterate phone-hater, was on the phone continually, asking favours of local food shops and businesses: the volunteer caterers needed food, the raffle needed donations of goods of all kinds, and the stables needed friends to perform.

Hour by hour it gradually came together. Our friends con-tributed their talent: Derrick Greaves painted pictures as a backdrop for the stage, John Neville sang and compered, Cy Grant, Richard Rodney Bennett, David Snell, Rhonda Gillespie, Frances Baines all played a part. John Williams not only played the guitar, he knocked nails into a wooden fence to pretty up the outside. I could not bear to be near as he happily hammered large nails, for fear of hearing the cry of pain that must surely come when he hit his thumb or one of those valuable fingers, but I was spared my agony; no cry came and the fence finally went up.

The eventual concert was a great success, bringing us financial support from the public and the Milton Keynes Development Corporation (who had appeared from out of nowhere on our undesignated doorstep), providing our first administrator, Lavinia Dyer, a lady commander of the ship, who saw that things were run smoothly during trying times, looking after the needs of artists who were performing for nothing or a pittance to help get The Wavendon Allmusic Plan off the ground, while also smoothing the temperaments of all concerned. Although many were in the business, like Quentin Lawrence, the TV director, and his son Stephen, Garfield Morgan, the actor, who lived nearby and was theatre manager for the early years, it was a mixed bag of expertise and willing hands from the village and friends and volunteers from the surrounding area.

WAP was launched, but it always needed more money, as charity always seem to. Fund-raising events for the Stables brought stars galore to grand balls and garden fêtes, but we could never have got WAP started without all our old and new friends – including Princess Margaret, who over the years has supported us so loyally, coming to concerts, opening the extension from a 150- to a 300-seater one, also being the main fund-raiser and presenter of awards to musicians of all kinds. The names of those who have given in some way to WAP are too numerous to mention, but I would like to give a heartfelt thank you all to those who had faith in our aims.

At one fête we not only had an autograph signing stand but a tent called 'Cleo's Clobber', the result of a vast emptying of drawers, closets, wardrobes and shelves – things I had no more

224

need of, but were too good to throw away. I had spent the night before writing out tickets with what I thought were reasonable prices, to pin to all the bits and pieces, from cast-off children's clothes to old work clothes of mine. On the day of the fête, as I came down the stairs with a large bundle of these goodies in my arms, the front door was suddenly flung open and a bright and cheerful voice called out, 'Cooeee!! Anyone at home? I'm here!!' Joyce Grenfell had arrived to lend a hand. 'What have you got there, Cleo? You look mightily weighed down, can I help?'

When Joyce saw my marked prices, she realized that here was someone who didn't know what a charity garden fête was about, and she immediately set about re-pricing and re-tagging everything. I was quite happy for Joyce to be a bossy-boots, and to let her preside over the hugely successful sale in the tent. If things were not moving she gave the crowd a shove, with a jolly pep talk in the style of St Trinian's, or with the ease and expertise of a barrow boy in full flight in Petticoat Lane.

Joyce was one of our biggest supporters, performing her one-woman shows at the Stables on several occasions. I had met her for the first time in June 1970, when we started rehearsals for *Where are the songs we sung?*, a musical birthday tribute to Noël Coward for the Aldeburgh Festival, with Richard Rodney Bennett and Benjamin Luxon. The show was devised by Colin Grahame, who was firmly established as the director of Benjamin Britten's operas by then, at Aldeburgh and elsewhere. We rehearsed at Richard's home, as he was going to do all the piano playing and arranging of songs that were new to us all.

One of the privileges of being a performer is the kick you sometimes get from meeting an artist you have admired from afar, especially if it's before you are one yourself. Such was the case for me with Joyce, the lady whose singing intrigued me enough to want to imitate the way she sang a certain tune by Richard Addinsell called 'I'm Going to See You Today'. Her sound was unforced in tune and true, qualities I found missing in so many before I became a professional singer. I loved the lilt of the song and the powerful way in which she expressed the lyrics (written by her). I became a fan, going to see her West End shows as well, to discover her comic side.

On meeting her at that first rehearsal, I found her to be as natural as her voice; a voice she was strangely unsure of, in a way that she most certainly was not about most things. Richard and I were constantly reassuring her that she was on pitch, as she called it, never thinking much of her own vocal ability. We got on well together immediately, despite a certain disparity of age and background, often falling about like a couple of silly schoolgirls if anything tickled our fancy. At one rehearsal of the Coward show the four of us had to sing sections of the song 'Mad Dogs and Englishmen'. Coming to the 'doo-wacka-doo' bit, an accidental slip of the tongue from Joyce made the phrase sound a little risqué and even more nonsensical than it actually is. We were all unable to contain ourselves when we realized the slip, breaking down into hysterical, helpless, leg-crossing laughter. The more we tried when we arrived at that section in the song, the worse we got, to the chagrin of Colin who had, up to the collapse, been directing our movements but was now sitting silently, patiently in the dark, waiting for the adult professionals up on the stage, behaving like one of Joyce's nursery sketches, to pull themselves together so that he could carry on. Several minutes elapsed, as we tried to resume, only to break down in a heap yet again. Colin, wanting to get on, became very cross and boomed out to us from the stalls, rather like a nursery school teacher, 'Very well, get it out of your systems and then maybe we can get on?' This should have brought us to our senses, but it was a hard struggle before we gained control.

This side of Joyce was very endearing: she was the oldest of us, and one would have thought it would have been she who called us to order, but she was the most collapsible of the lot, enjoying a good laugh and disliking anyone with airs or graces. We spent many happy hours together in the tea-shop near the hall, where we would sit and talk seriously about the show. Often, chatting about an awkward moment that had to be sorted out, she'd suddenly stop, midstream, put a hand on my arm and indicate with her eyes to listen to a couple talking near at hand; it was either an accent that had caught her ear or something that one of the 'woofers and weavers', as she called them, had said: ladies generally dressed from head to toe in hand-woven tweeds, crop-haired and rosy of face. Joyce always had an ear cocked, seldom missing a juicy everyday comment she could use.

Her last but one performance was at the Stables, a fund-raiser. Later on, we gave a concert in her memory, and many of her friends came to celebrate her life, in word and song. Reggie Grenfell gave permission for J.D. to set an undated poem Joyce had written, and I sang it at the end of the show.

> If I should go before the rest of you
> Break not a flower nor inscribe a stone,
> Nor when I'm gone speak in a Sunday voice
> But be the usual selves that I have known
> Weep if you must, parting is hell,
> But life goes on, so sing as well.

When, after a period of continual touring in cabaret, John asked me where I would like to go for a restful holiday, I was so exhausted that I said, 'I don't want to make any decisions, surprise me.' I flew from somewhere in the North to meet John at London airport, closing my eyes and ears to any clue that might tell me what he had arranged – I was hoping for a remote desert island. It was impossible to keep it secret once we got on the plane, which was an Air Malta one. It was an island all right, but not my idea of a dreamy desert one. I kept my disappointment to myself, as John explained to me the reason for his choice: it was a time when there were restrictions on how much money you could spend on foreign travel, and Malta's sterling currency enabled us to take a few more pounds out of the country.

We stayed at a newly built luxury hotel. It was a handsome place, living up to its luxury image, quite at odds with the tiny island, which could not be called luxurious. During the first week we made a leisurely tour of the island, discovering villages, cities, towns and beaches. There were caves of early man proudly shown to us on the island and some areas that had a history dating back to biblical times – and then of course there are the famous 'Knights'. Within the first week we both fell madly in love with the island, enough to send us on a house search.

We eventually found an old house in Birkakara, which we started to renovate with the help of Jusuf Hurst, the husband of actress Jean Kent, who had lived on the island long before it became a British tourist trap. There were a lot of British actors and actresses in Malta, most of whom we met at the innumerable parties we were invited to as soon as the word got around that we were inhabitants. In the end we found these parties so incessantly British that we opted out of as many as we could. However, we had a group of real friends who made our stays enjoyable: Jean and Jusuf were the closest, but there were also the painter Jason Monet and Doris, his Maltese wife, the actress Dawn Adams and her husband Jimmie White, both avid yachtsmen, and the two jazz-loving brothers, the marquises Pat and Joe Scicluna – all of whom were permanent residents and had close relations with the Maltese, either by birth, marriage or preference.

I have yet to meet a people as friendly as the Maltese who, unlike the land they have to work, are hospitable and warm, from the very young to the most ancient. Our family also loved the island: Alec and Jackie spent most of their long childhood school holidays there, both summer and Christmas, along with musician friends and our parents.

It was in Malta that I started writing seriously: falling in love with that hot, religious country inspired me to compose the first 'important' lyric of my career, as well as three more for the *Best Friends* album, our first with John Williams. We had been trying to sort all the lyrics out before our holiday, and on one of the meetings with John, at his home, I heard him playing the haunting melody 'Cavatina'. I was so moved by it, and by his playing, that I asked if it had a lyric, because if it did it would be wonderful to include it on the album. He said there were no lyrics that he knew of. I felt so strongly about the melody that I asked if words could be written: would he mind recording it again? John said he didn't and the wheels were set in motion by the publishers to get a professional to write some. But nothing had arrived before we left for Malta. All through our holiday the tune stayed with me. No matter how I tried to dismiss it, I found myself continually singing or humming it; while at the same time the first line 'He was beautiful', then 'beautiful to my eyes', persistently came into my head along with the tune. I didn't want the idea of using the song to fizzle out, so that was how I came to finish the song. But on the very day we went into the studios to record; someone finally sent a lyric round. I didn't like it but didn't say anything; as I wasn't a professional lyricist I had to leave the decision to those who purported to know best. Someone suggested that the names should be blotted out on the copies given to the publisher so that the choice would be an objective one. Later that day he looked at me, with what amounted to . . . pity? He had studied both lyrics and was wondering how to deliver the bad news to a budding lyricist, firmly convinced that his choice was not mine. It gave me great satisfaction to watch his face when I smiled and told him it was.

The album *Best Friends* with the song 'He was Beautiful' was a world success, with many other artists recording it, notably Iris Williams who had a big single hit in Britain. The song means many things to different people who have written to me; about how it has affected their lives or how the lyric describes a loved one, from a baby to a lost pet, and then of course there is the obvious question, about who inspired the words. My friend Marion Montgomery asks, 'Come on Cleo, who was he?' I reply, 'He's a compilation . . .'

Malta remains a loved island with many wonderful memories of family holidays: Jackie giving me my first flute lesson, when I was trying to encourage her to practise herself (it's since become a hobby of mine); Alec sculpting the soft Malta stone and becoming, along with John, producer, actor and director;

casting Jackie and me in the worst, funniest *Maltese Falcon* ever filmed with a family 8mm movie camera. Sea, boats, goats, poinsettia, pumpkins and grand Catholic churches, pervading the smallest of villages at every corner turn.

23

Show Boat

John and I were starting to collaborate and work together again, and this was a source of great delight to me. After my original break from the big band I had achieved my aim of becoming a solo artist, and promoters no longer expected me to be part of the package. It had taken a long time to kill that assumption, but we stuck to our guns; if they wanted me, I was extra.

One of our most satisfying collaborations had been the *Shakespeare and All that Jazz* album, where the music was honed by someone who knew my voice inside-out and exactly what it was capable of – on a good day. It came about not only because of my interest in the art of improvising and working on *That Was The Week That Was*, but after hearing the Lambert, Hendrix and Ross album *Sing a Song a Basie* on which the three singers sang the arrangements and improvisations of Count Basie's band and musicians. It was quite brilliant, both the singing and the lyrics put to big-band scores, and improvisations by all three, but mainly by Jon Hendrix.

I knew Annie Ross from the big-band days, when she had sung with Jack Parnell's band, and had always admired her style. We became friends and performed together many times in concert, and on the Edith Sitwell/William Walton entertainment *Façade*. We also did a show together devised by Ned Sherrin and Caryl

Brahms for the Stables. This was *Ladies Night*, the other ladies being Patricia Routledge and Elizabeth Welch.

Jack Henderson, the American artistic director of the London Camden Festival, became aware of my work through recordings (especially the Shakespeare record); he told me when we first met that he considered me to be one of the great twentieth-century Lieder singers. With the classical agents Basil Horsfield and John Daven, who had recently started working on our behalf, he asked us to put together a programme to prove his point for the 1966 Camden Festival. Highly flattered, I gave a great deal of thought to his suggestion, backed all the way by John, with his considerable knowledge of what I was or was not capable of. With the devoted musicianship of John and Laurie Holloway supporting me, we set about putting a repertoire together, and after many hours of selecting and rejecting, combined with long and arduous rehearsals, we found a programme to present to the public that we would be proud of. It caused quite a critical stir that took us to many important music festivals in the British Isles and Europe.

Although Basil Horsfield and John Daven worked in the classical world, they had extremely broad musical tastes, with a vast knowledge of all kinds of music. Their artists at that time included pianist John Ogdon, the great Welsh singer Geraint Evans, and many more famous names; later the list included Dame Kiri Te Kanawa. John Daven, who was an Australian, started spreading the news about me abroad, and contacts were made in that distant country for festivals such as Perth and Adelaide. But first I experienced the satisfaction of being in a smash hit musical in the West End of London for the first time.

All artists keep an eye and an ear open, or at least their managers do, for that one role or song that will open doors to further their careers. It is a hit or miss process most of the time, with luck being the prime factor. In 1970 I struck lucky when I was asked to play the role of Julie in the London revival of *Show Boat*, the great American musical. It meant I would be singing the song 'Bill'. When it was first produced, in 1927 at the Ziegfield Theater in New York, it was considered controversial because of the miscegenation theme that ran through it. But the magnificent songs and performances carried the day – Jules Bledscoe as Joe and Helen Morgan as Julie (Paul Robeson didn't play Joe until the London production in 1928). The music, an unknown quantity then, has since become one of the best-loved scores of any musical ever written, and all the songs have become standards, still loved worldwide.

The production I appeared in became the longest running *Show Boat* ever produced; it played 910 performances, from July 1971 to Sept 1973, at the Adelphi Theatre. Harold Fielding, the amazing showman and character of the London theatre at that time, and the management/producer of the show, had trouble right from the start of negotiations to put it together for the London stage, but the pre-hassles of big shows become half the fun for a lot of entrepreneurs in the business, and I dare say Harold loved the gambling side of it too; while Maisie, Harold's wife, kept an eye on the books for too much excess spending. Laurie Mansfield looked after my interests, relieving me of the in-fighting necessary to achieve a decent contract. It was the first big negotiation he did for me, and he gave me good advice, when I was uncertain whether I should accept the part, not sure at first whether I wanted to be involved just to sing one solo, albeit one of the great songs in the show. Laurie was convinced that it would be good for my career, and he was right.

What did intrigue me was the thought of playing, for the first time, a genuine mixed-blood Julie. In the past, only white women had played the role, both onstage and film. It was one of the carrots dangled before me – the chance of being able to break that mould. Wendy Toye, the great British director, fought for me to play the role and I wanted to work with her. Wendy's and Laurie's enthusiasm, combined with my gut feeling that the record of white versus colour for the role should be put straight at last, brought us almost to the point of acceptance.

However, there was still one more condition that Laurie had

to battle for on my behalf before I said yes. If I were to do the musical, I insisted, I wanted one more song. It was the last song written by Jerome Kern before he died in 1945, called 'Nobody Else but Me' and it was beautiful. Kern had written it for the 1946 revival of *Show Boat* on Broadway, when it had been sung not by Miss Julie but by the young ingenue Magnolia. Once that was agreed, I signed, and Benny Green, who was hired to do the rewrites, wrote a scene that incorporated the song without altering the intentions of the original script in any way. But it caused a bit of a problem with Kern's estate, who wanted nothing changed.

Elaborate sets had been built, costumes designed, fitted and made, cast assembled and after eight weeks of intense rehearsals in London (the show never toured), a week before opening the go-ahead for the extra song was still not forthcoming. Harold was going around tearing his hair out, but with his gambling courage in his hands and all fingers crossed, he sent a telegram to the States. 'The show will be cancelled if I don't get a yes on the song "Nobody Else but Me" by return' – or words to that effect. They conceded, though they insisted that Julie, after singing 'Bill', must leave, never to return again until the bows.

'Nobody Else but Me' became the song I looked forward to singing every night for a year, even though 'Bill' was the big popular show-stopper that everyone wanted to hear me sing. I had found my role, also my door-opening song, at last.

Harold Fielding was a stubborn man, a gambler who sailed close to the wind in business deals, large and small; it surprised me when I half won a small battle with him over who was going to pay my dresser, Hersey. I submitted that it was the management's place to pay the wages of the dressers for the show – after all I hadn't insisted on clothes that needed a dresser to get me on and off the stage. Our horns locked and Laurie Mansfield had to go through the toing and froing of renegotiation, as we both dug our heels in right up to the day of the first night. Harold really liked a contest of wills, and might possibly have said, go to hell, I'll put the understudy on, but Maisie thought things through a bit more and looked at her books, while everyone else, except determined me and Harold, were having fits up and down the corridors of the Adelphi. Laurie eventually came to the dressing room, pleased as punch with the solution of half and half from Maisie. I agreed, and the show went on.

It was the first time I had really used my clout, and I was quite enjoying the adrenaline it supplied. Once it was settled, Harold and I had a good relationship for the rest of the run. They seemed to have a dislike for Hersey, though, who certainly wasn't the run-of-the-mill, fuss-over-you motherly dresser, but looked more like a man in drag, which for all I knew she might have been. She had worked for me before, and it was she who approached me for the job – possibly one of the reasons why she was frowned upon. Anyway there was a resistance to her which I never fully understood. She was well known for enjoying a drink, but I experienced no trouble with that; she was always sober on the job, and extremely professional and loyal, guarding me from anyone she thought was an intruder and doing more than her job called for. She didn't socialize with the other dressers, so anything private wasn't spread around, but she kept her ears open for any delicious gossip that might amuse me.

The first six months in the show were sheer delight: the rest of the cast were wonderful socially and great fun to work with and we have remained in touch, particularly with the three Americans, Thomas Carey, Lorna Dallas and Kenneth Nelson (since departed). Thomas Carey, who played Joe and sang 'Ol' Man River', thought I was an American myself on the first day of rehearsals. Little did he know that when I sang 'Bill' during those rehearsals, I made a habit of slapping myself whenever I sang a long English A. As the lyric was written by an Englishman, P.G. Wodehouse, I kept feeling subtle distinctions within the song, for at times it felt so British. I didn't know at the time who had written it – it was only later that Benny Green told me the story of its entry into the musical. It had been written in 1918 ånd rejected twice from other shows and laid to rest, until

Kern knew it was right for Julie to sing in *Show Boat*. He had to get in touch with Wodehouse, who was now back in England writing his 'Jeeves' stories, to get his consent to it being used. He also had to think about the main lyricist's feelings on the matter, Oscar Hammerstein, who, I guess for the good of the show, also agreed. Anyway, when I sang 'He don't play golf or tennis or polo, or sing a solo or row, he isn't half as handsome as dozens of men that I know', there were times, during the first rehearsals, when I forgot my Southern accent, especially on the words 'half' and 'handsome'. In time my sore hand cured me and I managed to fool the American actors when they first met me.

When we got well into the run the cast became like a family. Although all the different agents and managers had done their job well, and fought for the best placing of their artists on the bills and posters, it was never upheld backstage; the singers and dancers in the chorus, principals and stagehands mingled happily in the most democratic way. The captain of this mixed bag of players was of course Wendy Toye, who had started in the chorus as a dancer, so always respected and fought for their rights. The good of the show always came first too. She had the terrifying job of working out the logistics, cutting where and when it was required, organizing and manoeuvring a large and sometimes unwieldy body of people (about a hundred). Temperaments and tantrums were never indulged, and some of the artists had to give up a song when the first dress rehearsal looked as if it would never end (unlike me, they had not got a line inserted in their contract that their solo songs were not to be cut).

Towards the end of the first six months I started to get antsie pants. Although I was talked about a lot onstage in my absence it was no satisfaction to me, sitting around offstage – I wanted to be doing something. During those months when I felt I was vegetating, I became a vegetarian. I also started to study Yoga, going regularly to classes in London while I was in the show; it was the start of a regime, with the exception of a couple of breakdowns on tour, that I have kept to ever since.

When my first six months were up, I left the show to tour for six months before returning for a further six-month season. Now that I had the reputation of being the star from the hit West End production *Show Boat* who sang the show-stopping song 'Bill', played *ad nauseam* on the BBC, the whole country knew about me. What had finally happened was a disintegration of my out-and-out jazz image. 'If she can sing that much-loved song to millions of people, to their delight, without upsetting them, then she's all right,' was the response of the powers-that-be.

24

Australia: Heat and Laughter

While I was out of the show, a concert tour was arranged for me and J.D. to travel for the first time further than Europe or the United States – a massive jump to Australia. We had no idea how we were going to be received there, so it was a journey into the unknown. Though a few Australian friends living in Britain tried to reassure us with stories about the friendliness of the Australians in general, it was still a nerve-wracking step to take. Our former agent had always said it was hard to get overseas tours together because of lack of interest. But along came entrepreneur Clifford Hocking, a Melbourne-based Australian who introduced us to the Aussie public with style and class as well as with the necessary amount of showbiz drum-banging. He had once managed a record store, and his knowledge of music and the arts was astounding. He had soaked up information on all the up-and-coming artists in a wide range of music, from classical to pop, and put it to good use.

Clifford had seen *Show Boat* and he was also impressed with the Shakespeare album. After lengthy talks with Laurie, everything was sorted out and he became the one to introduce me, John and our pianist John Taylor at the Perth Festival. (We used Australians, Derek Capewell, bass, and Graham Morgan, drums, on this first visit.)

Perth was the most perfect place to become acquainted with Australia. I have come to look forward to visiting the country so much that if a tour of it is missed out for any reason I feel a real sense of loss. Perth is miles away from anywhere else in Australia; it's the most isolated city of its size in the world. It is a stunningly beautiful place, with a gracious river, the Swan, running right through it – one of the reasons why a settlement was established there in the first place. Today the river lends Perth that leisurely, languid air that handsome rivers so often lend to boat-loving, fishing communities with a university.

Our journey was long and tiring, but when we arrived the media were there to welcome us and vie for our views on Australia, just minutes after we had set foot on land: radio and TV stations wanted to talk, and magazines take colour pictures. The feeling generated was one of great interest in and admiration for our music, which had been played on air over the years by Arch McKirdy, a lover of jazz, big bands and good vocal music whose choice was respected by his large listening audience. So thanks to the efforts of Clifford and Arch we found that there was interest in us in Australia after all. Australia, being so far from the UK, didn't always find it easy to attract artists in the seventies, and was starved of certain kinds of entertainment. Moreover there was a shortage of good halls to present it in. The public was ready to receive us with open arms and hearts, and they sure did.

It was a completely new experience for us all: although the majority of the population was still of British extraction then, the reception they gave us had nothing to do with the well-known reserve of the British Isles; from the time we landed, up to concert time and long after, we couldn't help being caught up in the enthusiasm and vitality of the Australian people wherever we performed. Perth became a reuniting experience for me too, when two of my former Southall workmates got in touch – Mrs Brooker and Sybil from my millinery and hairdressing days, neither of whom I had seen since my career started. Sybil was married with a family and Mrs Brooker was now happy and husbandless. It was a joyous reunion, and we spent hours talking of old times. Our other friendships built up and multiplied over the years – John even discovered a family Dankworth clan in Sydney he never knew existed.

The accent took a while to get used to, until the ear became acclimatized to the 'e' and 'a' sounds. To me it was slightly broader than a Cockney accent with an occasional touch of the American South. It intrigued me immensely, coming as I did from a place where an accent often stamped your place in society. Here, on the contrary, it seemed to be a leveller; I could discern no real difference in the sounds I heard from one district or city, unless it was someone from the old country, or a part of Europe. Fifteen years later, when Kurt Gebauer, our American road manager, was told to go to the 'chicken counter' to tend to some airport tickets, he was ready to tell them not to be funny, until we pointed out that they meant 'check-in counter'. It took him a long time to grasp that when someone told him they would put a letter in the 'litter box' for him, it would not be thrown away.

Perth holds good memories, from our encounter with Harry Secombe who made regular visits, creating warmth, mayhem, fun and laughter in seconds at any press conference he attended. Johnny Franz, Harry's long-time pianist (and my early A and R man at Fontana records) told of arriving late to do a concert with Harry as his car had broken down. He apologized profusely to Harry while at the same time cursing his darned Rolls-Royce for letting him down. In mock effrontery Harry, pulling himself up to his full, Welsh, defensive height, said to Johnny: 'A Rolls-Royce does not break down, it just declines to proceed.'

Which reminds me of another story about a Rolls-Royce (excuse me while I deviate – it's a good story). John and I were on the way to perform a concert when our Rolls-Royce 'declined to proceed' in Todmorden, England. John had to get out and push it to the side of the road, to the taunting shouts of owners of cars with lesser pedigrees that whizzed by us. John angrily lifted up the bonnet to stare helplessly inside, with not a clue about what to do, when a passing lad, aged about eleven, stopped by the side of the car, to stare at John staring at the engine. After a good study of the car he eventually spoke. "Ave yer broke down?'

'Yes! I have!'

'I didn't think Rolls-Royces broke down . . .'

'Well this one has!'

'Thur's a garage down t'road . . .'

John, seething by now at the mysterious stoppage and the innocently chirpy inquisitor, ignored the youngster's helpful remark and went on fiddling with wires.

Unperturbed, he continued to ask questions. 'Is that a pop star in't car?'

'It's Cleo Laine,' replied John, through clenched teeth and no eye contact.

The young boy's attention immediately turned from engine gaping to face gaping. I continued to bury my head into a pretend book-read; so he turned from me to ask John challengingly, 'What's Cleo Laine doin' in Todmorden, in a broken-down Rolls-Royce?'

The bonnet was slammed down. John got back into the car, tried the ignition and the Rolls at last decided to proceed. We made our escape, leaving the lad clutching his record shop plastic bag and gazing after us.

After the seething had died down we were able to laugh at the incident and feel compassion for the little lad. We realized that when he got home and told his story, he was unlikely to be believed, because he hadn't asked for an autograph.

On one visit to Perth we were told that Prince Charles was going to attend one of our concerts privately. For us, it was the last of a series of concerts before flying off to other parts of Australia. The last concert we perform in Perth is always an emotional event, with all our friends present to wish us God speed to our next port of call.

Flowers and streamers were thrown on to the stage, and the popular young – then unmarried – prince joined in. After the performance we stayed on to be presented to him. He had obviously enjoyed the informal evening and the audience had enjoyed having him amongst them unannounced. (It was at the time when young ladies would appear from nowhere to rush up to the prince and surprise-peck him on the cheek.) He admired the dress that I had worn that evening, and then asked me about the joke that had made me break down with laughter during the performance. I explained that it was a last-night inside joke, then told him the shortened story leading up to it. Here is the long version.

Before arriving in Perth we had appeared in Las Vegas, on a *Jerry Lewis Telethon* for children with muscular dystrophy. While we were there, we realized that our next concert before Perth was in Singapore, which had strict rules about the length of men's hair at the time. My pianist Paul Hart had hair way past the limits that Singapore allowed, so I said to Paul that if he wouldn't have his hair cut (which he wouldn't) there were only two solutions to the problem: a wig or a turban. Las Vegas was the place for wigs, so we went shopping. Paul, after long deliberation, picked an Afro wig, which he knew would look daft on his Anglo-Saxon features; he was making a point that anything other than his own hair would make him look utterly ridiculous. He was right. We all found it difficult to hide our amusement, collapsing hysterically at the sight of him. Although the hair was off his collar, the only way he would have been allowed entry, he did look absurd.

Luckily that visit to Singapore was cancelled, so we didn't have to go through with the hoax. But having spent money on this ludicrous disguise, Paul was determined to get his money's worth. As pranks are traditional for last performances, this was his opportunity. I walked on to applause to warm the heart, and the concert started quite normally. I'm sure Paul wasn't be-wigged when I walked on, but when I turned to look at him at some point in a song, there he was sitting at the piano with a big Cheshire-cat grin on his face and an Afro wig on his head; not only Paul, but my drummer, Kenny Clare, too. The sight of them both was too much for me, and the song I was singing turned into spluttering nonsense that could not be missed by the devoted fans, who eventually joined in the fun. It was an inside joke, but as it was a last night, everyone fell in with it, whether they understood or not. The young prince was amused, and gave me permission to kiss him before we took our leave. Just a little peck on the cheek.

Our first visit to Sydney was just as wonderful for different reasons. Arriving at the airport we were greeted by Clifford Hocking's public relations man, Adrian Rawlings, who looked like a contented Buddha in white. He continually dived into a plastic shopping bag to retrieve flowers from amongst his business papers, which he sniffed adoringly then popped back into the crushing plastic hothouse. Accompanying him on this first meeting was a surprise guest, the imposingly tall and large shape of the amazing traveller and blues singer Beryl Bryden. The last time we had seen Beryl was in 1968 in Czechoslavakia, just before the uprising, at a Prague European Jazz Festival; the time before that, in Holland. Beryl seemed to pop up everywhere, but to see her here in Australia was mind-boggling. She had, as always, been photographing everyone and everything since she'd arrived, had visited and dived at the Barrier Reef and sat in with all the traditional jazz bands at the working men's clubs that abound in Australia.

Adrian was no ordinary PR – he was a poet, a deep believer in the teachings of Meyer Baba and an Australian character, who spread love, and our concerts, with a lot of chutzpah all over the country. At that first meeting we realized he was not the usual staid publicity man when on arrival at our hotel he broke into a completely wild version of an old Bessie Smith blues, one I'd never heard before. Later I was to sing and record the song myself, in a slightly more subdued manner, at a live concert at the Carnegie Hall in New York.

Our hotel in Sydney has always been the Sebel Town House, the place where most entertainers seem to stay: it's unpretentious, and understanding of late mornings and later nights, which gives it an air of being home from home. The hotel overlooks the harbour and a park, situated not far from the centre of a district not unlike London's Soho, called King's Cross, which has a mixture of restaurants ranging from fine cuisine to grunge, mixed up with girlie shows, jazz and cabaret. Out one day for a stroll on my own, I was told in no uncertain terms to bug orf, by an irate young lady. Unaware of the reputation of the district, I had stopped to look in a shop window just a little too long for comfort, for someone who had regularly done business outside it long enough to consider it her own.

We appeared in Sydney long before the Opera House was built, but when it was finally up and running it was a venue we appeared in regularly, enjoying its opulence. Like no other building in Australia or indeed the world, its spectacular armadillo shape put Sydney and Australia on the international entertainment circuit map. The fine halls within the shape attracted the attention of world and home-grown artists, both classical and popular, which in turn brought about the building of first-class halls in other cities, so that the same artists who were drawn to the Opera House would continue by touring the country.

Even before all these wonderful halls were built, Clifford managed to entice international artists to visit, and was a concert pioneer in his country, touring artists in halls that were far from satisfactory. He introduced, as well as John and myself, performers like Stephane Grappelli, Paco Peña, Keith Jarrett and Gary Burton. The Adelaide Festival was one of the well-established festivals of the continent and had built a hall and performing complex long before the Sydney centre for the arts, but its exterior look, compared with the flying theatricality of the Sydney Opera House, was conservative and looked much like many another, even though its concert hall is excellent and one that I always enjoy performing in.

For our early first visits though, we performed in town halls, Masonic and university halls, sports arenas and buildings with corrugated roofs, the like of which, when we performed in the rain, presented counter-rhythms very difficult to compete with.

To explain why one becomes fond of a country that, for instance, celebrates Christmas, with all the trimmings, on the beach, partying and barbecuing in sweltering temperatures of 100 degrees and more, isn't easy. When first viewed the scene presents a ludicrous picture: Bermuda shorts, bikinis and sun protection warpaint stripes just don't seem right, when the calendar says December. I always want snow and crackling fires and the obvious seasonal changes; but after a few visits of being a whingeing pommie, the combination of warmth and unaching bones and joints plead with me to be sensible. I eventually capitulated; heat became nice.

I like the Australians' easy, gutsy, relaxed attitude and their love of outside life, which is understandable, given the abundance of magnificent beaches, the infinite variety of the landscape, trees, birds and animals. As I came to know the country's foibles, I grew to admire Australia and the Australians for their amazing adjustability and their willingness, from their early history to the present, to seek out the new and have a go. It's a hard nut who doesn't become fond.

Clifford, his partner David Vigo, and everyone who worked for them were not only great guides, hosts and advisers, but when things didn't go right, they were comforters too, always producing a solution to a problem. Collapses of parts of the body often occur when on tour, for reasons known only to the body – it's then that you need to have a sympathetic person on hand, who has a dentist, doctor, or chiropodist, in fact any body-parts magician up their sleeve whom they can lure off the golf course on a Saturday or Sunday – the usual days a part decides to collapse.

Once a tooth cap of mine, losing the battle with a crusty bread roll, decided to teach me respect at a concert later in the day. Spike Milligan describes the subject of teeth and their weaknesses perfectly in his comic poem 'English Teeth', and by chance I was giving a spirited rendition of the famous lines at the end of the poem, 'Three cheers for the brown, grey and black'. On the explosive word 'Cheers!', the cap blew out of my mouth, fragmented, never to be seen again. The concert continued till the end and mine was, I think, a performance a ventriloquist would have been proud of.

Melbourne was the city where Clifford's organization was based, so we seemed to do more socializing there on our days off. It was more conservative than Sydney, very Cheltenhamish, but bigger. On our first visits, night life was virtually non-existent, so after a performance, drinks and get-togethers were not easy to arrange.

After one particular concert, we had a visit from Lord Harewood and his new Australian bride, the former Patricia Tuckwell. We all wanted a drink, but the search that night, although exhaustive on the part of the team, revealed that there was some truth in what Sydneyites had described as Melbourne's stuffiness – at least after a certain hour. Until some bright spark suggested The Italian Waiters Club which, as he explained to us, was frequented by workers of all persuasions: off-duty night workers and early morning breakfast-eaters on the way to hard graft; there were no membership requirements, the only qualification for entry being that you were a worker with difficult hours. Well, we assured him we all fitted that bill, so with hope in our hearts, and empty stomachs, we proceeded to climb up a steep flight of stairs that led to a large, wooden-floored room, crammed with tables and chairs of no consequence, where groups of men sat either having heated conversations or heated games of cards or dominoes. The atmosphere was hot, bustling and it was full, but, as if by magic, before we could ask whether there was any hope of a table, white-aproned waiters produced the right number of chairs for the group, then a table, on which they placed half-pint tumblers.

When we had got ourselves settled, we began to take in this secret jewel – the sound of many European accents could be heard – not predominantly Italian, in spite of the name of the place. The aproned waiter stood unheatedly waiting for our requirements, while others dashed noisily about. The Harewoods, having already eaten, declined food, and the rest of us ordered spaghetti, which seemed the best bet and, of course, wine. 'You want wine? We give you wine.' No half-measures, the tumblers were filled to the brim, no vintage, no choice, except red or white: rough, drinkable and dangerous. Patricia and I must have been the only women in this haven for the night worker that night, but not an eyebrow was raised at our smart, bejewelled splendour.

My record career in Australia has always been a good one, starting with the *Feel the Warm* album, then the live album recorded in Melbourne at the Town Hall in 1972; both became gold albums. Later there were the John Williams collaborations, *Best Friends* and *Let the Music Take You*, and the James Galway album, *Sometimes When We Touch*. I have never been very keen on doing live albums, for many reasons, the prime one being the quality of the recording, which to me became questionable when extraneous coughs, shuffles, applause and laughter (which excludes the listener) are all left on, to be thrown into the atmospheric potage called value for money. And if quality sound (which should be the aim of all artists) is insisted upon for the recording, the sound in the hall can be badly affected, disappointing the public who made the effort to come to hear and see you in the flesh. So I feel someone always loses out.

In the case of the live Melbourne recording, I was told by Clifford and Bill Armstrong, the owner of Armstrong studios, that they wanted to record the concert and if I didn't like the result it would be forgotten as a commercial project, but we would have a keepsake. The final result was better than I thought it might be and the recording was of a very high quality, thanks to Bill and his company. But although it was a success, and others since recorded at concerts in Carnegie Hall have been huge sellers in the US and internationally, it is still not my favourite way of recording.

The love affair between Australia and me was strong enough to persuade me to do some things that I would adamantly refuse to do anywhere else, like eating maggots. I indulged in this delicacy after a concert in Adelaide. The day before I had been introduced to an Aboriginal lady by Adrian, who wanted me to meet and be greeted by the members of an Aboriginal club, with a 'cook-in': this is where they slow-cook food in a hole in the ground. I had a delightful afternoon of dance, talk and normal food, leaving with a little more knowledge than I had had previously about the life of the Aboriginal people. Some of the young people I met that afternoon came to hear me sing the next day, bringing gifts, one of which was canned wichetty grubs, in other words maggots. I think I partook of the offering without a trace of what was going on inside my head and stomach transferring to my countenance. As I popped it in my mouth the experience turned out to be a tasteful surprise.

At the same venue, the Adelaide concert hall, I experienced the singer's nightmare, when I announced I was going to sing a group of poems halfway through the concert and forgot the words of the poem that started the group. I launched into T.S. Eliot's poem, 'Lines to Ralph Hodgson esq.', with great gusto, singing the first line, 'How delightful to meet Mr Hodgson, everyone wants to know him' as if I had known it all my life; it was firmly imprinted on my mind. But easily as I began, just as easily I came a cropper, when my mind refused to put the next stanza through my mouth. I fuffed about for a while, hoping it would all click into place eventually, but I knew I was facing a blank wall that loomed up at me, and was not going away, and would remain blank until I did something about it.

I looked around at John, who most times could help me out with a forgotten lyric, especially if he had done the setting, but I could not get his attention. My other rescuer was the bass player Daryl Runswick, who, I hoped, might have noticed my plight, but he was otherwise engaged with his bass line. So I called a halt to the mess I was in and told the by now stunned audience that I thought I should try that again. Once again the intro was played, once again I sang the same lines, once again I ground to a halt. I stopped and started two or three times without any success and the boys were unable to get me out of the mire, so I apologized to the audience, telling them the song didn't seem to want to be sung so I'd get on with the other poems and come back to it.

All the other poems came instantly to mind without a hitch, and thankfully so did the rest of 'Lines to Ralph Hodgson esq.' when I went back to it. In the audience that night was the then Premier of South Australia, Don Dunston, who knew the poem and 'wanted desperately to help me out', he said, when we met later after the concert.

25

Breaking into America

Our first visit to Australia had exceeded our wildest dreams, making both of us bold, daring and ambitious gamblers. Encouraged by the enthusiasm shown for our music first by the American Jack Henderson and then by Clifford Hocking, the Australian, John felt we had something to offer to the world concert-going public, and that America should be our next adventure.

With very little knowledge of the American musical business world, our reputations known only to a cult few, we went to New York and John plunged himself into trying to convince mainly classical agents and managers what they would be missing out on if they didn't book us for a concert in New York as soon as possible. The concert programme that we were doing at the time was based on the one given at the Camden Festival, London, so it was extremely eclectic and we thought would only appeal to someone with a wide knowledge of all kinds of music. So the classical moguls seemed the obvious beings to go to.

John put his English reticence to rest and rushed in where angels not only fear to tread, but where they'd also be pretty damned scared so much as to put their hand on the handle of the door without an invite. Most of his chutzpah fell on stony ground anyway, but he was prepared for that: he was after all going to all the renowned entrepreneurs in the business, most of whom didn't know what a Cleo Laine was, until J.D. put them in the picture – then all they could say was 'Oh! she's a cabaret artist.' Well, I am many things but I have never considered myself to be primarily a cabaret artist, in fact I would say it was the medium I was most uncomfortable in.

In despair at finding a sympathetic ear or results from his trekking about all day, we went to dinner with an American friend we had met in London through a great friend of Duke Ellington's, Rene Diamond. Rene gave strict instructions to her friend Anita Porter that we were to be looked after grandly when we were in New York and Anita stuck to her instructions. When John told her about his unsuccessful meetings of the day, she had an immediate suggestion to make that was quite the reverse of what John had been going for. She suggested getting in touch with a man called Ron Delsenor, who was at that time a successful rock promoter. Ron was contacted and an appointment was made.

I don't think J.D. held out much hope, but by the time they met he was well geared up to the fast-talking, very-little-modesty style of the New York music world, and 'laid it on the line', as I do believe they say. Ron listened until John had come to the end of all that he had to say about me and not until then did he say: 'Oh I see! I get you, what you have is a class act.' So John agreed to a deal of splitting the expenditure of the concert fifty-fifty, and sharing any profits made.

So, together with Ron Delsenor at last I was going to be launched in New York, at the Lincoln Center's Alice Tully Hall, in September 1972, accompanied by British John Dankworth, John Taylor on piano, and Americans George Duvivier, bass and Bobby Rosengarden, drums. We did virtually the same programme we had presented in Camden Town and the cities of Australia. For the small audience present that evening I was a new experience, and when I say small, I mean, tiny, wee, minuscule. It was half full, and half of that half was papered (meaning they had been given their tickets). But we performed of course as if it were a full house.

John and Ron had created a memorable night for me, even if it was only one night. I said to myself as I stood waiting to go on: 'This is the ultimate of everything I dreamed of doing when I was a child' – with one big difference; it was like starting at the beginning of my career, but this time with all the know-how.

Before making my entrance, I took my usual deep breaths, blew my nose, cleared my throat, sipped some un-iced water and walked on. The audience applauded politely and I started singing, *a capella*, the first lines of the first song, 'I'm as restless as a willow in a wind storm, I'm as jumpy as a puppet on a string,' a slow, reflective and beautiful ballad, not the hit-'em-hard opener that most New Yorkers would expect to hear. When the song eventually opens out at the bridge with 'I keep wishing I were somewhere else,' John T., John D. and George D. subtly creep in to start accompanying me for the first time. It's then that it becomes one of those inexplicably magical musical moments that both performers and audience catch, if it is played and sung well.

I sensed the audience was holding its breath waiting for it all to come together, and then I sensed their happy releasing, when they too caught the moment and felt it had worked. Luckily I was in good voice and everything I and the musicians wanted to do that night seemed to come off without a hitch. Artistically it was a great success and the audience let us know how they felt about the evening, from start to finish with a standing ovation to warm the hardest of professional hearts.

Laurie Mansfield, our manager, stood proudly with us that night, agreeing to direct the lighting, working from a plot John had given him. I announced the encore, and Laurie gave the lighting instructions, which were 'Complete black-out onstage, spot on Cleo'. I stood waiting in that spot for what seemed an eternity for the piano accompaniment to begin. Something had gone awfully wrong at last. I turned to indicate to the two Johns that I was ready, but I couldn't see them well enough because the spot was blinding me in the black-out and they couldn't see me properly because I was in too much light. We had all forgotten that poor John Taylor had to see the music to be able to start to play it and inadvertently the reading light on the piano had been included in the complete blackout. I thought, 'Well that's it, finish as I started, *a capella*.' As I was preparing myself to do just that, John T. called out, 'I can't see the music to play!' Everyone laughed at John's plight, the lights went up and we finished in a blaze of glory.

For some reason the public always thinks breakdowns are planned as part of the act, even when it's explained after the concert that it was a collapse of either concentration or communications: the friends and fans who you see after the concert can't quite believe you didn't do it on purpose and insist that you keep it in. Of course it doesn't work if you try to do it again. Once when I was singing a Hoagy Carmichael song called 'I get along without you very well', the heel of my shoe caught in a crack onstage. I walked on minus the shoe, continuing to sing, and the next line came out, completely unrehearsed, as 'I get along without shoe very well.' 'Keep it in, keep it in!' everyone cried. 'It only works,' I had to explain, 'when my darned heel gets caught in a unsuspected crack on the stage.'

Clifford Hocking had flown in specially from Australia. During the after-show party Ron D. told John that the fifty-fifty arrangement for putting on the concert had lost $300. We paid our $150 happily: to us it had been worth every penny. Later that evening Clifford told us that if Ron did not want to continue he would be happy to take on the concert promotion. We talked with Ron about this and he said he was having trouble with his rockers at that time and could not commit himself.

Early next morning we bought the papers and read a review in the *New York Times* that many an artist would give her right arm for – gluing it into her scrap-book with her left. The fact that it was in New York where the public took notice of good reviews didn't hit home right away, so we didn't get too cocky about it. We had a meeting with Clifford, who said he wanted to put on a concert at Carnegie Hall in six months' time, if we were willing. We all chorused as one, 'Clifford! We couldn't fill the small Alice Tully Hall. How do you expect us to draw a crowd large enough to fill Carnegie Hall?'

'You go away and worry about the music,' he said, 'and I'll do the worrying about filling Carnegie.'

We went back to London feeling triumphant and in good spirits, I to spend a further six months in *Show Boat*, during which Princess Margaret brought her mother, Queen Elizabeth the Queen Mother to see the show. After the performance I went to Kensington Palace to have supper, where the Queen Mother was extremely knowledgeable about the music and past performers. When she left the gathering, she presented me with the bouquet of flowers that had been given to her at the theatre, saying that I was the one who deserved them, for the joyful evening I and the show had given her. It had been a joyful evening for me too: it was so relaxed and informal and I kept that bouquet for a long time.

John hadn't come to the supper because he was in Malta, avidly composing music for string quartets, and a piano concerto for the City of Westminster Festival, to be conducted by Yehudi Menuhin and played by James Walker. It was also during that six-month period that Alexander Cohen, the producer of the Tony Awards, was in Europe, filming snippets of musicals to make up a montage of American masterpieces that would be playing in different countries all over the world when the Tony Awards were shown from New York on national television in the US. When he saw *Show Boat* in London, he chose to film me singing 'Bill'. This helped my visibility in the States immensely, giving me a pretty good lift-off.

So it was Clifford Hocking who undertook our US concert work, starting with, yes, a full Carnegie Hall. He had taken care of his side of the business and delivered.

The New York Carnegie Hall concert was the first of all the other highlights I was to encounter in America. Our side of the deal was to be well programmed, thought out, honed and performed. It was an extremely moving experience, especially when I thought of all the famous artists who had done the same in the past, and had stood on the exact spot where I was standing, to start their first song, play their first concerto, conduct their first symphony, or perform in a classic jazz concert. The applause I received brought tears and goose bumps, reminding me of how I felt when I passed the audition that allowed me to enter, for the first time, into my dream profession. It was a one-of-a-kind peak, a never-to-be-repeated experience.

That same night they were selling my records in the foyer, all of them imports from England, and they were selling well; they were recordings from several companies, but I had recently signed with RCA London, whose head then was the American Kenneth Glancy. He had heard me singing at Ronnie Scott's jazz club and wanted to sign me up, but I was with EMI at the time. When I became free, he got his wish and I became an RCA artist.

The record they were selling from RCA London was 'I am a Song'. Being imported is not as advantageous as being pressed, released and distributed in the same country, and that was my next aim. John, Clifford, Laurie and I went to a lunchtime meeting at RCA to convince them that I should now be released in the US. I was the only woman at that meeting. However, though the lunch was good, no positive decision was reached.

Much later we discovered why: heads were rolling at RCA, so no decision-making was best for those company members at the meeting. A lucky streak was holding out for me though, for soon after that lunch Ken Glancy was made worldwide head of RCA records, and I was released worldwide. During Ken's reign, I made some of the best albums of my career, as, luckily, Ken was a music man, not a lawyer or accountant. Not only were my records released, they were distributed well. I recorded live at Carnegie, had billboards on Sunset Boulevard in Los Angeles for the album *Born on a Friday* produced by George Martin, and many more advantages, like being treated with special care on the road.

Because Clifford was an Australian, he had to have an American running the business. Vince Ryan was the man he chose, a classical concert promoter from New York, so together with Laurie Mansfield and his US representative, Fred Harris, they started getting tours and talk shows all over the country, mainly on the strength of the write-ups and US-released records. For a year or more we zigzagged across America doing what we had done at Alice Tully Hall, establishing ourselves on the concert circuit. Back and forth across the Atlantic we went, to stardom and success in Great Britain and a mixture of successes and fantastic failures on the road in the US.

One early failure was when we came into contact with a cowboy promoter working out of Grand Rapids, Michigan, who thought he might make a killing on the strength of the New York reviews by booking us into a vast sports' arena. His mode of operation was to spend as little money as possible to publicize the event, hoping the community would react as New York had done, and would respond in their thousands after reading a quote of how the Big Apple had reacted to us. It didn't work for him of course: only about 400, if that many, turned up, and for some reason he seemed to blame us for the sparse audience attendance in the unsightly, forbidding space.

Nevertheless we proceeded with the show. John and the boys opened with a few numbers before I came on, so I was not aware of the gaping void that I would have to confront. Always the protector and diplomat, John announced 'Well . . . you are not the largest audience we have ever performed for, but you are one of the most receptive . . . It would be nice if the people at the back came down to the front, though. It would be a lot cosier, don't you think?' The audience agreed with him; it broke up the cold atmosphere and when I walked on it didn't look as bad as it had done for him and the group when they had started. That audience was wonderful and very enthusiastic and we all ended up having a great time.

Although Grand Rapids didn't come out in their thousands to see us initially, the state of Michigan has been good for us,

257

Detroit being the prime example, brought about by the faith shown in us by the Director of the Michigan Opera Theatre at the Music Hall Centre, Dr David Dichiera. After one concert booking he continued to have us back, until we were able to do a week, branching out, eventually, into musicals.

The Dichieras introduced us to many delightful people, making us and our other Detroit friends part of their family. The nice part about touring is the gathering of new friends, both the famous and down-to-earth fans who become part of your life and who convince others they should become devotees too. John had a surprise fiftieth birthday in Detroit when Donna Nicholson, a friend of ours, arranged a visit to a hotel whose featured cabaret star that week was Sarah Vaughan. He knew nothing about it and was not only surprised but overjoyed at the reunion, after many years, as he had accompanied her when she toured Great Britain with his big band. It was a happy occasion for J.D. Sarah, as always, sang like a dream, but the icing on the cake for John was when she sang 'Happy Birthday dear Johnny' along with the rest of us, then presented him with a birthday cake. When the show was over we went to her suite and finished the night out, reminiscing, eating cake and drinking birthday champagne.

The combination of RCA's record-plugging efforts, David, newspaper reviews and the column and television show of friend Shirley Eder, opened up other venues in the district, such as the open-air Meadow Brook Music Festival Theatre run by Stuart Hyke. We became regular summer visitors, by ourselves on a glorious hot summer evening breaking the house record when over 12,000 turned up, some to picnic on the grass before the show, others seated in the covered auditorium. They could be magical evenings, when you were in competition with birds, bees, and sometimes flying creatures interested in the workings of the singing mouth. To keep interest alive and kicking, Stuart Hyke liked to ring the changes, asking us who we would like to share the stage with. So we would suggest friends of ours and if they were free on the day, often the response turned out to be positive. The list of friends who made memorable music with us on the Meadow Brook stage reads like a musical *Who's Who*: Chick Corea, Mercer Ellington and the Ellington Orchestra, Michael Feinstein, James Galway, Marian McPartland, Gayle Moran, Mel Tormé.

Shirley Eder, who came to most of these events, must have interviewed and become close to hundreds of stars in show business. So it was Shirley who threw a party for us and Peggy Lee, when we all happened to be in town at the same time. Peggy was narrating and singing in *Side By Side by Sondheim*. It was the first time I had met the great lady and we spent most of the evening sitting together talking shop, as if we had known each other all our lives. When we eventually broke up and left the party, I kept saying to John, 'Pinch me, have I been sitting all night on the same couch with the lady who wrote and sang 'He's a Tramp' and was in the film *Pete Kelly's Blues* with the great Ella Fitzgerald? And did she say how much she enjoyed, knew and admired my work? Or have I been dreaming in the cinema again? Wow!!! I'm really awake!'

The opportunities David Dichiera presented to me bolstered my musical stage experience, as I appeared for him in two of his productions during the opera season: a bonus I had not thought would come my way until he suggested them. *A Little Night Music* was a favourite Sondheim musical of mine, and to be given the chance to portray Desiree was an opportunity I couldn't resist. David gathered a cast together that excelled itself nightly. We had great fun together with Ron Raines, Louis Otey and Gloria Caponne, piling into cars desperately seeking out our other friends appearing in town on our days off.

Mark Murphy, a jazz-singing friend of John's and mine, was one of those who we avidly searched for one night, to introduce his music to Ron, Louis and Gloria, who were not jazz aficionados. The whole evening was taken up trying to find the club he was performing in. We eventually came across it just as the show was coming to an end, but having come this far we went in to enjoy the last set of Mark's innovative jazz singing.

259

We were all sitting comfortably and at last relaxed, imbibing the music and a much-needed beverage, when Mark, who had just been told we were in, announced our presence – something Americans do, and like. I'm never inwardly prepared for this, and get highly embarrassed, wishing I could drop through the floor, as when they ask me to come up and join in a song – everything goes to jelly.

Mark's next announcement was: 'Cleo, how about coming up and joining me in a song?' My throat took on the texture of sandpaper, my makeup was a mess: I'd done too much laughing in the car. I stood up, however, and joined Mark onstage. 'What shall we sing, Cleo?' asks Mark. It was a rhetorical question, as he'd already counted in a blues number before I set foot on the stage, and was ad libbing the lyrics: 'Welcome Cleo, welcome to the club'. Luckily the blues give you plenty of options: if you don't know the lyrics, you make them up, scat or pretend to be a trumpet. I held my own until I felt my tired voice succumbing and went into an apologetic ad lib: 'Sorry Mark, I've got a frog in my throat.' I repeated, 'I'm sorry Mark I've got a frog in my throat, I am so unhappy, 'cos I'm sounding so remote.' Fairly awful, but as always everyone thought it was a wonderful evening and we should keep it in. Oh! and Gloria and Louis fell in love and got married.

The development of my career in America was beginning to shape up much as it had for me in England in the sixties. I was starting to get unexpected phone calls. One call out of the blue when I was back in England was from Norman Granz, the famous record producer of jazz, asking me if I would like to be Bess to Ray Charles's Porgy, on record. 'Would I what?' I said, not believing what I'd just heard. Norman repeated, 'Would you like . . .' 'Yes, yes, I would like,' I replied, still not quite believing my ears. I was to fly back to the US almost immediately. The proposed recording was to take place in Los Angeles, with a large jazz orchestra, strings and the Reverend James Cleveland Choir; the musical director was Frank DeVol, who was also doing the arrangements.

This was one project I didn't have to lock myself away to learn, as I had sung most of the known songs at various times in my career, except two, the beautiful 'They Pass By Singin',' and 'Strawberry Woman', which Norman wanted to include. So I was virtually ready to go, as soon as Frank DeVol had finished the scores. I was excited and eager to get to work, when I got the next phone call: Frank DeVol had had a heart attack, so the recording was going to be put on hold. Although I did not know Frank, I had great concern for his well being and really assumed the whole venture would be cancelled. Ten days went by and I got the next call: 'Can you come over immediately? Frank has recovered sufficiently to go into the studios; he's finished the arrangements, he's all set to go.'

Once again I couldn't believe my ears, and was more than ever concerned for Frank, thinking that he should not be working so soon. I guess Ray Charles had the same message, and we all met for the first time in the RCA Recording Studios in Hollywood.

Ray and I got on with each other right away. The atmosphere in the studio was one of joy bordering on love, for the music and for the artistry of all concerned, and the recording was finished on schedule. The big band read like a jazz dream: names popped out of musicians I had admired on record for years, like Joe Pass, Lee Ritenour, J.J. Johnson, Harry Edison, Ernie Watts, Bud Shank, Bill Perkins, Vic Feldman, to name but a few. I had even recorded a solo by one of them: Britt Woodman, the Ellington trombonist, on the instrumental 'Sonnet to Hank Sank', from Ellington's' LP *Such Sweet Thunder*.

The music of George Gershwin is always wonderful to sing and Ray and I relished every tune and every word. Words for Ray, if he didn't know them, had to be read in braille, which intrigued me; I wondered if fingers misread sometimes, as eyes often did. It depended of course on the expertise of the reader's fingers. I surmised that, as a pianist, Ray would have a head start. I certainly made more goofs than him when I had to read lyrics.

261

The finished recording brought nominations for Grammys in the jazz, soul and pop categories. Ray and I got together again when he came over to England to appear as a guest artist on one of my television specials for ATV, performing parts of *Porgy and Bess*, and also our own repertoire.

Ray and I did one other eventful engagement together for a racehorse breeder in Kentucky, the Gentry Stables, where we were both flown in to entertain the buyers of the magnificent creatures on display. The event took place in a marquee on the lawn, beautifully decorated with flowers and bunting, together with hundreds of elegantly laid tables. It was a swish do, with nothing spared. They had flown us from our last performance in St Johns, Newfoundland, which had taken us fourteen hours, changing to and from four different airplanes and airports to get there. When our bedraggled caravan arrived, they looked after us as if we were the ones who were going to spend the multi-million fortune on their horses.

On the first evening of the entertainment, Ray discovered, just before he was due on, that he had lost his braille watch, and he would not perform until it was found. John and I had already done our part of the evening, so there was a hiatus, while everyone backstage waited for all possible avenues to be scoured, by Ray's and the Gentry's entourage. It was retrieved at last, after a vast amount of sweating by all, in the hotel room. Ray then went onstage and the show proceeded, the glamorous audience unaware that they might not have heard Ray Charles sing 'Georgia' that night.

I was no stranger to Los Angelos – I had appeared there in concert and on their abundant talk shows, including the *Johnny Carson Show* several times. For that show, guests were always lodged at the Sheraton Universal, which was up a steep hill, and not very convenient for those of us who enjoy walking. But we were not going to be defeated by the hill, or by the fact that walking for pleasure in Los Angeles is regarded as daft. So down the hill we went, combining our walk with a search for food at the same time. It wasn't the most enjoyable of experiences, but it did exercise our stiff joints. We found a restaurant at the bottom and had a good meal, good enough to kill any desire to walk back up the hill, but no taxis were forthcoming. So, rather than hang around, we decided to brave the hill back. Cutting a corner, we found we had to walk through a landscaped area of trees and thorny bushes. Even though it was getting dark, we plunged into the shrubbery, making good headway and enjoying the wild country walk when, annoyingly, halfway up, we ran into a problem: no one had anticipated that maybe, someday, some foreign idiots would take the obvious short cut to get to the top, and the watering system had been turned on. Sprinklers were placed in such a way that nothing on that hill would be missed by them.

When at last we reached the entrance of the posh hotel, the combination of our entanglement with bushes, thorns, the dreaded sprinklers and eventually mud presented the sight of some extremely bedraggled itinerants. We did our best to skulk past the doormen, receptionists, and other more elegant guests, in a state that my mother would have described as 'dragged through a hedge backwards'. We escaped back to our rooms and had hot baths and lots of laughs.

As most places where we stayed in Los Angeles were nowhere near where we eventually wanted to get to, we decided that future stays would be in a place where we could do a flattish walk daily, without being questioned, watered or looked at suspiciously.

More seriously, the biggest thrill for me, Alec and Jackie, who were now travelling with us during school holidays, was the engagement at the Hollywood Bowl with Henry Mancini. What an experience! Once again a stage, that I'd seen in films in my childhood. The thrill for the children was the immense size of it, and the way the audience made it a grand, candle-lit eating occasion as well as a musical one. They were too young to appreciate the history of the grand arena, and they became so blasé that to amuse themselves during our performances they gave us marks out of ten for our efforts, which they wrote down in a book. After the Hollywood Bowl performance they showed us the marks they had given us. Being very critical of notes not hit right on the nose, or a not up-to-standard solo, they felt that neither of us in their estimation deserved ten out of ten. They were judging us the way an Italian audience would judge a favourite opera-singer who missed a note. 'Don't think you sang the end of the last song as well as the night before, Mum, you kinda slipped off the note,' and so on. Well, I guess we were bringing up musical children and training their ears along the way, so we couldn't complain.

The party given for us by Henry and his beautiful wife Ginny was much more successful for the children: they were able to brag when they arrived home that they had met Quincy Jones, Johnny Mathis and other celebrities, and more important, that they had been invited to swim in a private Hollywood pool, go to Disneyland and swim in the Pacific Ocean. Vivid memories for me, but I bet they can't remember a thing. Leonard Feather, the walking, talking, writing encyclopaedia of jazz, and his wife Jane, also gave us a party when we arrived in LA, an evening filled with wonderful music and a lot of old friends from the past.

On one occasion at the Bowl we almost made history when it started to rain during rehearsal – so hard that they had to cover microphones up, and precious instruments were protectively put away. It continued pouring so hard that Ernest Fleischmann came to tell me that I might make the history books: the concert might be rained off (at that point we only had twenty minutes to go). The last time a concert was rained off had been forty-five years before, he said. I didn't make history, for the rain stopped with ten minutes to go before a mythical curtain rose, never to start again for the entire concert. Amazingly, such was their faith in Los Angeles' weather, the audience didn't leave but sat patiently under umbrellas. They knew the rain would stop.

26

Wet Feet, Sheep and Long-lost Relations

It was in LA that we were surprised and delighted to see Dudley Moore again after such a long time – when he came to see us at the Greek Theatre. Backstage, after our show, we had the great idea of asking him to be our special guest for our second season at the London Palladium. The first one had been so successful, with our friend John Williams, the classical guitarist, as the special guest, that we wanted to keep the standard of musicianship as high for the next year, and Dudley was so right, both as a musician and as an entertainer.

We were thrilled when he agreed, but he was waiting for a film to come up and couldn't give a definite answer for a week or two. In the end we sadly had to relinquish our star guest to the film *Ten*, and Dudley became a super star. The show went on without Dudley, who was replaced by a trio of great British jazz musicians: Kenny Baker on trumpet, Don Lusher trombone and Jack Parnell on drums.

Once upon a time, it was me who made a phone call. Out of the blue I phoned Dudley and said, 'Fancy making an album?' 'OK,' he said. We began to plan what to do; he made his lists and I made mine. Then we found a weekend when we were both free and wham! we had an album to be proud of, called *Smilin' Through*. Dudley asked for Ray Brown to be the bassist,

265

as he had recently worked with him and Nick Ceroli on drums. We certainly had no problem with that request: Ray was an all-time idol bassist for both me and John, who was doing the arrangements and producing the sessions.

It was a weekend of hilarious fun, and one wonders now how we got any serious music done. John and Dudley played off each other as they used to in the big band and the Cool Elephant Club in London. Once musicians get on a kick they won't leave it alone until it's drained dry. Dudley is a master of this word play if he has someone to feed him, as his comic partnership with Peter Cook showed. How can you keep a straight face when Dudley, seeing John jotting down some music, asks, 'What are you doing, John?' John replies, 'It's in the wrong key, I'm transposing it.' Dudley, in a Northern accent: 'Making a transposition, eh? My aunt had one of those once. Took 'er to the hospital, they did, transposed her from B-flat to E. Painful bloody business. You could hear her screams all over the neighbourhood.' J.D.: 'Hmm, very sad. I understand they removed her coda, too . . .' Then there's their classic 'Dying Swan', that evolved at the Cool Elephant Club. This begins with them starting to play Saint-Saëns' 'Le Cygne' seriously, John on saxophone for twenty bars, the last four of which they repeat over and over again, going down a tone each time. Not too funny so far, until you notice that with each lowering of pitch, the musicians seem to be sinking to the floor; an illusion, you may think, until you notice that Dudley is now off the piano stool, almost under the piano, John is on his back and the bass player is on his knees. The drummer is nowhere to be seen but an occasional thump comes from the hinterland. They are all still playing, or rather whimpering, as they slowly collapse into a painful mess, and the Swan feebly, finally dies.

All through the 1970s, while we were on the road in the US and Britain, we used the same musicians. The drummer was the renowned workaholic Kenny Clare, and the pianists, one after the other, were John Taylor, Tony Hymas, Paul Hart, Bill Le Sage and Mike Hatchard. Daryl Runswick also took over the piano chair, but was our main bass player for most of the time we worked with the British musicians in the US; later, much later, son Alec became my bassist. With these wonderful musicians we travelled the world, dashing back and forth across the Atlantic to teach at the Wavendon Allmusic courses, to do my television shows, appear at Royal Command Performances, and get caught in snowstorms one minute, heatwaves the next, then torrential rain on the way.

Talking of rain – one day we were to perform at Wolftrap, the outside arena near Washington DC. John was writing music in our hotel room, and we had ordered a room-service breakfast. When the waiter came with the food, all was as it should be, except that he was shoeless. Neither of us had noticed at this point, John because he was too engrossed in his work and it was too early for me to notice anything. But the waiter was anxious to explain the reason why he wasn't shod. 'The corridor, it's flooded,' he said, 'Oh,' we replied, still lacking curiosity about that or his unnoticed feet. He persisted: 'Aah . . . that's why I'm barefoot'. 'Oh! we hadn't noticed,' we said, staring down now at his shoe- and sock-less feet, not all that pretty for breakfast. Then he was gone, and we looked out of the window to see the cars down below parked in a swimming pool; the rain was bucketing down. John thought he should get in touch with the other musicians to tell them a rescue job might have to be put into operation, as we had hired cars down there which now seemed in danger of being swept away, with a few of our possessions in the trunk. So a rallying point was arranged. My last pictured memory was the ridiculous image of Kenny Clare and J.D., trousers rolled up past knees, shoeless of course, wading out to a car that had a drum and music in it which had to be saved from destruction. When Americans joke about the persistent rain that they encounter in England, I have to point out the times when I have felt that it was ark-building time in the US; but they do have better summers.

This was not the last image of Kenny Clare I have; many more ridiculous moments occurred to keep that hard-drinking, chain-smoking, Humphrey-Bogart lookalike drummer alive in my memory. Kenny was the most experienced flyer in the band: often when we finished a tour and made our way towards the exit and home, he would continue on to Europe to join a big band, returning later to the US to work for someone like Tony Bennett. So I generally stuck close to Kenny at airports when we had any waiting around to do before boarding a plane. He always seemed to judge to the last second the right moment to make a move, so I never moved until he did: while the others panicked and stood in long lines, we sat calmly keeping an eye on the bodies slowly disappearing into the tunnel leading to the plane till he assessed it was time to go. We read our books or talked about him giving up smoking: he always agreed with me that he should, but never achieved it.

When John and I went to see him when he went into hospital with cancer, his first words to me were, 'I know what you're going to say, Cleo . . .' 'I told you so?' I replied cheerily. 'Oh! Kenny, how could you think such a thing of me?' He truly believed he would be out in time to do the next gig with us, apologizing for missing a recent one; but he never recovered. He left a large gap that hasn't been filled – as a drummer or as a travelling companion. He was remembered by a host of his fellow musicians who performed at a memorial concert given at the Wavendon Stables, where a fund was created in his name to help young musicians.

Washington DC holds many fond memories for me. It was at a Kennedy Center concert that we first met Ben Stevenson, the artistic director and choreographer of the National Ballet Company. The company was in financial difficulties and sadly all Ben's efforts to save it failed and it was eventually disbanded. Ben, however, moved on to be artistic director of the Houston Ballet, and commissioned John and Benny Green to rewrite and expand the *Lysistrata* ballet that was done for Bath, allowing me once again to enter the world of dance. It was to be a completely new production, right down to renaming it *Lady in Waiting*. Ben was to direct and choreograph, and it came to fruition in 1984.

Wet Feet, Sheep and Long-lost Relations

My admiration for the dedication of dancers to their art was reinforced, as we worked relentlessly together to make a good production – the dancers not only danced, but sang too.

It wasn't all work, as the world-renowned Texan hospitality was prodigious and the dancers and I revelled in it. During our stay in Houston we were entertained in some of the grandest establishments I have ever seen, all with a down-to-earth informality that is quite delightful and at times very amusing. At one grand reception, given at the top of a lush hotel in a suite that had more windows than walls, the usual cocktail small talk was in flow, mainly about the production in progress, comments on my beautiful English accent and the fact that some of the guests had all of my records, and so on. Though not very good at small talking myself, I usually make an effort and dive in. I participated by starting a conversation with a gentleman who seemed to be left out of the hubbub going on around him. I thought I'd bring him into the party spirit, so gazing out of one of the vast picture windows, I started rather weakly by commenting on how flat the landscape was here in Houston. 'Yep!' he said. 'Flat as piss on a plate.' Slightly shocked by this reply, but not wanting to show it, I replied in my best imitation of Joyce Grenfell, 'Oh, how quaint! I've never heard flat described quite like that before,' and carried on chatting about nothing in particular. Later, having worked around to other corners of the room, I noticed the same gentleman standing in much the same spot, on his own again, but with a smile on his face. He's probably had a good time, I thought, shocking and shaking things up.

I have never gained much pleasure from shopping for working or any other clothes, so if a fashion comes around that makes it hard to get my act together I get even frustrated by it, such as trying to find the correct underpinnings for dresses designed for bustless, bra-less lassies. As I could never fit that description, the see-through fashion fad became a problem, but I fell into its trap one day and became the proud owner of a Zandra Rhodes' creation that needed nothing underneath to be successful. I couldn't believe this applied to me: I had always had a problem

269

disguising bras, until I discovered Frederic's of Hollywood's amazing array of boob halters. There, I'd recently discovered the stick-on bra, purported to give an uplifted silhouette to the more mature bosom.

I had a concert to give at the Kennedy Centre. Nothing venture, I stuck on the new stick-ons beneath Zandra's dress. They transformed me a treat – I had the proudest bustline without straps. I stepped on to the stage with a light spring in my walk, feeling released and wonderfully rejuvenated.

To start my first song, I took a good lung-expanding breath, and knew immediately I was in trouble when each time I inhaled I heard the noise of ripped paper coming from the vicinity of my high-flying bosom. With further breathing and a noticeable failure to counter the laws of gravity one side, it gradually dawned on me that the ominous sound was glue coming unstuck from expanding flesh. I continued singing, and tried to ignore what was happening under the see-through silk, though I did find myself taking smaller and smaller gulps of air. But small air-intake interfered with my singing, so I threw vanity aside for art and let it all hang out. I never tried the stick-ons again.

At a benefit for the United Nations, I wore a more sensible dress: it was an important do, as after the concert we were all invited to the fund-raising dinner and dance, where we would be hobnobbing with Henry Kissinger, George Shultz, Elliot Richards and others of that ilk. The music for dancing was by the amazing Lester Lannin orchestra – amazing for the fact that they played all night without a note of music in front of them, from show tunes to standards to jazz and rock and roll. It was a very impressive performance, as the standard of playing was extremely high in all departments, even though its main purpose was music for dancing, which I'm happy to say I did with wild abandon that night, with the help of my young US guitarist Larry Koonse. It isn't easy to find musicians eager to get on the dance floor, John being one of the reluctant ones, unless it's a slow. But Larry was raring to go and go he did.

It was like one of those movie scenes where all the other

dancers make space to watch the experts, but this was more like gay abandon brought about by a little champagne-drinking than expertise. The smaller group within the orchestra had taken over to do the rock and roll set, and Larry and I took to the floor, doing a dance that didn't resemble any known routine: it was probably nearest to a sort of jitterbug at first, a dance that Americans are rather adept at, then we broke away to do our own thing. Getting carried away, Larry got down, starting to break-dance with a frenzy that John Travolta would have been hard put to keep up with, doing all the street tricks he had up his LA sleeve. Eventually his choreographic ideas dried up, but rather than disappoint his audience, he finished by showing off his youthful strength with a few sets of push-ups. The society gathering was suitably impressed by my partner's and my efforts and we left the floor satisfied with our workout and impressed with the music.

Happily a large circle of friends has grown for us over the years: there are few cities in the world where some of them don't turn up when we perform. With most it's the easiest thing of all to start just where we left off, without having to go through all the preliminaries again. These friends are mainly musicians, artists in other areas, ex-students from the Wavendon courses, friends and family who love our music, and make our gypsy existence very pleasurable. Some have met at our concerts, becoming friends themselves, making the circle a continuum, as our caravan wanders the world.

Over the years we have integrated our UK and US musicians whenever and wherever we could. On a trip to Hong Kong, our American tenor player Ray Loeckle was appearing with us in a concert with James Galway when Ray's instruments came under scrutiny. For some reason known only to Raymond, they have lost all of their golden lustre. Now, with the colour of pewter bordering on gangrene, they are at a disadvantage when comparied to John's alto, and even more to Jimmie's real gold flutes. During the rehearsal for the show, Ray's flute became the subject of interest: Jimmie actually picked it up and blew it. Handing it back to Ray he said, 'You know Ray, the right agent could get a good part for that flute in a horror movie.'

In Fukuoka, Japan, we were all highly amused, when out walking the streets, by the unusual signal for a go-ahead to cross the road; it was a crazy rendition of 'Coming through the Rye'. We could never figure out the reason for the use of this particular tune, any more than why there should be a cable radio station in the hotel that played nothing but different arrangements of 'Auld Lang Syne' all day. We tried to catch it out by switching on at different times of the day, hoping that with a change of pace we might get 'I belong to Glasgow', but it never let the fans of the New Year melody down, at any time of the day. For some strange reason both songs are in the all-time top ten of Japan.

The American musicians and their wives are lovers of a strange assortment of animals of one kind or another, a combination of the exotic and homely, so cats, dogs, sheep, pigs and gorillas can often be the animated topic of a conversation or practical joke. Larry our pianist and I adore gorillas and all primates, joining societies, buying and receiving gifts from videos to toy monkeys, and of course zoo visits wherever we might be in the world. Larry's wife Bobbe is a pig lover, collecting anything piggy; it's difficult to pass a pig now without the urge to purchase it. Ray loves sheep, becoming emotional when he sees a full field; the tour of New Zealand was more than he could bear. So on Ray's first trip there, we arranged a surprise visit for him.

Dunedin was the place we hatched the plot, to take place in the hotel lobby before we left in the morning. But during the night it rained so hard that the promoter, who was also the sheep farmer, phoned to call it off: a bespattered sheep, to be practical, was going to be a bit of a handful to manage. Ray never knew about the failure, but never a group to let a good practical joke get off the hook, on our second visit to New Zealand we tried again. During the interval of our last concert, a sheep was nonchalantly carried backstage to wish Ray a happy birthday. The effort and secrecy that went into getting that one sheep carried up the stairs, for us to see Ray's reaction, was well worth it. 'You guys really know how to make a fella happy,' he said, almost weeping.

All told, over the past twenty-odd years we have visited thirty-nine of the fifty United States, returning again and again to most of them. Northern California, particularly San Francisco and its environs, is a particular favourite of mine. We had had some early, very successful concerts there, so it was not a surprise when we were invited to appear at the Fairmont, the grand hotel atop Nob Hill, for a season at the Venetian Room; a room designed like most of the posh hotels, all the grandeur out front for the customers, with the usual sleaze backstage. I had to walk through the panic of a kitchen trying to get the last orders for puddings served, before the cabaret started. My waiting moments before entering to perform were spent ducking and weaving, to avoid spills from trays filled with creamy delights, that just might land on the first-night creation, messing up the grand entrance, from whence a few minutes before the soup and fish courses had been the main attraction. It was quite an art, and as the days passed I became expert at it.

We had done quite an extensive tour, leading up to the stay in San Francisco. Stuart, my eldest son, had just been through a divorce, and was feeling very low, so John and I invited him to tour with us to keep his spirits up, and be our gofer. Later Alec and Jackie joined us when school broke for the summer holidays, so it turned out to be a family trip across the US, ending in that jewel of a city on the bay. One of the good things about an engagement in an hotel if you don't live near at hand is that you don't have to worry about accommodation for your entourage, as our children, along with our British musicians, were housed, fed and watered.

It was on this engagement that John decided that Alec should smarten himself up; after all, he was the son of the star attraction, and to enter that grand lobby with holes in the knees of his jeans long before it was fashionable and a Harpo Marx flapping sole on his shoe was not to John's liking, so he frogmarched him on a search for clothes in an effort to make him look presentable for the first night. I told him he wouldn't have much success, I had given up long ago. They returned several hours later, Alec with his dress code still intact, split jeans and disintegrating shoe, John a broken man, and no new clothes.

The first night came around and between Stuart, Elliot Ames, our smart American road manager, and the boys in the group they managed to tidy Alec up enough for him not to be thrown out into the night air of foggy San Francisco as that vagrant fan of Cleo Laine. The Dankworth table overflowed with support that night for their mum. Jackie, the only girl, dressed prettily for the occasion and looking very grown up, although not quite grown up enough; asked by a waiter what she wanted to drink, for some unknown reason she said, 'A Pink Squirrel, please'. He didn't hesitate: 'How old are you, miss?' She didn't hesitate either: 'I'll have a Coca-Cola, please!' She now had the full attention not only of all her male escorts, but a trio of young American ladies sitting at the table packed in next to them. The English accents intrigued them so much that they couldn't, apparently, contain their curiosity. Typically American, they asked very directly: where did they come from, were they fans of Cleo Laine (big joke) and so on.

The American girls thought they were being sent up when they were told they were the children of the lady who was about to sing for them, and had to be convinced; once reassured it was the truth, they became a very cosy group, for the evening and for the rest of the week. One of the girls, in fact, got seriously cosy with son Stuart, who decided not to return to England with us. Not long afterwards John and I inherited Sharon as a daughter-in-law, along with her darling son Christopher; a year or so later Stuart and Sharon gave us another beloved grandson, Thomas. They settled in the town of Sonoma, fifty miles north of San Francisco, which has become another home from home.

It turned out to be an eventful time at the Fairmont; John received a charming letter from a Mrs Edwin Dankworth asking that, as the name Dankworth was not a common one, was it not possible that John and her husband were related? While we were in town, could we possibly meet for lunch? We took a few days deciding whether the lady was a crank or not, then arranged the meeting. We were delightfully surprised by the couple we met, who turned out to be genuine relations. During the lunch we were to discover that Ed's grandfather was the brother of John's grandfather, making them second cousins. They did look similar, and Kitty, Ed's wife, had done her research well, going right back to the Lutheran exit from Germany. It seems only one brother came to Britain; the rest went to the New World and they were prolific. Dankworth is an unusual German name, as the spelling has not been anglicized as so many think.

So through our San Franciscan cousins we were introduced to relations galore on John's side. We see more of Ed and Kitty than most of the other cousins because, Sonoma, where we have a home, is not far from theirs in Alameda. But a visit to Milwaukee becomes a big family event. Knowing that there would be a dozen or more relations attending my last concert there, John and I thought we would amuse them by performing the Gershwin song, 'My Cousin from Milwaukee'. It's a fun lyric, but in retrospect not too flattering to sing to a real-life cousin, but they all seem to have a good sense of the ridiculous and saw the joke. Ted, who is Ed's brother, and his family live in Washington: another brother, Dick, in Reno.

Cleveland, Ohio, was the place, in 1982, where a vast number of Dankworths assembled for a family reunion. It confused the hell out of the hotel telephone operator who, when our manager called to be put through to Mr Dankworth, asked which one. 'John,' he replied. Desperately the operator asked again, 'But which one, there are so many!' Realizing she was panicking he said, 'Oh, just put me through to Miss Cleo Laine.'

27

Family and Friends

The seventies ended handsomely for me, as I was honoured with an OBE presented by the Queen at Buckingham Palace with Jackie and my sister Sylvia present; and I was chosen to perform for the Royal Command in the presence of the Queen Mother, another happy event to remember. The next year saw me in a production at the Comedy Theatre, London, that John had written for me, based on the life of Colette – a great delight for me, but not for the critics. Directed by Wendy Toye, the cast included Kenny Nelson, who played all the men in her life, and John Moffatt, who narrated the story between quick dress and scene changes.

But at the end of 1979 I had a phone call from Sylvia's son, Maurice, telling me my father had been diagnosed as having prostate cancer – the doctor had told him, but not Sylvia. Once I was told, I had to know exactly what it entailed so I got in touch with his doctor. I said I had read somewhere that prostate cancer was containable with certain drugs, but he informed me that he thought my father's had spread. It also transpired that Pa had been skipping taking his pills because they were giving him bosoms. He also had serious bronchitis – all in all he was not in a good state. Sylvia had to be told it was serious, and that she must make sure he took his pills, so I went to see them both, taking a walking stick along for him, as the last time I'd visited him he had been using a bit of old stick to push himself out of his chair. The new walking stick pleased him immensely and he used it to walk about the room for a while, till I said we had to sit and talk.

We had to convince him to take his medication. I told him I'd seen macho men with a lot more flesh in that area than many women: 'They'll just think you've started weight-lifting in your old age.' That might have done the trick once, but this time he wasn't convinced and during a quiet moment he looked up at me and said, 'I think I've left it a bit late, haven't I, Clemmie?' I tried to reassure him that we would get a second opinion from a specialist about what was ailing him. When we were about to leave, he, sitting in his chair, looked at us both and said, 'When you hear the thunder don't run under a tree.' We were nonplussed at first by this *non-sequitur*, till I hit on the answer to the riddle, which was a musical one: together we sang 'There'll be Pennies From Heaven For You and Me'.

Once again my sister was the main care-giver to this now frail, crumbling old man, and saw to it that he ate his food, took his pills, and kept clean and tidy. He had never been compliant, and a few months earlier this proud old reprobate would never have allowed himself to be ordered about. Only a short time ago Stuart's wife, Sharon, had been creased into helpless laughter and disbelief when, on a visit from the US, she watched him climb over from the back seat of the Rolls-Royce to the front, like a three-year-old in a tantrum, insisting that he'd rather sit up front with Harry to be taken home. Opening the door and doing it the normal way was much too simple. He was leaving the Old Rectory after showing off his tangoing, singing and flirting. Even at eighty-six he could make his grandchildren roar with laughter at the drop of a hat with his outrageous antics.

As I'd promised, I eventually arranged an appointment with a London specialist for a second opinion. Through the examination-room door I heard his agonized moans as he went through another investigation. The doctor told me to leave well alone, as there was no hope: he should not have any more poking about done, and he should be allowed to go with dignity, but the visit seemed to cheer Pa up, as the specialist told him he would make him comfortable; something was being done, he thought. The journey there and back home was physically very painful for him, and for me it was devastatingly sad. I was remembering him standing up proud as punch when he came to hear me sing, digging people in the ribs, as he told them, 'That's my daughter up there!' Although he never told me himself, I know that he always had a twinkle in his eye when he saw me perform. He died in December 1980.

Around the same time John's mother at the age of eighty-two was found on her bedroom floor early one morning having suffered a stroke. Luckily she had been persuaded to move close to us a few months earlier, so she was discovered sooner than she might have been in her old home. She was swiftly taken to Milton Keynes hospital, with some hope of recovery, as she was talking and communicating reasonably well, but she had a second massive stroke soon after, which disabled her to such an extent that she was unable to eat, talk or respond to anything. Ma Dankworth passed away in February 1981.

The parents who had passed on their joy of music to us, keeping it forever alive in the home, had left us orphans. To celebrate the musical influence they had had on the lives of their children, grandchildren and friends, on 26 April 1981, we gathered together – the relations of both families, and all their children, sang their praises at a black and white party at the Old Rectory Stables Theatre.

New York was the main meeting place for me and my Jamaican/American cousins. My pa's sister, Aunt Rebecca, was the only one I knew personally as I had met her in England a couple of times, and we corresponded. (She died in 1993 at the age of ninety-three.) I never met any of the other seven brothers and sisters. But when I started to work in North America, Pandora's box opened to reveal as many if not more cousins than John.

Dear cousin Daisy and her family and her brother Vincent (an actor/writer) are the closest, because she's the keeper-in-touch of the US family, so when I'm in New York we try to get together, and when there is a concert or club date Daisy and her singing daughters come along to give full support. Pandora revealed cousins in LA, New Jersey, Carolina and Rochester: a healthy mixture of intellectuals, doctors of religion, entertainers and plain ordinary folk. Canada was less fruitful, introducing me to only two of my mother's brother's children. I knew Gladys was a cousin immediately we met after a concert in London Ontario: she had my mother's looks. We didn't see much of each other after that first meeting, as we didn't play regularly in that area as we did other Canadian towns and cities, but we do keep in touch.

All the different family strains are interesting to see, but I find it hard to work out who belongs to whom. Daisy has supplied me with the Campbell family tree, naming everyone living and dead. She came to visit us, with her daughter Kim, well before my father died, sitting down with him to do what every son and daughter should do with their parents: ask them questions about their family and life with a tape-recorder on. When I learnt she had done that, I felt guilty that I had not even thought of making that kind of effort with either of my parents – but the guilt doesn't stop there. Later I had more reason for remorse when back on tour in the US with Jimmie Galway, I carried in my handbag the tape of the interview that Daisy insisted I listen to. I hadn't got around to it, but was looking forward to hearing all the gossip. I can't remember the exact location, except it was an outside venue with very little security. Jimmie, always concerned about the safety of his gold flutes, had asked me earlier, when he was rehearsing his pieces, if I was going to be in the dressing room all the time, and if so, could he leave a flute with me. His flutes remained his property, but somehow my handbag didn't remain mine. Daisy was understanding, but nothing I said could make up for the loss of something that for her held a great deal of sentimental value – a fun talk with her uncle Alec and a visit to England.

The record *Sometimes When We Touch* was the reason for
the tour with Jimmie Galway in North America, which set
the seal on our friendship and brought about an album that
became very successful the world over. The work of touring
and concertizing helped me to get over the sadness of the early
part of the eighties, bringing everything back to life again instead
of dwelling morbidly on the past. I was happy to be out and doing
again and getting great satisfaction from it. American theatre
work started to come my way, too, notably first *The Mystery of
Edwin Drood*. This was a great fillip for me, as I still hadn't got
over my feelings of despondency. The children had been acting
as they were supposed to, very rebellious teenagers, and John was
beginning to spend more of his time with symphony orchestras,
notably the LSO, so I was feeling lowish, when the invitation to
do a workshop for Joe Papp's Shakespeare in the Park Company
came my way.

During a break from touring, we stayed with our friends from
Philadelphia, Harriet and Bill Chanoff, at their home at Long
Beach, New Jersey, giving me a few restful days to dwell on
the invitation while we took long beach walks, visited bird
sanctuaries, ate fish suppers, listened to non-disturbing music
and happy friendly conversation. After that break we spent
some further time off in Sonoma, walking the hills and glorious
state parks that abound in the area, and I was beginning to feel
renewed and adventurous again. I made up my mind to say yes
to this opportunity.

It was one of the best career decisions I have made, for many
reasons: first to work for Joe Papp, second to get to know some
wonderful artists, and third to be in from the start of Rupert
Holmes's inspired creation of book and music. Although it was
hard work, once it became a positive production for the park, I
revelled in every minute of it.

Finding an apartment in New York that was halfway decent, at
a reasonable price, presented a problem. After looking at several
that were affordable on a long-term basis, I despaired at ever
finding something. Eventually the Shakespeare Company found

a place near the Public Theatre where the rehearsals were going to take place, in the famous Gramercy Park Hotel. Though in a dilapidated state, it retained a little of its grandeur and I had a certain amount of service, which was comforting during the heavy rehearsal periods. John was with me for a short period, writing for the LSO pops concerts, but I was soon to be left to fend for myself.

The morning after John had left, I experienced my first withdrawal-from-J.D. incompetence, when I felt like making myself a cup of coffee. J.D. had left me a new, unopened tin, and I thanked him for being so thoughtful as I removed the plastic top, thinking the next step would be just a tab-pull away to remove the seal. But it required a tin opener. The tin opener he had bought was a mystery, I sat trying to work the bloody thing out for what seemed like hours, to no avail. In desperation, I phoned Kurt, our manager, living in New Jersey, hoping that he would be able to solve my problem by remote control. 'Hmm . . . I always have trouble with those,' he said, when I explained what sort it was. He went to look for his to demonstrate. He couldn't find it, tried to explain, but it was a dismal failure. I put the phone down none the wiser. In the end, I had a cup of instant decaf instead, then went shopping. I bought freshly ground, leaded and decaffeinated coffee, along with a tin-opener that didn't require you to have a degree in engineering to manipulate it.

After that false start I managed, with the help of numerous friends and Daisy, not to be on my own if I didn't want to be – but with so much work to do it was heaven not to have to think about anything but my immediate needs. My co-stars were George Rose, Betty Buckley, Howard McGillen and Patti Cohenour, with George the one who held it all together. During rehearsals he was also playing on Broadway in a play called *Aren't We All*. He turned out to be my special buddy for the whole run: we went everywhere together. He had a great knowledge of all kinds of music, from listening to his vast and varied collection of jazz to opera recordings, recalling the words of music-hall songs, obscure musicals and films without thinking, all this combined with a theatrical memory that was like a computer.

Before and after we got to Central Park in the Delacorte Theatre the weather in New York was like a sauna, and was difficult to cope with: sleep was often hard to come by even with air-conditioning, and the energy level was not always easy to maintain. I went walking a lot in a park near the Gramercy, one that you could only get into with a key from reception. It wasn't very big but I walked round and round it, learning lines and songs, protected from the harassment of the alcoholics and drug-users of the district. When it poured with rain it brought refreshing relief to get soaked as I walked around, only for the humidity to return tenfold soon after, but I got used to it eventually.

Towards the end of July 1985 I moved into Clifford Hocking's flat at the Phythian Building on 70th Street, and felt immediately at home. On Sunday the 28th we started rehearsals at the Delacorte Theatre in the Park. It was all starting to come together, building up to the opening. Though the heat and humidity was often unbearable, after the enclosed spaces and air-conditioning, being outside gave most of the cast a feeling of release. Protection from the sun was essential, other advice was never to walk home alone after dark, watch out for fast bikers and your possessions and spray yourself with bug repellent.

It was a wonderful experience working for Joe Papp in Central Park. He achieved the impossible by being a showman, banging the drum continually on behalf of Shakespeare in the Park, while never losing sight of the need to nurture new plays and musicals, such as *Chorus Line* and indeed *Edwin Drood*. After the opening night (it was a limited run), we waited for the reviews to appear; and although they didn't say we were God's gift to the musical theatre, they were more than kind. Joe sensed that with a few rewrites and a lot more hard work, it would be able to transfer to Broadway. He gathered us all together and gave us a rousing pep talk, ending with the exortation to give him a smash hit.

What was amazing about that company was that we all believed we could deliver and did, because we gave him his smash hit, on 2 December 1985 at the Imperial Theater Broadway.

The period 1985–86 was one of wonderful happenings. Son Alec and his wife Linda presented J.D. and me with a grandchild in the delightful form of little Emily, Jackie's acting career seemed to be successfully taking off, I was nominated for a Tony award for my role as Princess Puffer in *The Mystery of Edwin Drood*, the cast and I did a number from the show in Macy's Thanksgiving Parade, and while I was in the show, won a Grammy Award for the album *Cleo Live at Carnegie – The Tenth Anniversary*. I received a dozen roses from Ella Fitzgerald with a note 'Congratulations gal! It's about time.' When it seemed certain I was going to be in New York for a lengthy stay our management company bought an apartment overlooking Central Park, which meant I would never have to look for another apartment or stay in a New York hotel again, and it meant I could put people up. Elisabeth Welch stayed with me at the time New York fêted her and her one-woman show. She was divine company, a laugh a minute, and her memory for dates and lyrics was unchallengeable. As I found out when I swore we opened in *Cindy Ella* at the Arts Theatre and she told me, 'You're wrong, gal, it was the Garrick.' Still not convinced she was right we had a bet. I asked Tony Walton, the designer, who looked through some old records for me and said, 'You have lost the bet I'm afraid, Cleo, she's right.'

Elisabeth won the off-Broadway Award for her show and became the belle of New York that season. The Sonoma family, J.D. and Jackie came to spend the Christmas holidays together and to see the show. For Sharon and her two boys, Thomas and Christopher, it was their first visit to New York, so it was a magical experience for them, also a bitterly cold one, coming from California. On Christmas Eve we had a family meal at our local restaurant, the Copper Hatch, where I was known. Like most restaurants in the city it was serviced by actors or singers waiting for their moment to arrive – which it did one day for a girl called Mary, who waited on me and John regularly. We had long talks about singing or acting and the disappointing auditions she went to, but she was always optimistic. Then she disappeared, and when I enquired after her they said she'd just moved on. Entering the theatre one evening later, Mary was there, talking animatedly to the stage doorman. 'Mary!?' I said, wondering if something was wrong and she'd come for help. 'What are you doing here?' 'I'm understudying you and I'm in the chorus,' she said without a blink of an eye. To say I was surprised was an understatement. I congratulated her on at last passing an audition, and of course saw her daily from then on. I often wondered if she had been clever enough, once she found out who and where I was, to study me and my English accent and go for it.

At the family Christmas Eve meal at the Copper Hatch the children were fussed over and fêted with all the goodies of the season, then given mugs to remind them of their visit. After the meal we decided to walk a few blocks to show them our neighbourhood. We were on the West Side and started from the café down Amsterdam Avenue, towards the Lincoln Center. Halfway down two men came out of a bar and before we had passed, wished us a merry Christmas, which for some reason broke into the song, so we joined them, possibly because we had had a little too much seasonal cheer. While the boys and I sang with them on the corner, someone came along and pressed a couple of dollars into Thomas's hand. By the time we got ourselves together to explain that we weren't buskers they were gone. We passed it on to the two men who obviously needed it more than Thomas, who nevertheless protested loudly about the loss of his good fortune at the start of his first visit to New York.

I stayed with the show for a further six months, discovering New York with friends and by myself, meeting stars who came to see the show, like Barbra Streisand and Ginger Rogers, whom I had supper with, and performers who were also appearing on Broadway. I was in the 'Broadway Softball League' singing (not all the words) the national anthem along with others at the opening of the season in Central Park.

On one occasion Joe Grifazi, an actor friend in *Drood*, asked if I would like to come after the show to hear his wife play at a club in Greenwich Village. I've never been too anxious to sit in a smoky atmosphere when I have so much daily singing to do, but to be friendly I agreed to go along with the group he was getting together. The soprano saxophone playing I listened to that night was some of the most imaginative, moving and creative jazz I'd heard in a long time from any player, male or female, and kept me enraptured all evening. I had never heard of Jane Ira Bloom before Joe proudly introduced me to his wife that night. She became a real friend and a musical colleague on record and live performances – she did a season with us at the Blue Note jazz club in the Village and also played on my record *Jazz*, along with Clark Terry, Gerry Mulligan, Mark Whitfield, and my US group.

I became a Broadway baby in every sense of the word: tarts and policemen said hi! nightly as I entered the stage door, and taxi-drivers yelled 'Heh! Cleo! How ya doin'?' The theatre district became a village and the convenient next-door J.R.'s the local eatery for many of the *Drood* cast.

It was there I discovered I was allergic to crab, after eating soft-shell crabs. It was some time before I realized that the reason for the closure of my throat, which obviously affected my singing, was due to these hard-to-resist tasty little devils. George and I used to visit weekly, whether we needed him or not, the greatest throat man in New York, Mr Grabsheid; he looked after all the Broadway stars as well as opera singers, who used to fly in from all the opera houses in the States for his treatments. It was Grabsheid who told me to lay off the crab. He was quite a character, just like his compatriot in London, Mr Alexander, both taught by Alexander's father in Vienna.

Standing in his white coat in the doorway of his office, a tall impressive eighty-year-old, he commanded in a throaty guttural voice, such as he would use to his beloved dogs and which it

286

made my throat ache to hear: 'Come!' Once in his sanctuary the next command was 'Sit!' then 'Open!' and last, 'Say Ahhh!'. After all those commands and analysis of the chords, he'd give an order you didn't dare disobey: 'No . . . rrrett vine! No . . . dairy product! No . . . chocalaate! No . . . Tea! No! Crap!' Then you got your treatment and you felt better. George and I loved him; when he died we, and many more singers, lost a great friend.

The Tony Awards' celebration, produced by my old friend Alexander Cohen for the last time, brought *The Mystery of Edwin Drood* many accolades, running away with best musical, best book of a musical, best score, for the multi-talented Rupert Holmes. And though I didn't win the best actress in a musical award (losing to Bernadette Peters) the nomination brought a fair amount of kudos. Princess Margaret came to see us, after she had finished her official Royal Ballet duties, paying a visit backstage that knocked all the Americans out, and I went to supper with her at the home of designer Carolina Herrera. We ended up singing Spanish songs, Princess Margaret and I doing the English lyrics, Oscar de la Renta and the others the Spanish. It's amazing how many Spanish songs have been translated into English, we got through quite a few that night.

My contract up, I decided it was time to go home. J.D. and I had been separated far too long and my hair was also fed up with being encased nightly under someone else's: it wasn't the kind that sprang back to life or any presentable shape after long-term imprisonment. It had spent almost a year under turbans and fancy headgear of one kind or another and I felt like seeing my bush for a change. Lots of new creams and potions were now being sold to make my kind of hair behave since it had become fashionable, and I was dying to try them all out.

My friends Jim Sindoni and Dr Sol Fox gave me a last-night party at Sol's handsome brownstone and although it was sad to say goodbye to all the friends I had made I knew it was time to move on.

I came back to England and must admit I didn't find it easy

to settle down at first. We were together on the road again, but John was the one tied up now with the LSO and the Wavendon Easter Course, so I didn't see much more of him than I would have had I stayed in New York. However, I carried on doing my thing while he got on with his, and we saw Jackie together when she visited Luton with the RSC in *The Merchant of Venice* and *Much Ado about Nothing* with Fiona Shaw in the lead. Early in 1987 we did a tour of Canada and the US, visiting Vancouver, Minneapolis, Boston, Washington, Los Angeles (where we took part in a *This is Your life* for Dudley Moore), then back to Canada to the freezing cold.

It was a hectic time and on a freezing walk we decided that the time had come when we should take a holiday together without work intruding into our lives. The choice of where to go was solved when our good friend from early New York days, Sir Hamilton Whyte, wrote us from Singapore, where he was installed as High Commissioner, to say that we should come over to see him and Sheila, his wife, before they left, as his retirement was imminent, and he would have to leave this lovely post. So we packed our bags and went, on 23 March 1987, to Singapore, the journey culminating in a slow and stately drive in the old Daimler to the British colonial house, Eden Hall, which was to be our home for the next ten days.

We first met Ham and Sheila in New York in 1973, when he was still a Mr and we were doing an engagement at the Rainbow Grill in the Rockefeller Plaza. He was head of the British Information Services at the time, and was the most unlikely civil servant one could wish to meet: a red-headed eccentric Scot who sped around New York on a bicycle, looking ruddily healthy and slim. Sheila travelled the world with him, but loved New York best, finding it gave her more energy to keep up her identity as a painter. They came to support us at the Rainbow Grill along with the nephew of Duke Ellington, Stephen James, Anita Porter and Duke's sister Ruth, and during the season there, Lena Horne came, and so did Tony Bennett and Irving Caesar, the lyricist of *Tea for Two*. John used to worry when he knew Irving was in, as I always sang 'It's' instead of 'is' – a slight lyric change. So one night he drew the attention of a waiter (who spoke minimal English) and asked him to give me a message. 'Please tell Miss Laine that the lyrics of *Tea For Two* are Darling, this place *is* a lovers' oasis.' The waiter was puzzled but said, 'Yes, I think I've got that.' Before I came on, John asked if the message had been given. 'Sure,' said the waiter. 'I told her you loved her very much and would like to take her to a desert island; she was very moved.'

I always suspected Ham had a hand in recommending that I receive the OBE. He never told me, but he claimed to have been disappointed that I didn't get a Dameship, so that I could open my show with 'There ain't nothing like a dame'.

Our Singapore holiday with them was a life-saver, as we enjoyed the orchid gardens, the zoo – and the cricket (played by Ham, with Sheila keeping score). I was able to improve my flute-playing with daily practice, and we swam, walked, drove, shopped. That presented a few problems for John, as it was difficult for him to find articles of clothing large enough for his western frame. Buying a pair of trousers in a sale on one shopping spree, for some reason he didn't bother to try them on in the shop, and when he eventually got around to it back at the house, he found he was not narrow enough in the hips (Oh! I of the Dunlopillo hips was overjoyed to see this), but he wasn't too put out, thinking that Ham, who was decidedly more slender than he was, might like them. We were gathered on the veranda talking about the day's happenings, when John produced his scanty pair of pants for Ham's approval. Without a moment's notice Ham's trousers came off and he'd got one leg encased in the new ones, when a maid came in with a message for Sir Hamilton Whyte. With no time to insert his other leg and zip up, he stood to attention with the pants held up in front of him, one leg in and one out, trying to spare her embarrassment. When she departed we realized how ludicrous he must have looked – it was the material of farce, and we could not contain ourselves. After all that, the trousers were too big for him.

28

Into the Woods

When we left Singapore we were well on the way to getting back
to where we were before my incursion into Broadway, going back
on the road with renewed energy.

In June we toured Israel with the English band, including
Larry the American guitarist, son Alec on bass and Laurie
Mansfield, our manager. Alec's wife, Linda and baby Emily came
along too, and it seemed that our problems had been resolved: we
were once more a happy family. Jackie was now in the West End
at the Ambassador Theatre in *Les Liaisons Dangereuses*.

I did a Gershwin Night with the LSO with Michael Tilson
Thomas conducting, and the LSO pops season started. There
were also rehearsals for the Shakespeare programme we were
doing in August for the Edinburgh Festival.

Then Michael Emmerson, who had been appointed head of
RCA's Red Seal label, asked me to become one of his artists,
and I agreed. My first record with the company, in October,
was *Cleo Sings Sondheim*; we recorded it in New York with a large
string orchestra arranged and conducted by Jonathan Tunick. I
met Stephen Sondheim during the sessions, and he seemed to be
pleased with how it was going. At the time he was busy preparing
for the opening of *Into the Woods*, one of the songs from which, a
quartet in that production, he made into a solo for me to record,

the lovely 'No one is alone'. It was a hectic end of the year for us and the Stables Theatre too, with the 'Wavendon Awards Gala' at the Barbican with the Princess Royal attending, after which we returned to the US and the road again.

In 1988 I went into the Yorkshire Television studios to record a programme based on the recording of the Sondheim album, which brought about a reunion with Laurie Holloway, who was the musical director. I got a lot of satisfaction out of doing that show. Not long after it was finished, in February, we were on our way to Australia, touring all the provinces again. In Sydney we met up with Elisabeth Welch who was doing her one-woman show there, once again repeating the same rave reviews afforded her in her home town of New York. As is always the case with Elisabeth, we all enjoyed ourselves.

We decided to send a lasting plant to her flat instead of flowers for her opening night, telling our manager to order something lovely which would get to her before she went to the theatre, so she would know we were thinking of her. As John was meeting an Australian Dankworth cousin, I went to see her show by myself. Afterwards she came to our hotel, which was next door to her flat, for supper. As the three of us settled down to eat Lis said, 'Heh! I got a bone to pick with you, about that fucking tree . . .' Apparently a vast tree had arrived for her that morning and it had taken took two strong men to install it. We could only think that the reason why she'd got a tree instead of a nice practical pot plant was the difference between what you'd pay for a pot plant in the US or Britain and a large tree in Australia.

At the end of the year I was on the West Coast of America, in my favourite area, San Francisco, recording the album of songs written by women called *Woman to Woman*. John did all the arrangements and orchestrations and co-produced it with Kurt Gebauer. I don't know if it had ever been done before, apart from lady singer song writers doing all their own material, but it was extremely interesting to research. At first we thought we would have to water it down to either lyrics by women (which produced quite a few) with male music, or vice-versa, but in the end we realized it would be copping out. So we started doing our homework. People like Benny Green, Michael Feinstein and Ned Sherrin made invaluable suggestions and gradually it all came together.

There were songs that I had known for years, that I had grown up hearing my Pa sing, like 'Close Your Eyes', with words and music by Bernice Petkere, and 'I'll Never Smile Again' by Ruth Lowe, who also did both, but I hadn't given any attention then to who had written them until this recording had to be researched. Another 'both' song is 'Willow Weep for Me', a standard jazz tune, and I think John's orchestration of it is one of the loveliest on the album; but I hadn't known that Ann Ronnell wrote it. This album made me become less sloppy about noting who wrote the standard songs that I loved and grew up with. They were not all standards, though: we were able to find some contemporary songs that sat well on my shoulders. In fact one of the reasons the album came about was a song I sang in concert that so many people asked me to record, 'Come in from the Rain', written by Melissa Manchester and Carole Bayer-Sager.

We also included the Blossom Dearie/Linda Albert song, 'Inside a Silent Tear', which was a new song. Blossom always kept me informed about her songs, either by song copies or tapes; I love most of them and have recorded her suggestions in the past. This song was special, as was Peggy Lee's and Marion McPartland's 'In the Days of Our Love' and Gayle Moran's 'Your Eyes Speak to Me'.

One of the nice things about the woman idea was being able to use two paintings done by my gifted water-colourist friend Dee Knott on the album. I had originally wanted them to be on the cover but the record company had other more commercial ideas. I fought hard and at least got them on the back. I also asked the boys to dress up in drag for the album cover but they all declined.

We stayed in Sonoma while we rehearsed and recorded the album. Our Sonoma house is my refuge from the tensions of the road. High up on a hill, it overlooks the town in the Valley

293

of the Moon. It's very laid back and friendly – farm and wine country; not as commercial as the parallel valley, Napa, but vineyards have grown since we first visited Stuart and Sharon there, and it's catching up.

John and I walk a lot when we stay there: the countryside is some of the most majestic and breath-taking one can imagine, from the Jack London home in Glen Ellen a few miles down the road and other national parks in the district, to the local bike path down the hill. I love our daily walks for the variety of welcomes one gathers: from the very young to the ancient, they all acknowledge you either with a 'Hello, mornin',' a 'Hi', a 'Howdie, how ya doin'?, or 'Have a good (or nice) one, gonna be a hot one,' to a surprise answer from an elderly gentleman who answered my 'How are you?' with 'Rotten – I ache, I cain't walk and I wish I was dead.'

I feel at home in Sonoma; I even like to go shopping, something I avoid like hell in Britain. We enjoy our two grandsons, who are good company along with eldest son Stuart, and we love his amazingly energetic wife, who is a teacher, cook, runner, soccer player, skier – she has a go at everything, even music. Stuart has a freelance graphic design business and goes along with almost everything that Sharon does. Sometimes we see nothing of them when we are there, even though we are virtually in the same house, but if we are there and a birthday or an American holiday crops up we often make it into a family event.

The autumn of 1988 brought an enquiry from a management company in New York asking if I would be interested in joining the company of Sondheim's *Into the Woods*, to play the role of the Witch on tour before going to Los Angeles. This was a tempting offer, but I couldn't say yes, knowing it would mean another long separation from John, without us having talked first about how it might affect us. We decided together that it would be a wonderful thing to do and that I would regret it if I turned it down, so I said yes and, remarkably, without an audition, because James Lapine had seen me in *Drood*, I got the part. We started rehearsals in New York at the end of October, with James Lapine directing (the writer of the book and director of the New York production). Stephen Sondheim came to see how we were shaping up towards the end of rehearsals, when it was nearly time to go on the road. I thought the cast was magnificent, just as good as the one I'd seen on Broadway, immensely dedicated to getting it right. They worked non-stop.

Sondheim's shows seem to bring out this quality in a performer, myself included. It became an anxious family at times, with the very young seemingly word perfect, assured and confident, until James Lapine started pulling them up and putting them through their paces, while we older ones clung to the books longer, as a security blanket. Until James said they had to go, and then of course it was wonderful to see and hear it all fall into place, piece by piece, little by little.

Our first engagement was in Fort Lauderdale, Florida, where relationships blossomed. I had quite a few buddies in the cast: Charlotte Rae (Jack's mother), a well-known television actress/comedienne, and Rex Robbins (the narrator), a fine New York actor, but we were all pretty close, even down to the stage hands, who had to work like Trojans to get the set up in time for us to perform. The stage often turned out to be impossibly small for the scenery which had to be reorganized in such a way that it became in effect a different set for the actors to work in; this of course meant detailed explanations of what was going to be missing or different. The crew and stage manager had to work out these jigsaw puzzles in every new theatre.

We played several theatres in Florida before our long stay in Los Angeles. Stephen Sondheim came to Fort Lauderdale, putting everyone on their toes by his presence, removing any complacency that might have set in. Once again we worked towards the first night, 22 November, when a large sigh of relief was let out by all. Most of the time the audiences were elderly and the first half of the show was enough for them, as hunger set in, making them eager to get off to an early meal and bed.

I loved performing the show, especially in Florida. My

favourite spot was my nightly visit into the audience dressed in the witch's outfit, to do a scene that appeared to be magic on my part. James or the stage manager would reconnoitre the theatre and work out the best position for me: it meant that when I entered and left, I had to disturb half a line of sitting customers for it to be effective. The entrance of this strange creature into their midst, that they had so far only viewed at a distance, was shock enough, but when I had to almost touch them, it often brought about amusing horror. I didn't have any lines until I got to my spot, and I couldn't drop character and apologize for having to disturb them, so some interesting bits came out nightly, depending on whom I had to push past. Sometimes they were so horrified they couldn't move, so in my best evil voice I'd command, 'Shift ya feet, or I'll shift 'em for ya,' whilst waving my magic stick in their direction. That always got them to move fast, so that I could get in and out without holding anything up. Other times someone thought a little chat would be nice. When this happened the character allowed you to be rude and make your escape: if it was a child, I had a grumble about all the stupidity up on the stage and that amused them. I loved it. I was often told to cut it out, but how was I to get to my spot? I never had any written lines, so I remembered Doris Hare and got on with it.

After a Christmas break in Sonoma, more rehearsals and long walks with J.D. over New Year, on 3 January 1989 I flew from San Francisco to Burbank for the ten-week season. This was the key date of the tour, bringing all the bigwigs back on the scene, giving us the willies once again. If it hadn't been for the traffic and the smog I would have enjoyed the beginning of my stay; I had been found a hotel that had just opened, the Marriott, very grand and within walking distance of a park and good shopping, but the daily drive to work was occasionally very hairy. My driver, George, knew all the back doubles but had to allow more and more time to get me to the theatre, as traffic piled up on the freeways.

After the first night brouhaha, it's good to settle down into a routine for a while, and get on with it. John came and went, but friends took over – Niki Nanos, Charlotte Rae and Rex Robbins all gave me hospitality, and offered an open invitation to tag along on any of their outings. So I never felt abandoned, until I received the bombshell phone call from my son Stuart in Sonoma saying that my brother-in-law Geoff had called to say my sister Sylvia had cancer, and they'd given her only six months of life. It was such a shock I didn't speak for some time, and when I did, I think I said something as daft as 'Are you sure?' Of course he was sure that's what he had told him, he was phoning to prepare me for the inevitable.

I spoke to Sylvia a few minutes later and suddenly found we were holding on to each other because of grim death, with thousands of miles between us. Our phone calls from that time on were almost unbearable for both of us: she was courageously insistent that she was going to fight it and win, seeing faith-healers regularly, cheerfully saying they had just left and she felt so much better. Another day a phone call to her would hear her in utter dispair at her weakness, and I would say, 'I'm coming to see you'. Then she'd brighten up and say: 'Oh! Clem, I don't want you to, I'm not that bad, and anyway I don't want you to see me like this.' Once again we went for a second opinion – John being at home it fell on him to arrange it, together with our friend Jinnie Haynes, who introduced us to the head surgeon of Milton Keynes Hospital, Chris B. Lynch. He examined Sylvia, then arranged a visit to a London specialist, who sent her home with a ray of hope, saying that, at present, it seemed to be dormant; he would not prescribe any treatment for fear of setting it off again.

When I heard that news, to me it meant one thing: there was nothing he could do. Apart from our phone calls, during which there were moments of incredible closeness, as our hearts opened in a way that neither of us had experienced as sisters before. It was devastating to realize, helplessly, that these moments were coming to us too late. Feeling unnerved and impotent at such a distance, my enjoyment of the play started to dwindle and my own health began to give me trouble, as a general malaise crept in:

the voice suffered first, then I had trouble with my teeth. I put it down to my LA allergy, and looked forward to moving on.

After LA we were on the move constantly, making it harder to keep up to date, but Sylvia was hanging in there and I hoped I would get back to see her alive. The tour took us to Orange County, Denver, Tulsa, Des Moines, Urbana Illinois, St Louis, Cleveland and New Orleans, where John was able to join me. It's a city I have always felt at home in, from our first visit there, when we appeared at the Fairmont Hotel. On this visit I had to do a considerable amount of PR work for the show, and on one occasion had to go to the Public Radio station to be interviewed. John accompanied me and after the interview the conversation switched from the show to jazz, mainly about where to go that wasn't on the tourist beat. The interviewer recommended a place called the Glass House, where a band named the 'Dirty Dozen' played, but having become relatively famous in the jazz world, the band were often on the road and not there. However, he thought the second band was worth hearing too and recommended a visit.

We made a note of this information, and decided to go at the first opportunity. I had been designated a limousine and a regular driver called Laverne to take care of me, a job which he took very seriously indeed; if he thought a place that I wanted to go to was rough or beneath my status he'd say, 'Ah dow'n think ya'll should go, Miss Laine.' Most times I took his advice, and would have on this occasion if I had not been accompanied by John, Rex Robbins and a young lady friend in the company called Anne Rickenbacker (who, during the tour, was the artist who always painted the logo on the wall backstage, a tradition that tells the interested 'we wos ere'), and if we had not been told about it by a very upstanding member of the community. Mysteriously, when we made enquiries about the Glass House, people were not too forthcoming, which aroused our curiosity and interest in finding it. We eventually found out that on the night we were able to go, the 'Dirty Dozen' was indeed not playing.

When we told Laverne he didn't like the idea of me, or rather his car, going at all: it was well out of town and not in a very salubrious district, according to him. We had to talk him into it. 'Let's just go and have a look, Laverne . . . If it's not OK, well, we'll just come back.' Grudgingly he said 'Aw'rite' and drove us out into what seemed the boondocks, miles away from the comfort of the garish resplendence that was the French Quarter. Eventually Laverne turned a corner that revealed a shack looking nothing like the glasshouse of my imagination, but a haunt where the walls appeared to be pulsating with energy, light and the sound of the music. That was exciting enough, until the next unbelievable happening: before our eyes, out of the shack, a black man twirling a white hankie came dancing, at great speed, in an incredibly athletic but balletic style. He crossed the street, pirouetted around, hankie aloft, and whirled back into the vibrating shack. To our amazement this free-form dance was repeated several times by other just as efficent male terpsichoreans before we got out of the car. Laverne said he'd go on in and investigate; Rex accompanied him.

Laverne came back to say, 'I down think ya'll . . .' but Rex interrupted and said, 'It's all right, just music, listening and dancing.' We relied on Rex's good judgement and went in. Laverne didn't trust his brothers enough to leave his limo unattended and so missed an evening of raise-the-spirit music and dancing the likes of which we had never seen before. Strangely the women in the place did not participate and were not dancing, but Anne and I couldn't resist and joined the men and their free-form whirlings, much to their surprise. Without losing the happy dancing swing of bygone days, the young band, playing the instruments of a traditional band with the exception of a baritone saxophone, updated the New Orleans marching music of the street band, by playing modern jazz with infectious walking rhythms, predominantly led by the tuba and drums. They lived up to the name of 'Rebirth' with the music they played.

We stayed well into the early hours, enjoying and happily complying to the shout from the stage, 'Eeny one out theare buya band a sixpack?' when they took a break. We returned to the tourist trap happily renewed.

One day Rex and his wife Pat invited us for a meal between shows on a matinee day, booking a table at the historic and fashionable New Orleans restaurant, Antoine's, a place more to Laverne's liking than the Glass House. When we met outside the stage door, I noticed Rex's face drop when he saw John's attire. 'John, I'm afraid you have to wear a jacket at Antoine's.' This never pleased J.D. when the temperature was up in the hundreds. But he had a solution to the annoying problem: the shopping maniac remembered that on an earlier visit to the store across the street, he'd spotted jackets on sale. He'd buzz over and get one and be back in a jiff. While Rex and Pat went on to the restaurant, I hung about in the limo with Laverne. Surprisingly, within a few minutes John was back with a jacket that looked its price of nineteen dollars, I shuddered but said nothing; it was going to get him into the restaurant. Driving towards our destination I realized we were passing a shop where I had spied a pair of shoes that had taken my fancy and asked Laverne to drop me outside, saying I'd only be a few minutes. John came with me and we were indeed back in a few minutes, to find no sign of Laverne. Anxiously looking up and down the street we spotted him outside the car talking to a policeman. Worried for our driver, a lying explanation at the ready, we found it was not a misdemeanour that had got them talking, but a lockout: the officer was trying his darndest to break back into Laverne's limo for him. Since John had left the new jacket in the car, we were back to square one and by now late. I was wearing a unisex Mondi jacket that some males would take great delight in wearing (but not John): it was unshaped and silver grey, with padded shoulders – very with it. I said, 'We have to get a taxi and you'll have to wear my jacket.' I thought he looked great but he thought he looked naff, as he tried to hide his entrance into the elegant dining room. Laverne arrived just as we started the meal holding the green nineteen-dollar horror, in which John felt much more comfortable.

Into the Woods

We journeyed on from there to Miami Beach for a two-week stay, and at the end of the second week, after a performance, John told me that Sylvia had died. I arrived at Gatwick on 8 May 1989. Sylvia's husband and their children and grand children gathered together; Stuart, whom she had cared for in his early days, came from California; brother Alec and I held hands. She is remembered every time her award helps young black and white musicians or actors further their studies. The Sylvia Kendrick Trust Award was started with a concert in her memory at the Wavendon Stables and money donated by her Stevenage workmates and family.

The tour of *Into the Woods*, for me, finished in Detroit, at the too large but magnificently refurbished Fox theatre. Anne Rickenbacker got to work at once, painting the logo of the show halfway up the stairs, which we signed for all to see. Tears, hugs, kisses, cards and goodbye gifts made parting sad, but I was looking forward to being on my unrestricted way.

The rest of the year was a round of touring, taking in Britain, Holland, America and Canada. It's hard to decide which city in Canada I enjoy the most, all of them have their special qualities and if the date gives more than an in-out choice, we take full advantage of what they have to offer. The walks one can do are unsurpassed, as ports, rivers and parks are made the most of in many of Canada's cities: we have tried as many as time allows. I love Vancouver's parks and waterways; I've even gone up a mountain in a ski lift. It was there that I had the honour of being accompanied by the great Oscar Peterson, as a guest on his television show. It was a great experience for me, to have not only his masterly backing but the drumming of Louie Bellson and bass playing of Niels Pedersen – oh! what joy. I did notice, though, that there was a little competition in the singing stakes with Oscar and Louie, as when they play they both hum (or grunt) their solos or backings – amusing as long as it's not too loud.

The island of Victoria BC is a dream for the ecology-minded, in that it appears to be quite untouched by the sophisticated world-weary parts of the mainland. Our visits there are not very frequent, but when the name Victoria comes up in the itinerary I know I can look forward to a few days of clean air and beautiful suroundings where I can take full advantage of the walks, gardens and water.

On one visit I had the strangest visitation from my past, when a note came from front of house to say a Mr Samples was going to attend the concert and would dearly love to see me after the show if possible. I was dumbstruck. Could it really be that boy Samples whom my pa regularly kicked out of the house as a bad influence on his two youngest? I would have to wait till after the show to find out. During the concert I tried hard to see if I could recognize him sitting out there, but it was such a long time ago since I'd seen him I probably wouldn't know what he looked like now. I peered just the same, but as far as I could see there wasn't a single black man in the audience – my best bet for spotting him.

When the concert ended I got changed more quickly than usual in order to greet this mystery Samples. I certainly would not have recognized the smartly put-together gentleman who introduced himself to me. But he was certainly black, he called me Clemmie, and he knew something of my family history – so I greeted him like the long-lost friend that he was.

Both our personalities came to the fore when I couldn't resist questioning him about what was he doing here in Victoria. He had on his arm a very elderly lady, well-dressed and bejewelled, by no means in the broke category. She was obviously very fond of Samples, telling me how he looked after her every need. I became more and more curious, as I could see Samples's eyes twinkling wickedly in the same old way. Come on, I said, tell me all.

He had, he told me, got to Victoria on a merchant ship as cook, then he'd jumped ship – he didn't say what for; the lady was too close. He'd hung about, getting casual work until he saw an advert for a cook in the paper, put there by his now companion. She took up the story: 'Oh, he changed my life,

302

he not only cooked for me but took me out, shopped for me, looked after the house. Oh! we became the closest of friends, oh I do so want him to stay, for ever!' His smart appearance was her doing, he whispered confidentially in my ear.

I listened to each of them extol the other's virtues in turn, sincerely hoping that the Samples I knew had changed, and that this trusting old lady was not going to be taken for a ride. We have been back to Victoria two or three times since, but there has been no further sighting of Samples.

Window or mall shopping anywhere in Canada can be a bit chancy, and embarrassing if you look scruffy, as there are so many ex-pat Brits who tend to recognize you. John and I are easier to spot if we chance a shop together. John was the one to be accosted this time, when two ladies who, we found out, had been in Canada for thirty years, still with Scots accents you could cut with a knife, were not in the least interested in me, as one of them had met J.D. when she was seventeen in Glasgow and became all dewy-eyed over him again; he had two grasps to release himself from. Sometimes when I'm asked 'Am I Cleo Laine?' I say, 'No, I'm often asked that,' and sometimes they assume I'm a lookalike. Like the man in the jewellery store in Toronto – he was a bit of a wag – who when asked the price of the earring I had in my hand that had no price on, said, 'Oh! That's the free one: buy one, you get that one free.' Later he said, 'Now who can we pair you with, let me see, if you were a bit taller you could be Johnnie Dankworth's sweetie.' I owned up, said everyone thinks I'm taller than I am, and gave him tickets for the show.

The Christmas celebrations started early in 1989 when Princess Margaret invited us to Kensington Palace to join her carol party on 14 December. It had been a regular invitation, either to sing carols before Christmas or to sing in the New Year, depending on where we were in the world. Laurie Holloway and Marion Montgomery, the wonderful singer from the States whom we have known ever since they met and married in the sixties, make up the musical guests invited. I remember on one occasion John and I arrived late to find everyone waiting to begin the carolling. We were hurriedly introduced by the Princess to those present: 'Lord so and so, Lady do da, the Hon. what's it, you know my sister' and the like. I moved on and then did a realization gulp. We had kept the Queen waiting: she wanted to get away to her staff party at the Palace. There was a professional group of singers leading the performance. The Queen, Princess Margaret, Marion and I stood in a line in the front, not a bad group of singers; we could obviously hold a tune, as someone at the back could not. This man was singing louder than the ones who could, and it was becoming painful to the ear. It got so bad that as one the Queen, Princess Margaret, Marion and I turned, glared at him and turned back. Either the amalgamated dissent or the presence did the trick, and we were able to continue without any more discord.

29

Mother and Daughter

The year ended as it always does, with family and friends doing three Wavendon Christmas Shows that help top up the coffers for the year ahead. That is when the family starts to arrive – though sadly depleted these days. We feel the loss and, together with friends, remember.

Apart from the occasional business hitches the 1990s have been extremely happy years: some of the most satisfying, artistically, that I can remember. I began the decade by going back to my old roots, after a long absence, when I did a few nights with John's big band during his engagement at Ronnie Scott's Club. I can remember feeling during that short stint how much I had missed working with a power house behind me – it was a good feeling and I should do it more often. I didn't mind the commuting, the late nights or early mornings; as a natural latebird the sound of the dawn songbirds to which we often arrived home lulled me to sleep. But the smoke in the club eventually started to affect my voice. Although the music lured me and will continue to do so from time to time, clubs will never be my first choice of work, certainly in Europe, where to ask smokers who like to hear their jazz in a club to desist while the act is being performed is tantamount to asking them to go cold turkey for an hour, giving them withdrawal symptoms.

I have found that Americans are much more sympathetic about this and actually applaud the request when announced. The subject is a hobby horse of mine that I, along with many other singers, go on about interminably and without shame. The music and the band, with some of the best players in the country playing behind me, was great, though; what more could I have wished for in 1990? Well, in April I won a British jazz award, for best jazz singer; I gave classes at the Wavendon Easter courses; and at the same time I was having exciting early talks involving a possible collaboration with Mel Tormé, which became reality in June and July.

The talks included how the shows, if we did them, would be presented. Lots of ideas were tossed around, but the one thing we wanted to get away from was both doing our own thing without working together in some way. John and I had so enjoyed the format that had been worked out with James Galway when we toured together, as had he, that we suggested doing it the same way with Mel: entering together with an opening duet, then both staying onstage listening to the other during the solos, and coming together for duets when the pace of the programme dictated. Mel was very excited about the proposal: as an ideas man who loves to try out different programmes all the time, he was happy to go along with it.

Putting the programme together with someone like Mel presented no problems. I think Mel in his performing and recording career has probably sung every great song that has been composed, as well as some of the not so great, and he remembers them all. When we were on the road with him, rehearsals often turned out to be 'let's test Mel' time. I can't remember any occasion he was defeated by 'Do you know this one, Mel? – he would either start singing it or play it on the piano before the first bar was out.

John and Mel got on well together, respecting each other's musicianship and knowledge of past bands, musicians and recordings. Mel has a wide knowledge of the most diverse subjects: he is a film maniac, an author, a collector of antique guns, planes and trains (not the big ones) as well as music – a fascinating man with a great voice who never ceased to amaze me, night after night on our tour. His pure jazz ability with a song blew you away, rhythmically and improvisationally, one moment, then moved you almost to tears the next, with the loveliness of his warm ballad singing. For some reason our voices complemented each other; breathing as one, our duets at times were quite magical, felt by everyone, audience and musicians alike – quite an uncanny experience.

Starting in Chicago in June the tour we did took in Carnegie Hall and the Hollywood Bowl, receiving ecstatic reviews there and every city and town we went to, ending in Saratoga Springs New York, at the end of July. We had had such a good time together that we talked at once about going into the recording studio while it was all still fresh in our minds, but as always other commitments got in the way and we had to wait until another year and more touring before the album *Nothing without You* was recorded 12–13 March 1991 in Los Angeles – it was released in 1992.

In the meantime I had to get yet another album finished, with guests coming from far and wide all over America to participate; thankfully the logistics were being looked after (thus taking the weight off J.D.'s shoulders) by producer Ettore Stratta. It was a gathering together of old and new friends, like Clark Terry the trumpet player, whom we had got to know when Ellington regularly toured Europe, Toots Thielemans the jazz harmonica player, whom John first met in the forties when they played together at the London Palladium in Benny Goodman's band, and Gerry Mulligan, who had toured England and Europe for years with his new-sounding, fresh, imaginative group. These were all great masters of their chosen music and if they did nothing else they would go down in jazz history as movers and shakers of style and change. Added to that great roster was the superb soprano sax playing of my newfound friend Jane Ira Bloom, the young guitarist Mark Whitfield, and piano players John Campbell and Mike Renzi. Of course my beloved American group supported me as usual. With that line-up it was a labour of love for me from beginning to end.

Meanwhile we were still touring and that had its usual problems, like having to hang about at airports all over the world, losing luggage or equipment, cars not turning up, or hotels not ready for you after long exhausting journeys. But Kurt Gebauer, our road and business manager, always sorted it out. Kurt travelled with us everywhere, magically smoothing out chaos and obstacles in a wizard-like way when the road intermittently bore down on us, as it famously does.

In the bitter cold of Minneapolis, in winter, for example. The driver of the limo that was taking us to the hall for the concert left the car outside the front of the hotel to call us from the front desk. Leaving the engine running to maintain the interior heat, he waited in the lobby for us to arrive. When we eventually appeared, we were pleased when he said he'd left the heat on and the car was right outside. Except that it wasn't there as we went out into the chilly night. Thinking the hotel porter had moved it for some reason, he asked, 'Sir, where's my limo?' 'No idea man, saw it there a minute ago,' the porter casually answered. It was then it dawned on the driver: 'Oh my Gawd! Oh hell! Christ, some bastard's stole my f. . .ing limo!! They've stolen my! . . . I cain't believe they'd steal my f. . .ing limo! I, yi! I cain't!'

All this as he walked in circles up and down. Eventually he threw his hat on the ground and stood still, staring into space. So did we stare into space. Because it was his thoughtfulness on our behalf that had caused him to leave the keys in the car.

There was no getting away from it; it had indeed been swiped, right under everybody's nose. Sadly we had to leave the demented driver, still pulling his hair out, wailing in the cold, while Kurt organized alternative transport for us all.

The most costly hiccough we ever had was an engagement for an important convention for IBM in San Francisco; it took place at the Masonic Hall, at the top of Nob Hill. We flew from England with all the music in order, and well prepared, to J.D.'s specifications as always, to perform with two horns,

John and Ray, and a rhythm section of Jim Zimmerman, Larry Dunlap, Larry Koonse and Jon Ward (drums, piano, guitar, bass). The day before, John called the boys for a run through in the afternoon to save time, as we had to fit in with the lecturers, one of whom was Dame Margot Fonteyn, which often shortens rehearsal time. Arriving early to take stock of the stage and the set up for the band, we found to our surprise that the stage was covered with music stands and seats to accommodate a large forty-five-piece orchestra. We asked if it could all be removed for our performance tomorrow, as it didn't leave us much space, or indeed look good. They informed us (to our utter amazement and horror) that the large orchestra had been hired specifically for the use of their solitary 'musical' stars – in other words, us; we were under an obligation to use them.

I would not have liked to have been John's or Kurt's stomach when they were told this news. That the generally efficient communication pipeline had cracked was obvious; but something had to be done and in a hurry. There were a lot of executive comings and goings, with neurosis at a very high level all round, when a solution to save face and situation thankfully presented itself. How Kurt and John figured it all out I have no idea, but the plan was this. First a midnight phone call to Alan Robson and Tod Wye at Wavendon, telling Alan to bring us the music by hook or by crook. The music needed (the list given), packed in a suitcase, a seat booked on Concorde leaving at nine a.m., getting Alan to New York virtually the same time he left; with half an hour to clear customs, he was then to catch the next plane to San Francisco, arriving, once again when he left, at twelve-thirty p.m. There he would be met and driven straight to the hall in time for us to rehearse with the orchestra at two p.m.

Miraculously it all went without a musical hitch, a plane or M1 delay, and the forty-five piece orchestra knew nothing about the trauma and hysteria created by their presence. John and Kurt looked just a little bit older after the ordeal, and Alan, although well fed and watered, didn't look too good either. All this happened in the days before the fax machine, which we often use today in an emergency, saving nerves, time and a considerable amount of cash.

I am exceedingly proud of the way my three children's careers and personal lives have turned out. Although it might not appear that way sometimes to them and maybe at times to others, they have always been uppermost in my mind and heart, even when I looked as though I had washed my hands of them. All three know that John and I are there. I could have been considered at times a Victorian mama in many ways, expecting obedience, good manners, consideration for others and a good report from school; but they had a lot of healthy neglect too, making them unspoilt and independent. The two boys, now men, have happy marriages and families of their own and share the caring and responsibility of them with two strong, intelligent working wives. Alec and Jackie, unlike Stuart, chose to enter the same profession as John and myself – music and acting.

Alec had rather more of an uphill struggle than Jackie with that career decision at first. After several early tries at piano and cello, Alec eventually failed the exam on clarinet to get into the Royal Academy, then chose, with our blessing, the electric bass. But he did very little work on it from then on. Although he did gigs with his schoolfriends and local musicians he was obviously not studying much, even though he had master tutors in Daryl Runswick, for bass, David Lindup for arranging and composition, and Ian Hall for harmony.

Frustrated with a year of compromise followed by wait-and-see, we listened to his excuses at lunch one day with little hope of any improvement and gave him two choices: either he could go and get a job in the local garage, or he could go to the Berkeley School of Music in Boston. He chose Boston. Although he was not completely happy there, often saying that he wanted to give up, in the short period that he was there he switched from electric to acoustic bass and learnt more about jazz than he had done from living in its atmosphere all his life.

I think one of the reasons he had problems was living up to

what people expected of him as the son of John Dankworth. This became apparent to us at another lunch one day when he asked whether we would mind if he changed his name, as when he did local gigs they would often announce him as our son, then expect him to do a brilliant solo. We sympathized, of course, understanding the pressure this would put upon any young student player, and asked what name he had in mind. I don't think he had given it much consideration, but after a moment's thought came up with, 'Well I was thinking about Coltrane . . .' We hid our laughter at his choice, asking him in all seriousness whether he didn't think that that name might bring him even more angst than he was having now.

Anyway, that phase passed and Alec at an early age became good enough for us to let him have the bass chair when it became vacant, giving him the opportunity to work alongside experienced musicians like Bill Le Sage, Kenny Clare, Alan Ganley, Daryl Runswick, Paul Hart, John Horler and many more. He eventually, wisely, broke the cord to go his own way, which he did successfully. Often now, when John and I do an interview on radio in the US, they have just played yet another CD with his name as the bass player on it. Then it dawns on them and they ask in surprised delight, 'Heh! you're Alec Dankworth's father?' I'm glad he didn't change his name.

I advised Jackie to train and get a reputation as an actress rather than a singer (she was good at that anyway) as she would find it difficult to cross over from singer to actress. Surprisingly she took my advice and went to the Guildhall School of Acting in the City of London. She had had flute lessons at both the schools she attended, St Christopher's, Letchworth, and St Paul's Girls School, London, along with singing and acting lessons, and she developed a good musical voice and strong acting ability at both schools. Both Jackie and Alec also attended annually the Wavendon Music Camps, founded and run by John's sister Avril. The children's camp is a stone's throw from the Rectory in the field behind the Stables, taking the whole place over for the three weeks they are in residence.

311

Cleo

When they were sent off to camp in their own back yard they were told they had to imagine they were miles and miles away from home, as the other children actually were, so they couldn't keep running back to the house. Jackie was always very good at this, so when she realized that she didn't have the money each child was asked to bring to put in the tuck-shop bank for her week's goodies, she wrote and posted a letter to John marked URGENT: 'Dear Daddy, would you please let me have a pound, love Jackie.' For some reason only known to Jackie she constantly lost not the normal one sock, but one shoe instead, which made her regularly late, while the household searched high and low. Camp was of course ideal for losing things, so wellies and runners were routinely sent, after a little note.

From camps, Jackie went on to the Easter and jazz courses, learning something new each year that strengthened her singing and musicianship, while at the same time she grew into a beautiful woman. Jackie was also the letter writer in the family, from her boarding school, and later on the road when she became a touring actress. I didn't realize this until much later, when a project I had nurtured for years came to fruition at the Stables.

It all started when I had thoughts of doing a mother and daughter show with Jackie. A talented Canadian writer Alexis Bernier wrote a play with lyrics that she hoped John would set to music, with us in mind. It didn't materialize, but it planted a seed in my mind that became an obsession. I found myself buying mother and daughter books whenever I went book-browsing: letters, poetry, short and long stories all went into an extra suitcase that was lugged around the world. I'd read, mark, make notes all the time without a clear idea of where it was all going, till John said, 'You've been at it long enough, do something with that bloody case full of books before we all get hernias.' I contacted my old friend/actress/director/writer Denise Coffey, and she helped sort out the material and wrote extra pieces, though was not free to direct.

Then Abigail Morris entered the scene, when she asked for a woman to play God in *Noah's Flood*, which she was going to direct at the Albert Hall for the 1990 proms. The powers-that-be got in touch with me to see if I was interested. I agreed, and the weeks following saw me walking the fields around the Stables declaring my lines: 'I God that all this world hath wrought, heaven and earth, and all of naught,' and so on. The girls in the Stables office thought I was in a demented state, 'Is Cleo all right?' they asked, 'She's doing very strange things in the field.' The prom performance was a success, because of Abigail, who not only controlled all the different forces involved, but brought new ideas and directed them brilliantly. I loved every moment – and decided to ask her to direct our mother and daughter project. She was delighted, and the idea gelled into *Suit Case Four*, which was produced at the Stables.

The surprise of the show was the second half. Abigail had gone through all the letters that Jackie and I had written to each other over the years, sorting and editing them into a potted history of our relationship, with songs interspersed, as we read the letters to each other. I hadn't realized how much we had corresponded over the years and had to get through some emotional moments during rehearsals.

Jackie was committed to so much other work about that time that after the week we did at the Stables we decided to shelve it to work further on it at a later date, but when that date came around Jackie was still tied up. So we did a one-day concert together instead and *Suit Case Four* remains closed for the time being. Jackie went on to do Sondheim's *Into the Woods* as Cinderella and *Sophisticated Ladies*, receiving great reviews for both. She has decided that now she can cross over as a solo singer and still be considered an actress, which I think she is doing successfully; it's a difficult feat the other way round.

Stuart the eldest remains close and is now a family man who loves and listens to music, but he followed a different drum, leaning towards the fine arts and developing his own business. He is also admired in Sonoma as the Englishman who started soccer camps, teaching young Americans the art and skills of the game he inherited from his father and which he played naturally as a child. I still get great joy from them all as well as the occasional heartache.

The year 1990 ended as always at the Stables, but before those concerts, we had an invitation from Princess Margaret to come to the combined birthday party of all the royals at Buckingham Palace. I wouldn't have missed it for the world, although I hate going through the what-shall-I-wear process, or the thought of having to buy or get something made. I rummaged through my old stock and picked out the black velvet dress I had had made for the *Edwin Drood* Tony Awards. Princess Margaret had arranged for us to have supper with Lord and Lady Sainsbury at their home before arriving at the Palace at ten-thirty p.m. Anya Sainsbury had been my other half in *The Seven Deadly Sins* so we had lots to reminisce about, and we also knew Bryan Forbes and his actress wife Nanette Newman, the other two guests, so it was an easy evening.

Our driver Geoff Bond drove us to London leaving plenty of time to search for a place to park. After a few turns around the square he happened to strike lucky when he found a spot almost outside the Sainsburys' house. He told us later that when he'd told his mother where he'd gone that Wednesday, she was very interested in all the details, so he told her where we had had supper before the do, and that he'd had to wait for us outside Sainsbury's. 'Thur were a slight pause at end of line when I told her this,' Geoff said, 'and then she said, "Why . . . d'thur live over't shop?"'

The Queen and Prince Philip greeted everyone as they arrived at the top of the stairs, shaking hands with us all before we entered the rooms leading to the picture gallery where dancing was to be the order of the evening. Before we got that far we had to pass through the crowded rooms where drinks were being served. This was the hard part of the evening for me, having to go into rooms full of people I didn't know, until, gradually, comforting known faces popped up to have a cheerful chat and I relaxed into the swing of it.

Mother and Daughter

Later on the dance floor we bumped into every royal known to man and woman in the British Isles. From right left and centre they came at you, on a dance floor with walls laden with Old Masters. Trying to be heard above the trumpets, the Queen stopped her dance and us as we whirled pass, to ask, 'The band's too loud, don't you think?' We defended it, diplomatically, saying, 'Well, they do have to please the youngsters too, Ma'am.' It was a very historic occasion: the royal world that night seemed happy and in a carefree mood, future events known only in their secret hearts. I knew how Cinderella felt at the ball for real that night, with the exception of not having to run away from my Prince Charming. I had breakfast with him, along with the *hoi polloi* and nobility, danced the last waltz, said goodnight to the Queen and Princess Margaret and whizzed down the stairs with both shoes firmly on feet and ground, to where our Geoff was waiting to drive us, sleepily happy, back home.

On the way I couldn't help comparing the difference between the ways in which the well-heeled upper classes and the not-so-well-off of my early pub-outing years let their hair down. They were not really dissimilar: with the exception of money, they both liked a knees-up, a good drink and plenty of nibbles and both were cliques who allowed only a peek not an entry. I decided I was not a natural party-goer and fell asleep.

30

Side by Side with John

The Stables Theatre, although primarily known for presenting programmes of classical, jazz and popular music, does occasionally put on theatrical productions, such as try-outs for one- or two-hander plays not requiring too much scenery, poetry, readings of Shakespeare by actors from Stratford or the National, and small musicals. Early on the vicar, the Reverend Chianchi, had involved the church in the W.A.P festivals by having our organized poetry readings there, read by Jenny Linden, Dame Sybil Thorndyke, Annette Crosbie and Derek Jacobi.

On the 150th anniversary of the 'Penny Post', J.D. and Benny Green collaborated on a show they called *Penny Black*, for the Post Office. This was directed by Wendy Toye, as was another show called *Mrs Pat's Profession*, based on the relationship between Mrs Patrick Campbell and George Bernard Shaw. Our good and resourceful friend Tony Field organized not only the intricate details of this production, but fed us too.

I played Mrs Pat, as I had done all those years ago in Nottingham. When Wendy, who had other commitments she had to honour, gave up her involvement in the play, she recommended director/actor David Kelsey, who was at the time playing H.G. Wells in the production. After Wavendon, Tony Field arranged a musical reading for backers at Drury Lane with

Julian Glover playing the part of Shaw brilliantly, but so far it has gone no further. But two productions have gone on from the Stables to the West End: *Colette*, also directed by Wendy Toye, and the David Kernan production of *Side By Side by Sondheim*.

Nineteen ninety-two started with a fright for me when John collapsed in Holland; he had been working relentlessly, performing successive weeks at both of the Ronnie Scott's clubs.

Without drawing breath, he flew to Holland to conduct a programme with the Rotterdam Symphony: included in the trip was a talk on orchestration to students at the Rotterdam Conservatoire of Music that he had agreed to do for the American trombonist Bob Brookmeyer, a professor there. During this talk he looked so green and ill that Bob thought he should see a doctor when he got back to his hotel. This he did and he was sent to hospital right away with suspected appendicitis.

All this was unknown to me until I received a phone call from John in hospital telling me what had happened. Although it was a shock, I was glad he was in hospital, being watched. Then in the middle of the night the second call came that made my heart die. This time it was from the hospital to tell me that Mr Dankworth was seriously ill: his appendix had burst unexpectedly in the night and he was being operated on at that very moment.

When I flew out to see him he was in a pretty state. It was a Godsend it hadn't happened while he was conducting; as it was, the burst in relative comfort had left him very weak. He was in no mood to talk, but thought he would make the Bermuda date we were supposed to do quite soon – I didn't argue with him, but flew out to Bermuda on the 4 February, alone, to perform at the festival there, with the American group. Larry Dunlap the pianist became M.D., sharing out the parts between himself and Ray Loeckle that I usually duetted with J.D. Had John been able to fly, Bermuda would have been ideal to restore his health, as the weather was balmy and the island so relaxing and unspoilt. I phoned him daily, finding that his recovery mood varied from day to day, from animated talk to complete silence. Although he knew it was impossible, he really wanted to be up and doing: it was the first time in his life he had been in hospital and he was not relishing the experience.

He was brought home by our driver Geoff, and looked after by Geoff's wife Bea until he was able to fly to San Francisco for Sonoma. He looked and was an ill man. But instead of resting in Sonoma, he insisted on going to Hawaii for the next date, even though everyone was prepared to relieve him of duties, and wanted him to have a restful holiday. Larry Dunlap and the boys, along with a young conductor, were on hand to do the work involved, but John insisted on going. This time I did argue – I didn't think he should be heroic – but it made no difference. He was as thin as a reed without its strength, as he had been drip-fed for ten days, with not much more than baby food after that, and here he was doing heavy duty aerobics, conducting a symphony orchestra, touring the islands, playing.

It was lucky he had time off when we got back to the US because he paid for all that needless exertion and became almost bed-ridden again. Gradually his health and weight returned to normal, and so did our relationship: we were able to argue once more with gusto, without any fear of upset. We all missed him terribly during this period of withdrawal, and welcomed his return.

After John had slowly and gently recovered, with some lovely sunny dates shared with Henry Mancini in Palm Desert, California, we returned to England to find an invitation for us to attend Neil and Glenys Kinnock's silver wedding anniversary party, with a request to honour them with a favourite song of theirs; John Williams had already accepted. We said we would love to – silver wedding anniversaries are, after all, getting rarer and rarer, and they should be celebrated.

It took place at the Parliament Chamber, Inner Temple, and was a lovely do, apart from all the non-stop, shop-talking politicians constantly nattering. It was the families of the two being celebrated and their more artistic friends and supporters that brought it down-to-earth, with a feeling of fun and celebration more than compensating for the natterers. John Williams played classical guitar pieces beautifully, then I joined him to sing 'He Was Beautiful' with J.D. and the trio, John Horler, Allan Ganley and Malcolm Creese. John Williams finished up playing some jazz with us, then the group took over and played for dancing.

Not long after that night, I received one of those phone calls again, this time from someone from our past, Harold Davison, who represented Frank Sinatra's concert tours. Frank Sinatra was coming over to tour Europe: would we do the Albert Hall with him? He added: 'I suggested you to Sinatra, and he said, "If she'll do it, go for it."' Although we had never met, I knew that Sinatra had been aware of me as a singer for some time, as I had appeared in Las Vegas twice when he was also there in the seventies. Which I will digress for a while to tell you about.

My first season in Las Vegas was with Bill Cosby, some time in the seventies. Cosby was one of the nicest and most generous personalities to work alongside, a relaxed and easy-going man who loved and supported jazz and jazz musicians. He was learning the bass at the same time that I was struggling with the flute, so our two dressing rooms emitted some very odd sounds before the entertainment began. His act was so un-Vegas-like in character: no high production, girls or sets, just him sitting on a chair talking to the audience for an hour, about everyday happenings in life that made the ordinary man/woman there respond to the serious absurdities of life with laughter. I think he might have got some material from the visit to the dressing room of son Alec, who was still anarchically dressed with noticeably large safety-pins in the bottom of his jeans when he was introduced to him. Bill Cosby, recognizing the rebel, couldn't help commenting, 'Were you there, when you purchased those jeans?'

I enjoyed a lot about Las Vegas, first the fact that it didn't pretend to be anything more than an American money-making city that twinkled like an overdressed Christmas tree, with a fairy on top without a bra; secondly there was the weather, which everyone warned could be disastrous for my voice, but which turned out to suit me down to the ground: I never felt so healthy. For the first time in years I didn't notice my aching English joints, and my voice survived two shows a night, seven days a week, non-stop for three weeks. And it was in Las Vegas that I had an unexpected visitor. After one of the shows the security officer knocked on the dressing room door. John answered and the guard said to him, 'Mr Cary Grant is here to see you.' Thinking one of our musicians was playing around John replied sarcastically, 'Tell him Napoleon isn't available.' The face of the messenger became very serious, and so did John's when he looked to see the screen idol walk in with his young daughter. He pushed past John, declaring, 'I'm in love with your wife!' Greeting me with kisses on both cheeks, he told me how much of a fan he was and how much he'd loved the performance, all in that Judy! Judy! voice. It was a visit to die for; how could I dislike Las Vegas?

And to top it all, I heard through the grapevine that Frank Sinatra was singing my praises from the stage and indeed in the local paper, and advising his audience to take me in before they lost all their money. So when the phone call came from Harold it was and yet wasn't a surprise, though I felt it was a shame that it had come so late in his career. It wasn't an easy decision to make, as I knew, even though I was told to the contrary, that it would not do much at this stage for my career. But I liked the thought of being able to say, 'Yes, I worked with the greatest popular singer of all time,' so everything went into action for the build-up to the event. Suddenly I had friends who popped up from out of nowhere, like the people who had met me at a party given by someone who was the cousin of a musician who was a great fan of John Dankworth's before he started his band in the fifties, and the people who had admired my singing right from the start and wanted to hear me at the peak of my career at the Albert Hall but had been unable to get tickets . . .

I found it all irritatingly amusing and got on with getting my act together. We asked, via our manager at the time, Laurie Mansfield, and Harold Davison, if we could meet Frank Sinatra

321

in the hope of doing a couple of songs together. This was on the cards during the early-talking stages, but it fizzled out later when we were told he was not up to learning new songs. I pointed out I knew all his songs and would fit in, but it was not to be.

On the day of the first concert, everyone assembled for rehearsal except Frank; his son Frank Sinatra Junior was to sing the songs as well as doing his usual job of conducting the band. Before we started, as I sat listening to all the familiar songs and arrangements being dissected, I said to John Flannigan, who had booked the musicians for the Sinatra organization for years, 'I thought you said Frank wouldn't be at the rehearsal? 'He's not,' he said, 'That's Frank Junior.' The similarity was so amazing, I had to go and see for myself. When introduced, I said how I admired him and his father, and he replied, 'I'm honoured that you give me top billing.'

Frank Junior was not an easy man to get close to, but as the week developed he became quite chatty, to the point where he regularly did up a difficult button on the sleeve of my dress before I went on. He took his job as conductor extremely seriously. One night I noticed he was looking rather concerned, and when I asked why, he said he was not making contact with the musicians: they couldn't see him properly so they had trouble following him. He wasn't complaining but was worrying about how he was going to solve this problem. The next night he was all smiles. 'Solved it!' I said. 'Yeah, I was up all night trying to figure it out, then in the middle of the night I woke up and said "That's it!" Come and see.' He showed me a fine pair of white gloves he'd bought, usually used for film editing, that he thought would allow his hands to be seen in the shadows. I wished him luck and secretly hoped he wasn't going to look like Al Jolson flailing about in the background. They seemed to do the trick though.

On that first-night day reporters and cameras buzzed around like bees in the comb of the Albert Hall, on the lookout for sweet happenings; someone interviewing me from the *Evening Standard* said, 'I get the feeling that everyone is scared of him, are you?' I answered honestly: 'No, I'm not, I'm just anxious about my dress designer, I'm not sure if he will get through all this security to adjust my gown in time for tonight.'

Frank Sinatra and I met for the first time on 26 May 1992 in my dressing room, not long before I went on. He asked me: 'Well . . . d'ya feel up to it?' 'Oh yes, I'm OK,' I replied, I suppose rather cockily. 'I'm not,' he said, 'I haven't sung for four days.' Really not a long gap, for me anyway, so I felt I had to reassure him. 'Well,' I said, 'All you have to do is walk out there and stand doing nothing – they will adore you.' I think he liked that. After the first night we all ended up at a very late party in Chelsea, and the next day I called in to ask him if he'd managed to get any sleep. 'Yeah,' he said, 'I caught up, but I won't do that again.' I replied, 'I bet you do,' and his relaxed lady dresser smiled and nodded her head in agreement with me. I knocked on his door every evening after that to say hello and ask how he was.

One of the highlights for me that week had nothing to do with Sinatra: it was when a tall, elegant Gregory Peck, looking even handsomer than in his films, came to my dressing room to tell me with the most distinguished speaking sound to fall on any ears how much he admired my singing. The week was worth it for that alone.

That week at the Albert Hall, I thought Sinatra sang as well, some nights, as of old, occasionally coming close to the impressive sound of his earlier days and showing a breath control, on certain phrases and songs, that was awe-inspiring. It became an interesting lesson for me, to watch what and what not to do, to pass on at some point to aspiring singers at the Wavendon courses.

He had created a style of singing that is classical yet popular, using the microphone instrumentally to enhance every aspect and asset his voice possessed, in a way few have achieved before him or since. I think these are the lessons to learn (whether studying classical or popular) from seeing or listening to him. At the same time he has created an almost classic stage persona, a stagecraft that is peculiar to him and when imitated by others is third-rate and laughable. This is the part that other would-be singers should admire, but not touch, from his casual approach – unless, of course, they are impersonators. On him it becomes art; on others it's a joke.

Frank turned out to be a charming man to work with, certainly not a scary monster. I was impressed when I heard him override one of his heavies who thought my musician, Malcom Creese, had got too close when he asked if he could take a picture of him before he went onstage. Frank said, 'No! You can have one with me,' and the camera was passed to the objector, who had to do the clicking. Not until the last night did I request a together picture, when he said, 'I thought you'd never ask!'

One night the Prime Minister John Major and his wife came to the show, and a photo call was arranged between them and Frank before the show started. Our American manager, Kurt Gebauer, found that the press officer who arranged it came from the P.M.'s office. He searched him out and asked, 'Is it possible for Cleo Laine to have a photo with the P.M.?' The press officer replied, 'Yes . . . on his silver wedding anniversary'; a sarcastic reference to the Kinnoch evening, which went way over Kurt's head. He hadn't told me he was making this request, but I wouldn't have said 'you'll be lucky' if he had. When Kurt did tell me later, I thought it a rather childish reply, but shrugged it off with 'That's politics.' However, I enjoyed the ambience and glitz of it all, and in the end I was glad that for a week I became part of Frank Sinatra's entourage.

It was good to get back on the road again, both with the British musicians in England and then over to the States and Canada with the Americans, doing mixed and interesting work by ourselves, in concert and at festivals, then joining up again with Henry Mancini for an enjoyable week at the O'Keefe Center in Toronto. After which the recording studio called again. Because of the critical success of the album *Jazz* we decided, supported by our record company, to do another album with guest artists. Over the years John and I have been close to George and Ellie

Shearing: George has often supported Wavendon's efforts by donating a solo concert when on holiday in England. I've always loved and admired his beautiful creative playing, so he was first to be asked when the decision was made. Keeping our fingers crossed we hoped that everything would work out after we proffered the invitation, as artists who willingly wish to join in often cannot, because of other commitments. George said he would be delighted to be part of the venture, if we could do it in New York. So George was the first guest signed, to be recorded later.

On our return to Sonoma at the end of August the serious work began – discussing repertoire, keys and routines for the album, and making contact with the other artists we hoped would play on it, then finalizing arrangements so that John could orchestrate and score in relative peace and I could get on with learning routines and new songs for the rehearsals coming up in San Francisco in September. This time the album was being produced by Kurt and John.

I first heard and met Joe Williams when he came to England as the featured singer with the Count Basie Orchestra. He and the band had a smash hit blues at the time called 'Every Day', and from then on I was a devoted fan. His reputation as a blues singer has never waned, growing stronger over the years. Because he was chosen to appear in the *Bill Cosby Show* as the father of Cosby's wife, his fame later spread as an actor, but he kept singing and made some pretty impressive recordings, which made me want to ask if he would be my singing guest.

It was a great thrill for me when he agreed to duet with me on the record. We all met up in San Francisco, along with the young guitar guest Mark Whitfield, who once again contributed some fine solos. Joe and I put down two songs, a blues called 'It's a Cryin' Shame' with a great tenor solo by Ray Loeckle, and a standard called 'What'll I Do', which Joe chose. He sings very much like his personality, relaxed and laid back, so the sessions were very easy-going and joyful.

When the work was finished in San Francisco, we flew to

New York, with a delightful break in Toronto before the next recording dates. There we met up with Dudley Moore, who was doing one of his favours for a hotel manager during the film festival; we promised to perform with him. To be with Dudley was a wonderful giggle as usual, catching up with news, even though we'd seen him in March when he did a gala performance at Wavendon for us. It was a lovely interlude and we went back refreshed and ready to go.

We finished the recording with George Shearing, doing two new songs, and another two with Gerry Mulligan, whom we had asked again, in New York, at the end of September – but lots more had to be done before it was finally put to bed, as they say in the business. We came back to the UK, first to talk with our new manager Deke Arlon, to arrange and sort out the coming years ahead together, also to find out if anyone was interested in the book I had begun in Sonoma and intermittently on the road, instigated by Faith Evans. When Faith, who is a literary agent, first told me I should write a book about myself I said, 'What for?' She replied, 'Well, if you don't, somebody else will, one day, and you might not like it.' So that's how I got jump-started, in Sonoma.

Nineteen ninety-three began with John and Alec forming a big band called the Generation Band, filled with young British jazz bucks who delighted the ear and eye; only two of the older generation played in it, John and Jimmie Hastings. They opened for the first time at Ronnie Scott's two clubs, full of hope, passionate fire, energy and new orchestrations. The hard work and headaches ahead were put aside in the joy of playing. I loved sitting on the sidelines, watching the build-up to the explosion come into fruition. While this youthful group was being celebrated, we were gathering together the friends, musicians and family of David Lindup to celebrate his life in music at the Festival Hall. David, who died very suddenly at the beginning of 1992, was a great loss as a friend and musician to so many, and this was a way of showing our respect for his wonderful qualities and idiosyncrasies, along with a joyful evening of some of the vast amount of music he had created over the years, played by his peers. He was given a posthumous award for his music, along with other awards to young and experienced musicians for keeping the standard high and alive in music.

Youth reared its beautiful head again when Alec and Jackie got together to appear at the Pizza on the Park. For the first time in my life and possibly the last, I became a real stage mum and collected friends and family to cheer them on for their week in cabaret: Tony Field and Ted Algar, Jim and Nancy Marshall, Claire and Des Rayner, Deke and Jill Arlon, Elisabeth Welch, who adores Jackie's singing, and many supporters from Wavendon. I went in nightly with a new group of people and watched and listened to the group and singer become stronger with each performance. A proud start to the year for me to see one child being a leader, and another a wonderful original singer.

All that work and creativity started the year with a bang in England. The months after were filled with trips to Japan, New Zealand and Canada, concerts with Mel Tormé for the J.V.C. Newport Jazz Festival at Carnegie and New Haven and a season at the Blue Note, New York. I was writing, too – a lyric with John for a television film called *Money For Nothing* and another for the haunting theme played in the Public Broadcasting Service series about the American Civil War.

Now 1993 has almost ended and I am sitting gazing out of the window across to Central Park pursuing a recent pastime of mine. In New York, in the hills of Sonoma, and in the garden of the Old Rectory, I have for some months been doing what doesn't come naturally to me: typing. All these gazing places have helped in one way or another to get me as far as 1993 in the story of what I consider to be a fruitful, mostly happy life and career. John and I are here, stopping over in New York on our way back to England to spend Christmas at the Old Rectory. We came from Sonoma, in the Valley of the Moon where, miraculously, we spent the American pre-Christmas holidays – Hallowe'en and Thanksgiving – with the whole family, at one point or another.

Jackie and Alec were on their way to Hawaii, Hong Kong and Indonesia, so with a few days to spare, they and the group were entertained before they flew off. Jackie had arrived even before we did, with her boyfriend, Harvey, just before Hallowe'en, so together with Stuart and Sharon they'd organized their disguises for the party, which we went along with when we arrived.

As they'd decided to go as the Beatles, although none of them looked remotely like any of them, even with the disguises, John and I joined in: I hired a wig and added myself to the non-lookalikes in the unlikely shape of Yoko Ono, and J.D. became George Martin without too much effort. Nobody knew who or what we were supposed to be, even when we attempted to sing one of their songs to make it clear to the other ghouls present.

We had one more concert to do before Thanksgiving: our last concert of the year in America, at the San Francisco Jazz Festival, where we played a wide variety of music from Shakespeare to the blues of the great Duke Ellington, with a big band assembled by our pianist Larry Dunlap.

Thanksgiving we celebrated in the glorious state park of Yosemite. This time it was a three-generation family outing: John, me, Stuart, Sharon, Thomas and Christopher. Yosemite has climbs to take your breath away. At times I envied young Thomas, who at fourteen was deer-like as he raced impatiently ahead of our ancient legs. Then I realized he wasn't really taking in the surrounding beauty as he bound up and down without effort. I had once, like him, gazelled up and down mountains and hills without really looking. Now it was time to take in the sights in a leisurely way, John and I spent our short time there well, dividing it between climbing with one group and valley-walking with the other.

But all too soon we had to face up to the packing and exit for New York and then London, a long journey, thankfully broken by my having to do a television appearance on PBS, the public television channel; which was showing the Leonard Bernstein musical *On the Town* in which I had taken part. It had been recorded earlier at the Barbican in London at the begining of the year, and they were transmitting it during their autumn fund-raising campaign.

Right now from my cosy distance the New York skyline is looking breathtakingly beautiful under a blanket of snow. Tops of trees hold my gaze for the moment, but soon I will be closing up the machine that has given me moments of anxiety bordering on trauma, when for example I have accidentally hit a wrong key that wiped away weeks of torturous typing. Then John and I will wander out to eat, relax, and take a walk around the New York streets, to look at the amazingly beautiful window and street decorations that are twinkling and sparkling in a way no one in the world does better – in preparation already for the next holiday, Christmas. Tomorrow the scene will change to an English country garden where once again Wavendon will hold our attention until the Christmas holidays descend, leading us into yet another exciting year ahead.

Discography

1955	*Cleo Sings British* (10″)	Esquire
1957	*Meet Cleo Laine*	
1957	*She's the Top*	MGM
1959	*Valmouth* (original cast)	Pye
1961	*Jazz Date* (with Tubby Hayes)	Wing
1961	*Spotlight on Cleo*	
1962	*All About Me*	Fontana
1963	*Cindy-Ella* (original cast album of 1962 Christmas production, Garrick Theatre, London)	Decca
1963	*Beyond the Blues*: American Negro poetry, read by Brock Peters, Gordon Heath, Vinnette Carroll, Cleo Laine	Argo
1964	*Shakespeare and All That Jazz*	Fontana
1966	*Woman Talk*	Fontana
1967	*Façade* (with Annie Ross) British reissue: Philips	Fontana
1968	*If We Lived on Top of A Mountain*	Fontana
1968	*Soliloquy*	Fontana
1969	*The Idol* (soundtrack, composed by J. Dankworth: two Cleo Laine vocals)	Fontana
1969	*The Unbelieveable Miss Cleo Laine* ('Sampler' of Fontana tracks)	Fontana
1971	*Portrait*	Philips
1972	*An Evening with Cleo Laine & the John Dankworth Quartet* British limited edition reissue: Sepia	Philips
1972	*Feel the Warm*	Philips
1972	*Showboat* (single LP)	EMI-Columbia
1973	*I Am A Song*	RCA
1974	*Live at Carnegie Hall*	RCA

331

1974	*Close-Up*	RCA
1974	*Pierrot Lunaire* (Schoenberg) Ives Songs	RCA
1974	*Beautiful Thing*	RCA
1974	*Easy Living* (Anthology of Fontana tracks)	RCA
1974	*Spotlight on Cleo Laine* (Anthology of Philips/Fontana tracks; double album)	Philips Int'l
1975	*Cleo's Choice* (1956–57 singles) Abridged issue on Quintessence Jazz	
1975	*Born on a Friday*	RCA
1976	*Live at the Wavendon Festival*	503
1976	*Porgy & Bess* (with Ray Charles)	London
1976	*Return to Carnegie*	RCA
1976	*Best Friends* (with John William)	RCA
1977	*20 Famous Show Hits*	Arcade
1978	*Gonna Get Through*	RCA
1978	*A Lover & His Lass* (reissue of *Cleo Sings British* plus 8 Dankworth 7 tracks)	Esquire Treasure
1978	*Wordsongs*	RCA
1980	*Collette* (original cast)	Sepia
1980	*Sometimes When We Touch* (with James Galway)	RCA
1981	*One More Day*	Sepia
1982	*Smilin' Through* (with Dudley Moore)	CBS
1983	*Platinum Collection* (Anthology of RCA, Arcade tracks; double album.	Magenta
1984	*Let The Music Take You* (with John Williams)	CBS
1985	*Cleo at Carnegie*	DRG
1985	*That Old Feeling* (issued first in Australia: Interfusion L38195)	CBS
1985	*Johnny Dankworth and His Orchestra* The John Dankworth 7 – featuring Cleo Laine 1953–1958 (6 Cleo Laine vocals)	EMI
1986	*Wordsongs*	Westminster
1986	*Mystery of Edwin Drood*	Philips
1988	*Cleo Sings Sondheim*	RCA
1988	*Showboat* (Re-issue of 1972 Cast Album)	EMI
1989	*Woman to Woman*	RCA
	Jazz	RCA, Victor, (BMG Classics)
	Blue and Sentimental	RCA, Victor, (BMG Classics)

Index

Index

337

Ingram, Rex, 51
'Inside a Silent Tear', 293
International Artists, 210
Into the Woods (Sondheim), 291,
  294–301, 313
Ionesco, Eugene, 146, 181, 211
Israel, 291
'It's a Cryin' Shame', 325
Italian Waiters Club, Melbourne,
  247–8

Jackson, Fred, 172
Jackson, Pieter, 172
Jacobs, Derek, 317
James, Stephen, 288
Japan, 272, 327
Jarrett, Keith, 245
Jazz album, 286, 324
Jazz Jamboree, The, 123
Jazz Journal, 138
Jerry Lewis Telethon, 243
Jessie (maid at Cliftonville), 39
Joan (factory worker), 62, 73
John, Elton, 289
Johnny Carson Show, 262
Johnny Dankworth Big Band: J.D.
  decides to form, 120, 123; C
  signs contract, 123–4; Johnny
  Dankworth Seven incorporated
  into, 124; J.D. does most of
  writing for, 124–5; opens in
  Nottingham, 125; success
  of *African Waltz*, 134; more
  successful than the singers, 134;
  C decides to leave, 142, 143;
  at Oxford, 151; Dudley Moore
  and, 151–2, 167, 184, 266; in
  United States, 152–8; Louis
  Armstrong plays with, 158;
  Lee becomes pianist, 167; J.D.
  re-forms, 171; at Edinburgh
  Festival, 196; at Nether Hall,

200, 215; film-writing subsidies,
  204; at Ronnie Scott's, 305–6
Johnny Dankworth Seven, 128,
  135, 141, 191, 202; C first
  hears of, 89; C first sings with,
  91; C's first date with, 95–6;
  treatment of a singer, 99–100;
  renames C, 101; weekly
  broadcast, 102; and 'Birth of the
  Cool' band, 102; characters of,
  106–7; passing time while on
  the road, 107–8; first television
  appearance, 108, 109; tour of
  Germany, 108, 117; Savoy
  Hotel gig, 113–15; told of J.D.'s
  decision to form a big band,
  123; incorporated into Big
  Band, 124
Johnson, J.J., 261
Jones, Quincy, 156, 264
Jones, Thad, 137, 159
Jones Beach, 154
J.V.C. Newport Jazz Festival, 327

Kathy (in Southall), 60, 62
Katz, Dick, 189, 197
Keaton, Kathy, 182
Kelsey, David, 317
Kendrick, Callum (C's nephew),
  119
Kendrick, Geoff (Sylvia's husband;
  C's brother-in-law), 103, 126,
  141, 177, 180, 220, 297, 301
Kendrick, Sylvia Beryl (nee
  Campbell; C's sister), 1, 8, 34,
  36, 52–3, 62, 126, 127; birth,
  5; appearance, 7; character, 8,
  17–18, 48; lessons with Mme
  de Courcey, 12; first concert
  performance, 14–15; helps in
  parents' boarding houses, 18;
  at school, 23, 48; ice-cream

Index

Index

Index

351